Routledge Revivals

Stagflation: Volume 2

Demand Management

First published in 1983, this is the second of two volumes on the causes and cure of stagflation. The authors deplore the contemporary unemployment due to the failure of governments to adopt Keynesian measures for the expansion of economic activity, but recognise that in contemporary conditions such measures would lead to an unacceptable and explosive inflation of money, wages and prices. They therefore advocate a dual strategy of financial policies for a steady expansion of total money incomes combined with individual wage rates set at levels to promote employment.

The book is of importance for all those concerned with macroeconomic theory and policy. The description of the meaning of a New Keynesian policy and of the arguments for it have been written in a way which should be intelligible to policy-makers and students, and not only to economists with technical training. Professional macroeconomists will be interested not only in these sections but also in the fully specified macroeconomic model used to analyse New Keynesian policies in economic terms and to carry out a counterfactual re-running of history. In addition, the unusually detailed exposition of the application of control techniques to a difficult multivariable control problem also makes the book of interest to control engineers who wish to acquaint themselves with recent generalisations of classical frequency response methods.

T0298603

Demand Management

David Vines,
Jan Maciejowski
and James E. Meade

Routledge
Taylor & Francis Group

First published in 1983
by George Allen & Unwin

This edition first published in 2011 by Routledge
2 Park Square, Milton Park, Abingdon, Oxon, OX14 4RN

Simultaneously published in the USA and Canada
by Routledge
270 Madison Avenue, New York, NY 10016

Routledge is an imprint of the Taylor & Francis Group, an informa business

Publisher's Note
The publisher has gone to great lengths to ensure the quality of this reprint but
points out that some imperfections in the original copies may be apparent.

Disclaimer
The publisher has made every effort to trace copyright holders and welcomes
correspondence from those they have been unable to contact.

A Library of Congress record exists under LC Control Number: 83008828

ISBN 13: 978-0-415-66859-0 (set)
ISBN 13: 978-0-415-66831-6 (hbk)
ISBN 13: 978-0-203-81463-5 (ebk)
ISBN 13: 978-0-415-67049-4 (pbk)

Stagflation. Volume 2
DEMAND MANAGEMENT

DEMAND MANAGEMENT

David Vines, J. M. Maciejowski,
J. E. Meade
University of Cambridge

London
GEORGE ALLEN & UNWIN
Boston   Sydney

George Allen & Unwin (Publishers) Ltd,
40 Museum Street, London WC1A 1LU, UK

George Allen & Unwin (Publishers) Ltd,
Park Lane, Hemel Hempstead, Herts HP2 4TE, UK

Allen & Unwin Inc.,
9 Winchester Terrace, Winchester, Mass 01890, USA

George Allen & Unwin Australia Pty Ltd,
8 Napier Street, North Sydney, NSW 2060, Australia

First published in 1983

British Library Cataloguing in Publication Data

Vines, David
    Demand management.
1. Supply and demand   2. Economic policy
3. Macroeconomics
I. Title   II. Maciejowski, J. M.
III. Meade, J. E.
339.4'7   HD82
ISBN 0-04-339030-7
ISBN 0-04-339031-5 Pbk

Library of Congress Cataloging in Publication Data

Vines, David.
    Demand management.
(Stagflation ; v. 2)
1. Demand (Economic theory)   2. Keynesian economics.
3. Macroeconomics.   4. Great Britain – Economic policy
– 1945–   . I. Maciejowski, Jan Marian.   II. Meade,
J. E. (James Edward), 1907–   . III. Title.
IV. Series.
HD5710.S7 vol. 2 [HB842] 339.5s [339.5'3] 83-8828
ISBN 0-04-339030-7
ISBN 0-04-339031-5 (pbk.)

Set in 10 on 11 point Press Roman by the Alden Press
and printed in Great Britain by Billing and Sons Ltd, London and Worcester

Contents

Preface

The economic strategy of what we call 'New Keynesianism' consists of two elements: first, financial policies should be designed to keep the flow of total money expenditures on the products of labour on a steady expansionary growth path and, second, against this financial background, money wage rates should be set in such a way as to promote output and employment in each sector of the economy. A first volume on Wage-Fixing, which considers the needed reform of wage-fixing institutions, has already been published. The present volume is devoted to the design of fiscal, monetary and foreign-exchange-rate policies for the control of the money demand for the products of labour.

The present work consists of three main strands which, while they are closely intertwined, do nevertheless constitute somewhat separate contributions to the whole. The three authors of this work have co-operated closely on all the parts of the work; but each of them has been mainly responsible for one of the main strands.

(1) J. E. Meade has been primarily responsible for Chapters I–VI in which the theory of demand management, and its implications for control policies, are discussed in general terms.

(2) J. M. Maciejowski has been primarily responsible for Chapters XII–XIV, which describe techniques of feedback control and their use for the design of economic policies.

(3) David Vines has been concerned with the application of these control techniques to the United Kingdom economy – or rather to a dynamic model of the UK economy, since for better or for worse we do not constitute the government of the country. The construction of a suitable model, the application of the control policies to it and the analysis of the results constitute the basic economic content of the volume. The tip of the vast iceberg of the work in fact involved is displayed in Chapters VII and VIII and Appendix A.

In addition to these three main strands we are indebted to the Institute for Fiscal Studies for organising a small informal committee to consider the practical difficulties involved in making frequent and prompt changes in rates of tax of the kind that our control rules might require. As a result of this committee's deliberations we include in this volume: Chapter IX on indirect taxes, drafted by J. E. Meade with the help and advice of the late Dorothy Johnstone, leading expert on customs and excise problems; Chapter X on the income tax, which is a reproduction of work by John Kay and Irene Cameron of the Institute for Fiscal Studies; and Chapter XI on taxes on wages, drafted by D. Vines with some technical help from a representative of the Inland Revenue, Mr R. A. Blythe, who is, of course, in no way committed to the opinions expressed in that chapter.

The project as a whole has been sponsored by the Department of Applied Economics of the University of Cambridge. It has been supported by the Social Science Research Council who have financed the secretarial expenses, the appointment of Mr David Vines, Fellow of Pembroke College, Cambridge, as a Research Officer of the Department of Applied Economics, and work done by Dr J. M. Maciejowski while he was lecturer in Mathematical Engineering at the University of Warwick. The Nuffield Foundation have also helped with the finance of the work of Dr Maciejowski, now a Fellow of Pembroke College, Cambridge, and a member of the Control and Management Systems Division of the Cambridge University Engineering Department. The Treasury have been of the greatest possible help to D. Vines in his use of the Treasury Model for the design and construction of the smaller model used in the present volume, and in giving assistance with computing. Mr Keith Singer provided very valuable programming assistance in the construction of the smaller model. Mr Martin Weale has given us a number of helpful suggestions concerning Chapters II–VI.

We are also indebted to the Science and Engineering Research Council, and to the Cambridge University Engineering Department, for access to the Cambridge Linear Analysis and Design Programs, the use of which was essential to the work described in this volume.

Finally, we would like to thank the staff of the Department of Applied Economics and Mrs P. Lister for their most efficient help in the preparation of our work.

Cambridge   DAVID VINES
January 1983   J. M. MACIEJOWSKI
                                                          J. E. MEADE

Part One

The Policy in
Theory and Practice

CHAPTER I

Introduction

This work is concerned with the nature, the causes, the consequences and the cure of stagflation, that ugly state of affairs in which the economy is both stagnant with heavy unemployment of people and other resources and also simultaneously suffering from a rapid inflation of money costs, prices and incomes. Already in the introductory chapters of an earlier volume we have given an outline sketch of our analysis of the problem.[*]

We there suggested that a basic feature of the phenomenon is a general attempt on the part of the various agents in the economy to obtain standards of living that in combination exceed the supply of goods and services available for their consumption; that these overambitious claims take the form of increases in money incomes that outrun increases in productivity; that this necessarily leads to a rise in money costs and money prices, and so in the cost of living; that this results in further wage claims to offset the rise in the cost of living, leading to still further rises in costs, prices and the cost of living and thus to a vicious circle of explosive inflation of money costs, money prices and money incomes; that sooner or later the authorities must take steps to put a stop to this explosive inflationary process by restrictive fiscal, monetary and foreign-exchange policies designed to damp down the rising levels of total money expenditures; and that this reduction of demand results in decreased output and employment, which will have to be prolonged and severe if it is ultimately to break the overambitious claims that have caused the trouble.

In Volume 1 we suggested that the best way to tackle this problem was by means of what we called a New Keynesian policy. By this we meant (1) that the apparatus of demand management (that is to say, the combination of budgetary, monetary and foreign-exchange policies) should be so operated as to keep the total of money expenditures on the goods and services produced in the country on a steady growth path, expanding at the moderate rate of, say, 5 per cent per annum, and (2) that, against this background of a steady but moderate expansion in the total money demand for the products of labour, wage-fixing institutions should be so reformed as to ensure that pay in the various sectors of the economy was settled at rates that served to promote employment in each sector.

The main body of Volume 1 was devoted to a discussion of the various ways in which wage-fixing institutions might be reformed so as to meet the requirements of such a New Keynesian policy. Similarly the main body of

[*]See Chapters I and II of *Stagflation, Volume 1* on *Wage-Fixing*.

the present Volume 2 will be addressed to the problems involved in using financial policies so as effectively to maintain the total money demand for the products of labour on a steady predetermined growth path. The questions that this demand-management problem involves were not discussed in Volume 1 but were enumerated on page 7 of that volume in the following words:

> By what means should total money expenditures be controlled? By monetary policy? By fiscal policy through raising and lowering rates of tax and levels of public expenditure? By changes in the rate of foreign exchange or other measures to affect expenditure on UK exports and UK import-competing products? What should be the precise measure of total money expenditures which it was aimed to keep on a steady growth path? Should it be the Gross Domestic Product (i.e. the value of all goods and services produced for consumption, investment, government use, and exports)? Or would it be preferable to aim directly at keeping the total money demand for labour (i.e. total wage and salary earnings) on a steady growth path? Above all, in view of the dynamic interrelationships in the economy between taxes, interest rates, foreign exchange rates, prices, outputs, and employment, what are the best rules for operating the monetary, fiscal, or other controls for the purpose of keeping the chosen measure of total money expenditures on its target growth path?

The study of these questions that follows consists of three main strands:

(1) In the investigation of demand-management policies one must consider the relations between monetary policies, budgetary policies and foreign-exchange-rate policies and their effects on the balance of payments and capital investment as well as on the total level of money expenditures. These relationships and their implications for control policies are discussed in Chapters I–VI in general terms.

(2) The choice of precise rules for setting tax rates, interest rates and foreign-exchange rates in order to control the performance of a dynamic economy requires the techniques of control engineering. The relevant techniques, and the way we have used them to devise policy rules, are described in Chapters XII–XIV.

(3) A description of how the UK economy might have fared had such policy rules been applied to it is given in Chapters VII and VIII. Such an exercise in rerunning history of course requires a dynamic economic model and the one that we have used is described in Appendix A.

In addition to these three main strands, Chapters IX–XI describe the practical difficulties that would be involved in making frequent and prompt changes in rates of tax of the kind that our control rules might require.

The present volume must be regarded as an interim report on a subject on which much further work needs to be done. We are conscious of the following six major limitations of the present analysis, which raises problems on which we are continuing to work.

(1) The model of the United Kingdom economy used in this volume could itself be developed to serve our purposes more completely. In particular, it needs to be expanded to cover the movement of capital funds in the balance of payments (and thus to integrate the effects of interest changes fully into the system on the lines discussed in Chapter V). In addition, the production function needs to be modified to consider the effects of interest-rate changes upon investment, along the lines discussed in Chapter V.

(2) In the present volume we consider as the basic demand-management target the maintenance on a steady growth path of the Money GDP (i.e. of the total of domestically produced money incomes). This target is much more ambitious than attempting to keep not the level, but the rate of growth of the Money GDP at a predetermined figure. Moreover, for a New Keynesian economic strategy it might be better to take as target not the total Money GDP but only the earnings component of the Money GDP (see Section 2 of Chapter III).

(3) In the present work we have designed rules for tax rates that depend solely on what is happening to the Money GDP and rules for the foreign-exchange rate that depend solely on what is happening to the current account of the balance of payments. But in reality there are three 'weapons' of financial policy (typified by the rates of tax, of interest and of foreign exchange) and three 'targets' for financial policy (typified by the level of money incomes, the overall balance of payments and the proportion of the community's resources devoted to capital accumulation at home or abroad). A revision of the rules that took into account the effect of each of the 'financial weapons' on each of the 'financial targets' might appreciably increase the effectiveness of the policy (see Section 5 of Chapter V).

(4) A major question is whether the particular control rules derived from the particular model examined in this volume are robust enough to be reasonably effective, indeed not to do more harm than good when applied to another model – or, above all, if applied to the actual United Kingdom economy. We have not yet undertaken any systematic enquiry into the robustness of our rules to meet deviations from the assumed underlying relationships.

(5) In our work we have not allowed for the fact that the adoption of a publicised New Keynesian policy may cause people to react to various developments in ways that differ from their previous

reactions in the absence of those declared policies. For example, we have assumed that consumers would react in their purchases to a rise in VAT in the same way as before, even though it were now announced that a rise in VAT was to be operative only so long as it was necessary to damp down an undesired inflation of total money incomes. If the consequential rise in the price of goods is expected on these grounds to be only temporary, there would be an added reason to postpone purchases; and to the extent that our model did not take such reactions into account the proposed rules for changing rates of VAT would be misjudged. It is uncertain how far such influences are at work and difficult to know how to measure their effect. But they may be very important.

(6)   The model of the UK economy on which we have based our work is essentially one in which output and employment depend upon Keynesian effective demand. It makes simple assumptions about the production function: (a) total output is assumed to respond to changes in demand so long as there is unemployed labour; (b) incentives to invest in new capital equipment are modelled so as to ensure that there is always a margin of unused capacity; and (c) output per head is assumed to grow exogenously at a given rate. Such simple assumptions are reasonably adequate for our present purpose, which is to examine whether finely tuned controls of total demand can prevent substantial *short-run* fluctuations of output and employment; but a more sophisticated production function would be needed if the purpose of our analysis were extended to take into account the *longer-run* effects on output and employment of the important technological revolutions (in micro-electronics, robotics, information techniques, etc.) through which we are now passing.

It may well be asked whether the publication of their results by three miserable sinners who have left undone so many things that they ought to have done serves any useful purpose. We make bold to justify our publisher's action. To remove the deficiencies enumerated above will require prolonged work. Meanwhile there are in the real world a number of urgent decisions to be taken about policies for demand management, a state of affairs that justifies the publication of an interim report if that report has any serious contribution to make to the current discussion. We feel that, even in its present form, it has contributions to make under each of the following nine headings:

(1)   In the first place, the theory of policy that we set forth in Chapters I–VI provides a systematic exposition: of the relationships between monetary policies, budgetary policies and foreign-exchange-rate policies; of their effects on the total level of money expenditures, on the balance of payments and on capital investment; and of the

implications for demand management. For reasons explained in Chapter II, this particular package of policies seems to us more desirable than either Orthodox Keynesianism or monetarism.

(2) A central issue is whether fine-tuning through frequent and prompt feedback variations of financial instruments (rates of tax, interest and foreign exchange) has any real contribution to make to a successful management of demand. Our study suggests that it can be helpful; we have in fact found control rules that, given the dynamic properties of our model, do in fact keep Money GDP very closely on its predetermined growth path in spite of the exceptional turmoils of the period studied, which include a fourfold rise of oil prices, the development of North Sea oil and the impact of the great world recession on the United Kingdom economy.

(3) Our study of these matters provides an instructive exercise in the development of control-theory techniques for their application to dynamic economic systems, a matter that consciously or unconsciously is in fact at the heart of all demand-management policies, no matter what theory of policy is adhered to. Indeed, we would recommend Chapters XII–XIV as providing a basic text for any economist who for the purpose of considering macro-economic policies wishes to familiarise himself with the relevant elements of control theory.

(4) As stated above, we have not yet systematically investigated the robustness of our fiscal rules; but our study makes it clear that if fiscal fine-tuning is to be tried it is most important in the interests of robustness as well as of direct effectiveness that adjustments of tax rates should be made with the minimum of delay in response to deviations of the Money GDP from its target growth path (see Section 1 of Chapter VIII). For this purpose some changes in the administrative arrangements for income tax and/or for national insurance contributions would be most desirable. A change from the present cumulative to a non-cumulative system for PAYE would be of outstanding assistance (see Chapters IX–XI).

(5) Our study also suggests that while fiscal feedback fine-tuning can play an important part, this does not preclude simultaneous attempts to control the situation by the forward planning of tax structures or of various governmental expenditures. Indeed, an appropriate arrangement might well consist of two elements: (a) an annual review at the time of the budget at which the whole structure of taxes and of further expenditures was planned ahead with the object among other things of keeping the Money GDP on its planned path, combined with (b) the use of fine-tuning adjustments of certain taxes in the period between one annual review and the next to help to correct unforeseen deviations that occurred during that period (see Section 3 of Chapter VI).

(6)   Successful stabilisation of the Money GDP through finely tuned fiscal measures will necessarily depend, as our study confirms, on a willingness to face, and ability to finance, large fluctuations in the balance of overseas payments. We can hope to make prompt adjustments to total money expenditures, which will lead to prompt fluctuations in the demand for foreign goods and services; but the readjustments then needed to the balance of payments by changes in the exchange rate will work only slowly because of the slow response of the channels of international trade to changes in relative prices (see Section 1 of Chapter VIII).

(7)   Another cost of successful stabilisation of the Money GDP through finely tuned fiscal measures is the need to face frequent temporary variations in the real value of take-home pay. The more closely one aims at keeping the Money GDP on its target growth path, the more marked and frequent must be the upward and downward adjustments of the tax rates used for this purpose and so of the post-tax real value of any given money wage (see Section 1 of Chapter VIII).

Nor is this simply a matter of short-run fluctuations; we have to face an even more important problem of longer-run variations in real living standards, owing to the fact that the balance of international trade adjusts only slowly to the foreign-exchange measures taken to control it. During a period of balance-of-trade deficit, our policy implies that tax rates should be low in order to stimulate domestic consumption demands and thus offset the low demand for UK products in export and import competing markets; with the subsequent restoration of the balance of trade, taxes must be raised in order to restrain consumers' demands to offset the restoration of net foreign demand. As a result, under our policies during the period 1975–77, when UK balance of payments was in deficit, the standard of living would have risen much more than could be justified merely by increased domestic productivity; but it would have had to be cut back very sharply in the years 1978–81 as our balance of payments was restored to equilibrium. This problem, and its possible treatment through the structural forward planning of elements of expenditure on UK products other than consumers' demands, is discussed in Section 3 of Chapter VI.

(8)   Volume 1 on Wage-Fixing considered various reforms of wage-fixing institutions that might result in setting wage rates so as to promote employment and output in each sector of the economy. Our present study on demand management has dealt with wage-fixing simply by attempting to answer the question: what precise quantitative response of money wage rates to the levels of available unemployed labour would be needed to keep the unemployment percentage at a suitably low level? Clearly there may be a yawning gap between the precise wage response that this volume on demand management

suggests as being needed and the wage responses that might result from the various institutional reforms discussed in the volume on wage-fixing. We have done nothing directly to close this gap and indeed cannot clearly see how one could set about trying formally to do so. But our present study gave us some surprising comfort to be somewhat less disconcerted by the existence of this gap than we had expected to be.

In the first place, the response of wage rates to unemployment that our present study indicates as being desirable takes a perfectly straightforward form (see Section 1 of Chapter VIII). It has one outstanding feature: while money wages are geared to a more or less stable expectation of price rises, they do not respond at all to actual fluctuations of the cost of living, but only to the level of unemployment. It is not suggested that this is at all an easy reform to achieve, but it does in fact reproduce the basic feature of the reforms discussed in Volume 1. Moreover, there is evidence to suggest that the needed degree and form of response of wages to unemployment is not totally unrealistic. The Treasury Model of 1980 contained an equation that purported to describe the actual influences affecting wage settlements. It comprised an influence of the level of unemployment in restraining wage settlements, which is a great deal weaker than that which our study indicates to be desirable, and also an influence on such settlements of actual and thence expected fluctuations of prices (i.e. of the cost of living). If this Treasury Model equation, *but with a stabilised price expectation*, is applied to our model in place of the ideal wage response suggested by our study, the results remain quite satisfactory (see Section 1 of Chapter VIII). In other words, there is some reason to believe that the basic need in wage-fixing reform is to shift the emphasis away from actual fluctuations in the cost of living without requiring any unrealistically increased degree of influence of the availability of unemployed labour on the final settlement; and this is entirely consistent with the conclusions of Volume 1.

All our results rest on the crucial assumption that wage-fixing is reformed in this way, so that rates of pay are set so as to promote output and employment rather than to offset changes in the cost of living. Indeed, to adopt our fiscal controls of expenditure without any reform of wage-fixing arrangements could make the outcome even worse than it is at present (see the Note to Chapter VIII). Thus the present volume may be regarded as an essay on the potential benefits to be reaped if a suitable reform of wage-fixing arrangements can be achieved — our exercises suggesting as a result for 1982 an unemployment percentage of 4 per cent instead of 12 per cent with a level of real consumption some 7.5 per cent higher than with present policies and institutions. Persuading people to accept the necessary changes will not be easy, but the prize to be gained is of the greatest value.

(9)   The application to our model of our tax rules and of the desired wage response does in fact result in keeping the Money GDP very close to its planned path and the unemployment percentage very close to 4 per cent (instead of rising to more than 12 per cent) between 1972 and 1982. In other words, it successfully achieves its targets: it maintains employment — indeed finds employment for a 4.8 per cent larger number in 1982 than 1972 in spite of the world recession and in spite of an adverse movement of prices of imported primary products; and it does so without ending up with a deficit on the current account of the balance of payments.

In these circumstances, the application of our control policies necessarily calls for a marked worsening of the terms of trade, since the increased demand for imports due to the expansion of home activity is compounded by a world recession in the demand for our exports and by a worsening of the price of imported materials relatively to our manufactures. To prevent a deterioration of the balance of payments, our export and import competing products have had to be made much more competitive relative to foreign products. The resulting deterioration in the terms of trade has had the effect in our controlled economy of causing the real standard of living to rise between 1972 and 1982 by less than could otherwise have resulted from the rise in the productivity of domestic industry and the development of North Sea oil. However, the maintenance of high levels of output and employment far outweighs the worsening of the terms of trade resulting from our control policies, so that the standard of living in 1982 would be markedly higher in our controlled economy than under present policies (see Section 2 of Chapter VIII).

The deterioration in the terms of trade in our controlled economy has nothing to do with the particular choice of a New Keynesian policy or with the use of our particular finely tuned controls. Any set of policies that maintained full employment in 1982 would have to cope with these same implications of the structural changes that occurred in the world economy between 1972 and 1982. What it does illustrate is the enormous additional advantage that we in the United Kingdom would have enjoyed if the world recession had been avoided — or, in other words, if all the developed countries had simultaneously and in concert adopted policies with the same effects as the New Keynesian economic strategy that we have recommended for the United Kingdom.

CHAPTER II

The Case for New Keynesian Demand Management

The basic subject matter of the present enquiry is to examine the feasibility of applying financial policies effectively for what we have called the New Keynesian demand management, i.e. for the purpose of keeping the money expenditure on the products of labour on a steady growth path. It is, however, important to understand why we have chosen to concentrate our enquiry on this particular brand of Keynesian demand-management policy. We have already outlined our reasons for this choice in Chapter I of Volume 1. But it will be useful to summarise and somewhat elaborate these reasons before we turn to our main subject matter.[*]

1. Three Competing Strategies

The evil of stagflation consists of (1) output and employment being too low and, simultaneously, (2) the rate of rise of money costs and prices being too high. To control simultaneously these two aspects of the economy requires the use of at least two independent sets of policy instruments. One of these consists of the weapons of financial policy that can affect the level of the total money demand for goods and services, and the other consists of the various influences that can be exerted to affect the level of money wage rates and of other money costs, and thus the level at which money selling prices are fixed. In Volume 1 we have discussed at length the various forms that policies affecting money wage costs may take; and in subsequent parts of this volume we shall discuss at length the various forms that financial policies for the control of the demand for goods and services may take. But for the time being we will talk only in general terms of demand-management policies and of wage-fixing[†] policies. We have then these two sets of policy instruments to use in attempts to remove the two evils of unemployment and of rapid inflation.

---

[*]These reasons are discussed in a different but complementary way in Meade (1981).
[†]Selling prices of domestic products depend, of course, upon profit margins as well as upon wage costs. In Volume 1 we have discussed the importance of restraining excess profit margins, but have explained that the basic problem in the present stagflationary situation is the control of wage costs, since profit margins are already at an exceptionally low level. See Volume 1, *Wage-Fixing*, Chapter I, Section 8.

The fundamental feature of New Keynesianism is the suggestion that demand-management policies should be used to maintain the total of money expenditures on the domestic output of goods and services on a steady path with a moderate rate of growth, expanding demands if money expenditures fall below and restraining demands if money expenditures rise above this target level; and, against this financial background, money wage rates and thus, with given profit margins, money selling prices should be so set as to promote employment, since the extent to which a high level of money expenditures will lead to high prices rather than high output and employment will, given the level of profit margins, depend upon the levels of money wage costs.

But this is not the only way in which the two instruments of demand management and of wage-fixing can be applied to the two objects of full employment and of the control of inflation.

An alternative Keynesian strategy is that financial policies should be operated with the purpose not of keeping total *money* expenditures on domestic products on a predetermined growth path, but rather of keeping *real* economic activity (output and employment) at a predetermined full-employment level, raising money expenditures and so the demand for the products of labour if employment falls below this level and restraining demands if, by rising above this level, it causes an inflationary excess demand for resources. We call this the Orthodox Keynesian view about demand-management policies because it was the way in which Keynes himself regarded the matter during the 1930s; and, broadly speaking, it was the predominant view for a quarter of a century after the Second World War (1945–70). An implication of this view, which became fairly widely accepted during the postwar period, is that if the maintenance of economic activity at some predetermined full-employment level leads to an unacceptable inflation of money costs and prices, then some form of 'incomes policy' is needed in order to control inflation or, in our present terminology, wage-fixing must be used to control inflation. Thus we designate as Orthodox Keynesianism the use of demand-management policies to maintain employment at a high and stable level and the use of wage-fixing to control inflation.

It would be wrong to draw the dividing line between the use of financial policies to control the level of total *money* demands (New Keynesianism) and their use to control *real* economic activity (Orthodox Keynesianism) too sharply in so far as actual postwar policies were concerned. While the main emphasis was on their use to maintain real economic activity, this was increasingly tempered by consideration of the need to restrain an inflationary threat.[*] In this case we can think in terms

---

[*]An even more important factor tempering the use of financial policies exclusively for the maintenance of full employment was the recurrent threat of a balance of payments crisis due to an excess demand for imports, an excess demand which could be checked by a reduction in the total of money expenditures on all goods and services.

of a mixed strategy, the current financial policies being so designed as to achieve some compromise between the maintenance of full employment (which might call for some expansion) and the control of inflation (which might call for some restriction).

There are in fact very powerful and very sophisticated arguments in favour of such 'compromises', that is to say, of taking into account the effect of financial policies on both the objectives of full employment and of avoidance of inflation. When there are two policy instruments (such as demand management and wage-fixing) to be employed to achieve two objectives (such as full employment and the avoidance of inflation), the control engineer will argue that, for reasons that we discuss below, it is inefficient to devote the use of one instrument exclusively to the achievement of one objective and the use of the other instrument exclusively to the achievement of the other objective. The efficient procedure is to take into account the effect on both objectives of any given combination of both instruments and to search for the combination of policies that will jointly produce the best attainable combination of the objectives. Any systematic attempt to devise a strategy for policies on this basis we may call Cross-Linked Keynesianism.

We have then three possible policy strategies:

(1)   Cross-Linked Keynesianism, which seeks a combination of demand-management and wage-fixing policies to achieve a desired combined outcome for employment and inflation, taking into account the effect of each policy 'weapon' on each 'target' outcome.
(2)   Orthodox Keynesianism, which links the use of demand-management policies solely to the promotion of employment and the use of wage-fixing solely to control inflation.
(3)   New Keynesianism, which links demand management solely to the control of total money incomes and wage-fixing solely to the promotion of employment.

Does it really matter which strategy is adopted, if one successfully attains both full employment and a control of inflation? To illustrate the idea that it is all a fuss about nothing Professor Abba Lerner once related the following anecdote. A kind father called his son and daughter to him and said: 'Here, Tommy, is a penny to buy me a newspaper and here, Mary, is a penny to buy some sweets for Tommy and yourself.' So the children went to the shops and came back with a newspaper and a packet of sweets. 'Well done,' said the father, 'You have done just what I told you.'

We consider these important international aspects below (see Chapters III, IV and V). For the time being we concentrate on the domestic aspects of the choice between using demand-management policies to stabilise the level of *real* economic activity and their use to stabilise the level of *monetary* transactions.

'Well, Daddy,' said Mary, 'Not exactly, we spent my penny on the news-paper and Tommy's penny on the sweets.' The father was furious at their disobedience and sent them both to bed without any supper.

It would, of course, be a matter of complete indifference if each method would equally certainly and with equal speed and ease lead to the same final equilibrium – a set of conditions that presumably applied to Tommy's and Mary's pennies. But there are at least three reasons why the analogy may break down in the case of the 'expenditures' of demand management and of wage-fixing on the 'purchases' of full employment and control of inflation: the different strategies may not in fact lead to exactly the same final outcomes; one instrument may be more effective in its use for one purpose than for another so that it is not a matter of indifference how the weapons and targets are married to each other; and there may be a number of conditions that are not strictly economic – namely, political and administrative – that in fact tell in favour of one strategy rather than another.

In the light of these considerations we will devote the remaining pages of this chapter to a consideration of the relative merits and demerits of each of the three possible strategies in order to give our reasons for preferring New Keynesianism and for devoting the rest of this volume to a study of that strategy.

2.   The Merits and Demerits of Cross-Linked Keynesianism

Analysis of the dynamic economic model is likely to show that, with various time lags which must be taken into account, expansionary demand-management policies are likely to lead to some increase in employment and to some increase in inflation, while rises in wage rates are likely to lead to some decrease in employment but to some increase in inflation, and vice versa. The control engineers' analysis is thus likely to result in rules that instruct those in charge of demand-management policies to expand in order to fight unemployment or deflation and to contract to fight overfull employment or inflation. In the case of a clash of objectives, the rules will instruct them how much relative weight they should put upon each objective. And similarly the rules would instruct those in charge of wage-fixing as to how much relative weight to put on the two objectives of employment and of control of inflation in deciding whether, and if so how much, they should encourage wage restraint or wage increases. The rules would thus instruct both sets of policy makers – the demand managers and the wage fixers – to give due weight to both objectives in the formulation of their policies, though these weights would not be the same for both sets of policy-makers. The best weights to be allocated to each control instrument for the attainment of each policy objective would depend upon the effectiveness of each instrument in the control of each

Table II.1

| | States of the economy[1] | | | |
	A	B	C	D
(1) Existing state:				
Inflationary (+) or deflationary (−)	+	+	−	−
Overfull employment (+) or unemployment (−)	−	+	−	+
(2) Restoration of equilibrium requires:				
Expansionary (+) or restrictive (−) demand management policies	?	−	+	?
Inflationary (+) or deflationary (−) wage-fixing	−	?	?	+
(3) Orthodox-Keynesian rules prescribe:				
Expansionary (+) or restrictive (−) demand-management policies	+	−	+	−
Inflationary (+) or deflationary (−) wage-fixing	−	−	+	+
(4) New-Keynesian rules prescribe:				
Expansionary (+) or restrictive (−) demand-management policies	−	−	+	+
Inflationary (+) or deflationary (−) wage-fixing	−	+	−	+

[1] See text for explanation.

objective, upon the relative importance attached to the attainment of each objective, and upon the relative cost, if any, incurred in the use of each instrument.

From this analysis it is easy to see that, if it could be properly applied, the great merit of Cross-Linked Keynesianism over its two rivals would be its greater efficiency. This is illustrated in Table II.1.

Column A of the table relates to a stagflationary state of the economy in which inflation is combined with unemployment, as is shown in section 1 of the table. Section 2 of the table then describes the nature of the demand-management and wage-fixing policies that will ultimately be needed to restore equilibrium in the sense of obtaining both full employment and the target rate of inflation of money prices or incomes. Wage restraint is clearly required, since it will tend both to increase employment and to restrain inflation. It is not so obvious whether an expansionary or a contractionary change in demand management will be required. It may well be that, with given demand-management controls, such as the existing levels of budgetary expenditures and of tax rates, interest rates and foreign-exchange rates, the degree of wage restraint needed to restore full employment would have to be so great as to cause an undesired deflation of money prices and incomes, in which case wage restraint needs to be combined with demand-management expansion. On the other hand, with unchanged demand-management controls, the degree of wage restraint needed to restore full employment may be insufficient in itself to restrain inflation, in which case demand-management contraction needs to be combined with wage restraint in order to attain the final equilibrium.

Both Orthodox Keynesianism (section 3 of the table) and New Keynesianism (section 4) will prescribe wage restraint, in the former case to control inflation and in the latter case to promote employment; since both anti-inflation and anti-unemployment influences are desired in the stagflation of column A, such wage restraint is unequivocally desirable. But Orthodox Keynesianism will unambiguously prescribe demand-management expansion as a means of promoting employment, even though the wage restraint needed to control inflation may itself be enough to promote the demand for labour beyond the full-employment level; and, if this were the case, the expansionary demand-management policies initiated to promote employment would soon need to be reversed in order to avoid an excess demand for labour. Conversely, New Keynesianism (section 4) would unambiguously prescribe a contraction of demand-management policies in order to restrain inflation; in fact it is possible that with existing demand-management policies the wage restraint needed to promote full employment might have to be so savage as to cause an undesired deflation of total money expenditures, in which case the demand-management contraction would need hastily to be reversed to prevent a deflation of money incomes.

Columns B, C and D of Table II.1 show the uncertainties that may arise in other economic situations. Thus column B shows the familiar old-fashioned inflationary situation in which demand-management restriction is needed to fight both inflation and an excess demand for labour, but in which it is uncertain whether such deflation of demand will need to be accompanied by wage deflation or by wage inflation to supplement the effect of the demand-management deflation on the demand for labour. Column C is the reverse position to column B and shows the familiar old-fashioned deflationary situation (e.g. of the 1930s); it indicates a sure need for reflation of demand but an uncertainty whether this should be accompanied by a stiffening or a relaxation of wage restraint. Column D illustrates the conceivable, but improbable, reverse of the stagflationary situation of column A — a fairyland in which an inflation of wage rates is greatly to be desired both to prevent a deflation of money prices and incomes and also to restrain an excess demand for labour, while there is uncertainty about demand management. We have examined the implications of the uncertainties arising in the stagflationary situation of column A. The same analysis can be applied, *mutatis mutandis*, to each of the columns B, C and D.

Thus the basic argument in favour of Cross-Linked Keynesianism is that it can avoid inefficient uses of the control policies. For this reason, if the instruments of control — tax rates, interest rates and foreign-exchange rates for demand management, and rates of pay for wage-fixing — could be raised and lowered without administrative or institutional difficulty, there would be a very strong case on efficiency grounds for using them on Cross-Linked principles. The instruments of demand-management control can, subject to any overriding political constraints, to some considerable extent be treated in this way. The authorities do possess the administrative–institutional competence to fix tax rates, interest rates and foreign-exchange rates at levels of their choice. But, in the absence of a revolution in present institutional arrangements that would transfer to some central body the power of fixing rates of pay, this is very far from the case for wage-fixing.

One consideration that must be taken into account is that the instruments of control needed to fight the macro-economic problem of stagflation are also necessarily used for a number of other micro-economic purposes. We can illustrate this in the case of tax policy, which, for reasons discussed later, we shall treat as the main weapon for demand-management control. The authorities will want to take into account the degree of progression of the tax structure and so its effect on the distribution of income and wealth and also the incidence of the tax on various commodities and activities and so its effects on the environment, on economic efficiency, on incentives and on many other matters of micro-economic concern. The present administrative–institutional arrangements do permit the authorities to determine a level and a structure of taxation that does allow for its effects both on the total level of demand (which is our interest in the present volume) and also on the other micro-economic effects mentioned above.

Rates of pay also have micro-economic as well as macro-economic effects. In particular, while the average level of rates of pay throughout the economy is of great importance in determining the general rate of inflation of money costs and prices and the general level of employment, differentials between rates of pay in different sectors of the economy have very important functions in aiding the allocation of labour between various regions, industries and occupations, restraining the demand for labour and attracting new recruits where labour is scarce and vice versa. Chapter VII of Volume 1 describes in some detail the formidable and, many would add, the undesirable centralised institutional revolution that would be needed to enable some central authority to put wage rates up or down, taking into account any desired adjustments of differentials, in the same way that the government can put tax rates up or down, taking into account any desired adjustment of tax structures.

In brief, while demand-management control can, and indeed must, be centralised, wage-fixing control cannot readily be centralised. It is desirable, if not unavoidable, to search for a decentralised wage-fixing system. This argues against Cross-Linked Keynesianism since it is virtually impossible to conceive of any decentralised system that would induce individual wage-fixing bodies to put weight on *reducing* wage claims

simply because the cost of living was *rising*. But this is precisely what is
involved in any use of wage-fixing for the purpose of controlling inflation.
The argument tells even more strongly against Orthodox Keynesianism
under which system the wage rate is to be used solely for the control of
general inflation. As we shall argue later, it tells in particular in favour of
New Keynesianism, where the purpose of the wage rate in each sector
could be defined as the promotion of employment in that sector.

In a free, open, democratic society it is desirable that the *raison d'être*
of any policies adopted by the central authorities should be readily
understood. This consideration also tells against the Cross-Linked solution.
As can be seen from the cases marked with a query (?) in section 2 of
Table II.1, the Cross-Linked rules will not permit a clear-cut connection
between each instrument of control and each objective. Thus (see Columns
B and C of section 2 of the table) wage restraint may be called for when
there is a scarcity of labour or when there is unemployment, and it may be
called for when there is a general inflation of money prices and incomes or
when there is a general deflation of money incomes and prices. Thus, even
if there were no more administrative–institutional difficulty in running a
centralised wage-fixing policy than there is in running a centralised
demand-management policy, there would remain a case against Cross-
Linked Keynesianism.

With Orthodox Keynesianism it would be much easier to explain to
the public that demand was being managed to maintain full employment
and wages were being fixed to prevent this from leading to an inflation of
money incomes and costs. With New Keynesianism it would be much
easier to explain that demand was being managed to prevent an undesirable
inflation or deflation of total money incomes and that wage rates were
being set to maintain employment. In a democracy in which the man and
the woman in the street need to understand what is afoot, there is a strong
case for ascribing to each authority a clearly defined responsibility on
which its performance can be judged – to the Treasury and the Bank of
England the duty *either* to maintain employment *or* the duty to control
inflation and similarly to the wage fixers (whoever they may be) the duty
to control *either* employment *or* inflation.

3.   The Merits and Demerits of Orthodox Keynesianism

In this case demand-management policies are designed to maintain real
economic activity at a full-employment level, expenditures on goods and
services being stimulated if employment is below this level and being
restrained if the demand for labour rises above this level.

In order to operate this system it is necessary to determine what level
of employment should be regarded as the target full-employment level.
There will, of course, always be some persons unemployed in a dynamic

economy in which the demands for various products are growing at different rates, technologies and the requirements for different skills are changing, the elderly are leaving and the young are entering the labour market, and so on. There will always be some frictional unemployment as people move from job to job and often some more concentrated pockets of what may be called structural unemployment as whole industries or regions decline and others grow. The problem is to determine what level of unemployment should be ascribed to these frictional and structural causes as contrasted with general unemployment due to a general deficiency of demand for the products of labour. Should an unemployment percentage of 1 per cent or 3 per cent or 5 per cent or 10 per cent be considered as compatible with full employment? The problem arises because markets, and in particular the labour market, are not fully competitive. It has been analysed at some length in Section 7 of Chapter I of Volume 1. The following is a brief summary of that analysis.

Over a large range of employments, wage claims are formulated by powerful monopolistic trade unions, operating independently of each other, and each of whose interest lies primarily in obtaining the best possible real standard for those in employment in the particular sector concerned rather than in expanding the volume of employment in that sector. Those workers who are outside these organised sectors will have to compete in any remaining sectors in which monopolistic wage bargaining is not so strictly organised. Competition here will drive down the wage, so that many workers are unable to find jobs at more than the unemployment pay that they receive when out of work.

It is, of course, true that the wage claims in the organised sectors are not wholly unaffected by the level of real economic activity and the difficulty of finding work in those sectors. But the level of economic activity and of employment opportunities may have to be very restricted before real wage claims in the highly organised sectors are sufficiently restrained to correspond with the amounts available from productivity increases. Wage claims are made to offset the current rate of inflation of the cost of living as well as to achieve some improvement in real standards. So long as the amount claimed to improve real standards exceeds the amount available from increased productivity, the rate of money cost inflation will increase. To take a numerical example, suppose the current rate of price inflation to be 10 per cent per annum, the current rate of increase of output per head to be 2 per cent per annum, and the claim for an increase in the real wage to be 4 per cent per annum. Then the money cost per unit of output will rise by 10 per cent (the cost-of-living wage claim) + 4 per cent (the real claim for improvement) − 2 per cent (the reduction in cost per unit due to productivity) = 12 per cent, so that the rate of inflation will rise from 10 per cent per annum to 12 per cent per annum. We define the non-accelerating inflation rate of unemployment (NAIRU) as the level of unemployment that would be sufficiently high to cause the claims for real improvement to be reduced to the rate of productivity increase (i.e. from 4 per cent to 2 per cent in the above example), so that the inflation of money costs per unit of output would not rise in an explosive manner.

With present wage-fixing arrangements in the very extensive organised sectors of the labour market by several independent competing monopolistic bodies, concerned primarily with the real standards of those employed in each sector independently, NAIRU may be high (e.g. 10 per cent); it would certainly be lower, perhaps much lower (e.g. 4 per cent), if the object of each wage-fixing body were to fix a wage in each sector that would promote to the fullest possible extent the level of employment in that sector. We may define the full-employment rate of unemployment (FERU) as what NAIRU would be if in the organised sectors each wage-fixing body were aiming at the promotion of the level of employment in that sector rather than at the highest possible level of real wage for those employed in that sector.

To have found such a satisfactory definition may be very comforting to the academic logician, but it will not be very helpful to the practical demand-management authorities who will be left with the problem of guessing what NAIRU would be if the wage-fixing institutions were radically reformed or, what comes to the same thing, of guessing what are the levels of frictional and structural unemployment. But if the analysis is correct, whatever the precise level of unemployment chosen to represent full employment, the maintenance of employment at that level by means of demand-management policies with unreformed wage-fixing institutions is likely to lead to an explosive inflationary situation with the threat of not merely rapid, but ever-rising rates of inflation. The prevention of such inflation in conditions of full employment will require a centralised incomes policy with all the difficulties and disadvantages of such a policy, which have been mentioned above and which are discussed at length in Chapter VII of Volume 1.

This is the great demerit of Orthodox Keynesianism: it involves a serious threat of explosive inflation the control of which, if possible at all, will involve a most difficult and undesirable authoritarian intervention in business arrangements.

4.   The Merits and Demerits of New Keynesianism

The main merits of New Keynesianism can best be noted by describing how this system avoids the main demerits of its two rivals.

Thus, unlike Cross-Linked Keynesianism, it does allocate clearly defined responsibilities to each of the main 'controllers' and it does this in what may well be regarded as a natural manner which could be readily understood by the man and the woman in the street. It calls on the Central

Bank (which is in charge of the supply of money) and the Treasury (which is in charge of the expenditure of money) to be responsible for control of the inflation of total money incomes; and it calls on the wage-fixers (who are in charge of setting the price for labour) to take account of the effects of that price on the demand for, as well as the supply of, labour.

This division of functions may well be regarded as a more natural one than that implied by Orthodox Keynesianism.

In wage-fixing, Orthodox Keynesianism inevitably goes against market forces (requiring wage restraint just when demand is high and prices are rising most rapidly and wage expansion just when demand is low and prices are falling), whereas New Keynesianism follows the market (requiring wage restraint where labour is plentiful and wage expansion where labour is scarce). It is for this very reason that New Keynesianism unlike Orthodox Keynesianism is compatible with a decentralised system of control. The great demerit of Orthodox Keynesianism is its consequential necessary reliance on a centralised incomes policy, the logical outcome of which is a very far-reaching authoritarian and bureaucratic intervention in business arrangements in order not only to control the general level of wage rates, but also to control differentials in an economy with a very large variety of methods of pay.

New Keynesianism also avoids the difficulty discussed above that Orthodox Keynesianism faces in having to formulate some predetermined notion of what constitutes 'full employment': is it at a 1 per cent, a 3 per cent, a 5 per cent or a 10 per cent unemployment percentage that the economy is left only with frictional and structural unemployment? How far should expansionary demand-management policies be driven in their attempt to reduce unemployment? This problem does not occur with New Keynesianism where the demand managers have the task of keeping the total level of money expenditure on domestically produced goods and services, and so the total level of domestically generated money incomes, on a steady, moderate, predetermined growth path. Some level for this predetermined rate of growth of total money incomes would, of course, have to be chosen. Is 1 per cent, 3 per cent, 5 per cent or 10 per cent a reasonable target figure? We discuss below in Section 4 of Chapter III the considerations that would have to be taken into account in making this choice; but it is bound to be somewhat arbitrary. But in so far as this is so, it is an arbitrary decision about ultimate equilibrium growth of all *money* costs, prices and incomes and is thus basically less important than the Orthodox Keynesian arbitrary decision about the full-employment level for *real* activity in the economy. With New Keynesianism the resulting levels of real activity in the economy will depend upon the success of the various micro-economic arrangements in the various sectors of the economy, including the setting of wage rates, in promoting real activity in the various sectors.

But it is here, of course, that the possible dangers of New Keynesianism arise. Orthodox Keynesianism relies for its success on a radical transformation of present decentralised wage-fixing arrangements into some centralised incomes policy. New Keynesianism relies upon a radical reform of decentralised wage-fixing so that in each wage settlement more account is taken of the promotion of employment in that sector. Failure on the wage front would wreck both Orthodox Keynesianism, whose full-employment target would have to be abandoned because of the need to grapple with an explosive inflation, and New Keynesianism, whose control of inflation would have to be abandoned because of the need to grapple with heavy unemployment. A major question is, therefore, which form of change in wage-fixing arrangements is the more difficult to achieve politically. If it were easier politically to arrange that trade union leaders should hand over to a central bureaucracy the fixing of wage rates than to persuade them to adapt a continuing system of decentralised collective bargaining so that more weight can be put on the effects of settlements on levels of employment, then in spite of its other disadvantages Orthodox Keynesianism might have to be preferred. But there is no obvious reason to believe that this would be the case.

5.   The Demerits of Monetarism

It may be asked how, if at all, a New Keynesian policy differs from the monetarist policy of the present government, which consists after all of a financial policy for keeping the stock of money (M_3) on a steady growth path and leaving the wage rate to market forces to promote employment. There are in fact two quite basic differences.

In the first place, the financial objective of New Keynesianism would be to keep the total *flow* of money expenditures on the products of the economy, and not merely the total *stock* of money, on a steady growth path. This is perhaps the basic Keynesian, as contrasted with the monetarist, feature of demand management. In the 1930s Keynes opposed attempts to promote employment by cutting wage rates largely on the grounds that in the conditions then ruling such a reduction of money wage costs would, with a constant *stock* of money, lead primarily to a deflation of all money costs, money prices, money incomes and money expenditures, and so to a corresponding reduction in the *flow* of total money expenditures, and thus to little, if any, increase in real outputs and employment. New Keynesianism aims precisely to prevent this deflationary effect of wage restraint by ensuring through demand-management financial policies that wage restraint does not lead to any reduction in the *flow* of total money expenditures, and thus does effectively result in increased output and employment. It is basic to this analysis that the objective of demand management should be the *flow* of money expenditures and not the *stock* of money.

Second, there is an even more important difference in the attitudes to wage-fixing arrangements. The monetarists in charge of the policies of the present Conservative government have tended to take the view that no radical change in wage-fixing institutions is essential to success. The assumption has rather been that the knowledge that the authorities are going to prevent any rapid inflation of the stock of money will sooner or later cause people to expect a lower rate of price inflation and thus will moderate those claims for increases in money wages that are made in order to offset expected increases in the cost of living. It is realised that the process will lead to a temporary reduction in output and employment before the reduction in the rate of growth of money expenditures is matched by an actual corresponding reduction in the rate of growth of money wage costs; but the temporary, regrettable high levels of unemployment will, it is argued, themselves powerfully reinforce restraint in wage claims.

In contrast to this, it is an essential feature of New Keynesianism to argue that New Keynesian demand management will be compatible with a high and stable level of employment only if it is combined with a radical reform of wage-fixing arrangements. The basic argument, which has been expounded at length in Volume 1, is that, if and when employment is once more restored to its pre-recession level, wage claims would probably once more be made at levels that exceeded the rate of growth of productivity unless there had been some radical reform of present wage-fixing arrangement. This would be so as long as wage claims continue to be formulated by monopolistic organisations that naturally put much more stress on the standard of living of their members who are in employment than they do on opening the occupation to the increased employment of outsiders. In this case, even if the present savage recession and heavy unemployment did temporarily effectively damp down the present wage and price inflation — and experience over the last few years suggests that this is a very slow and uncertain process — it would merely mean that the whole process of explosive inflation would start once more as soon as full employment was restored.

Moreover, there is reason to fear that the temporary but severely prolonged recession would make the resurgence of explosive inflation recur earlier and at even less satisfactory levels of employment than would otherwise have been the case. The recession will have caused severe cutbacks in employment, leaving fewer persons in employment in many sectors offset by a large number of unemployed outsiders, in particular of young persons who have failed to find jobs in replacement of retired workers and are, therefore, not even members of any trade union. This will mean that, so long as wage claims are made in the organised sectors primarily in the interests of those in employment, there will be a larger proportion of unemployed outsiders whose interests will be relatively ignored in making wage claims. A given degree of upward pressure on wage rates is likely to occur at higher rates of unemployment than was the case before the recession. Radical reform of wage-fixing arrangements will be even more urgent than before.

6. Some Further Implications of New Keynesianism

In Volume 1 a number of other features and implications of the reforms of wage-fixing suitable for a New Keynesian demand-management system have been discussed at some length. It would be tedious to repeat that discussion in this volume, but the nature of three such features may usefully be briefly summarised.

First, if wage-fixing is to be used primarily for the promotion of employment, it cannot at the same time be used primarily as an instrument for obtaining a socially desirable and fair distribution of income. Much stress is laid in Volume 1 on the need for, and the greater effectiveness of, instruments other than wage-fixing to achieve any socially desirable redistribution of income and wealth (see Volume 1, Chapter I, Section 8).

Second, it is not proposed that wage rates should be slashed or raised with excessive abruptness to meet all market fluctuations in the demand for labour in the various sectors. The argument is simply that wage rates should be gradually adjusted in the directions needed to promote employment, i.e. at a moderate average rate but with some degree of extra restraint where labour is plentiful and some degree of extra expansion where labour is scarce (see Volume 1, Chapter VIII, Section 3).

Third, there would have to be careful transitional arrangements in the movement from present conditions to an ultimately satisfactory New Keynesian demand-management regime. It might well, for example, be desired to end up with a situation in which the total of money expenditures on the products of labour was kept on a steady 5 per cent per annum growth path. But if one started from a situation with inflation running at, say, 10 per cent per annum and with an unemployment percentage of, say, 12 per cent, any sudden introduction of a mere 5 per cent target for the growth of total money expenditure would have catastrophic effects. As is argued at length below (in Section 4 of Chapter III), one would need a sufficiently relaxed control over the growth of total money expenditures over a transitional period to allow for the finance of an increased output of goods and services that did not require an impossibly rapid rate of reduction in the inflation of money wages and prices (see Volume 1, Chapter I, Sections 5 and 6).

Moreover, the commitment to achieve any given target for the next year's growth of total money incomes might at first be less than 100 per cent firm. The rate of growth of total money incomes could be first introduced as an important measure of the degree of success in financial management and then, as experience was gained in the methods of financial control and in the success of any reforms of wage-fixing arrangements, could gradually be transformed into the main, if not exclusive, firmly held target. Movement in this direction is the essential need.

CHAPTER III

Three Financial Targets: Money Income, Balance of Payments and Investment Ratio

1.   Introductory

We now confine our attention to a New Keynesian strategy. In this case employment is to be promoted by the fixing of wage rates at appropriate levels. This has been discussed at length in Volume 1, and no purpose would be served by repeating that discussion here. This wage-fixing is to be carried out against a background of demand-management policies designed to keep the total money expenditure on goods and services produced in the UK, and so the total money income earned in their production, on a steady growth path. This path for domestically produced money incomes we will call the money income target.

Up to this point we have discussed this target as if it were the only target with which we need be concerned in devising a set of financial controls through fiscal, monetary and foreign-exchange policies. But in fact it is not possible to overlook the effect of such a set of financial controls on the balance of payments and on the distribution of the national product between current consumption and capital development for future use. We must in fact think of a set of three targets – the total of domestically produced money incomes, the balance of payments with the rest of the world and the ratio of capital investment to current consumption – as being controlled by three sets of financial instruments – fiscal policy, monetary policy and exchange-rate policy.

Accordingly in this chapter we discuss the nature of the three financial targets, in Chapter IV the nature of the three weapons of financial control and in Chapter V the way in which the use of the weapons might best be designed for the successful achievement of the three financial targets.

2.   The Money Income Target: Coverage

We start with a discussion of the choice of the most appropriate money income target to represent the total of money incomes generated by the production of goods and services in the UK. Table III.1 illustrates the nature of the choice.

Items 1, 2 and 3 of the table together constitute the 'net domestic

Table III.1

1. Wages and salaries ⎫	⎧ received in respect of the production
2. Income of self-employed ⎬ . . .	⎨ of goods and services in the UK,
3. Net profits and rents ⎭	⎪ and before deduction of direct
	⎩ taxes on such income

4. Net domestic product at factor cost
5. *Add* depreciation allowances

6. Gross domestic product at factor cost
7. *Add* indirect taxes less subsidies

8. Gross domestic product at market prices
9. *Add* net income received from operations overseas

10. Gross national product at market prices

product at factor cost' (item 4). This represents the sum of the earned and unearned incomes (wages, salaries, profits and rents) received from employment in the UK of real resources of labour, capital goods, land and natural resources for the production of goods and services for sale for final use (1) by the government, (2) by persons or businesses in the UK for consumption or to add to their capital equipment, or (3) by foreigners. There are, however, two important respects in which item 4 under-estimates the amount that the final buyers of the goods and services produced in the UK will in fact have spent on those products.

Consider, first, a producer who is buying some new machinery to install in his business. This producer will deduct from his own gross profit (which he receives from the sale of his product, whatever it may be) a depreciation allowance to cover the reduction in the value of his old machinery. If item 3 of the table includes only his net profit, the total shown in item 4 will cover only the part of the total output of new capital goods that remains after deduction of the amount needed to make good the depreciation in value of existing fixed capital equipment. If it is desired to cover the sales value of all newly produced fixed capital goods instead of only the excess of that value over the fall in value of existing fixed capital goods, then item 5 ('depreciation allowances') must be added. This gives in item 6 what is called the 'gross domestic product at factor cost'.

Item 7 then shows the second major addition that must be made if one wishes to cover the total amount spent by the purchasers of the products covered in item 6. Items 1, 2 and 3 represent incomes received by the producers of goods and services before the deduction of any direct taxes payable by them to the government; but these items do not include any indirect taxes paid by the purchasers of the goods and services from the production of which these incomes were received. Thus the payment of VAT or of the excise duty on tobacco is included in the amount spent by the purchaser of the goods concerned but is not included in the incomes received by the producer and seller of the goods. Conversely, if the government pays a subsidy on the production and sale of a good, the amount received in income by the producers will exceed the amount spent by the purchaser. Thus item 7, the excess of indirect taxes over subsidies, must be added to item 6 to obtain the 'market price' charged to purchasers as contrasted with the 'factor cost' of the producers; this is called the 'gross domestic product at market prices' (item 8).

Item 8 relates to the value of goods and services produced by the real resources employed in the UK. But some UK citizens may own resources (whether labour, capital or land) that are employed abroad and the incomes received from abroad in respect of these resources do represent part of the national income; conversely, some of the real resources employed in the UK may be owned by foreigners and the income earned on these resources does not form part of the national income. To obtain the value of the product of the *nationally* owned instead of the *domestically* employed factors one must add to item 8 the net excess of income from UK resources employed abroad over income earned on foreign-owned resources employed in the UK; this is called the 'gross national product at market prices' (item 10).

Which of the items in Table III.1 would one like to choose as representing the value of the products of labour that one would aim through demand-management policies to keep in a steady growth path? The idea behind New Keynesianism is to keep on a steady growth path the total sales value of the domestically produced goods and services from which wages and other contractual incomes are derived, so that the fixing of wage and other contracts will not be subject to wild inflationary or deflationary influences. Indeed, it is hoped that wage-fixing for the promotion of employment will be aided if it is known that the flow of funds from which contractual earnings can be financed may be relied upon to grow at a steady rate, neither more nor less rapidly than, say, 5 per cent per annum. Such contractual incomes are in respect of resources used domestically, which suggests that item 9 of Table III.1 should be excluded.

Wage contracts are in respect of incomes, which are, of course, exclusive of any indirect taxes levied on the products of the labour concerned but inclusive of any direct taxes to which the wage earner may be liable. This suggests that item 7 of Table III.1 should also be deducted. It is the factor-cost rather than the market-price value of output that constitutes the fund from which contractual wages can be financed. If it is the factor-cost product that is stabilised, both direct and indirect taxation can be used as an instrument for demand-management control at any given level of contractual wage earnings. A rise in direct taxation means that people have a smaller tax-free spendable income to spend on products at unchanged market prices; a rise in indirect taxation means that people have unchanged spendable incomes that will serve to purchase less goods because of the rise in their market price.

There is little or no difference between the suitability of items 4 and 6 as objectives for demand-management control. Depreciation allowances depend upon the loss of value of existing fixed capital goods and represent fairly conventional assessments that are not subject to great variation from year to year. For the purposes of ensuring a steady growth of the factor-cost value of domestic production, item 5 makes no significant difference. The present volume is written on the assumption that it is item 6 of Table III.1 (namely, the money value of the gross domestic product at factor cost) that has been chosen as the money income target. In what follows we refer to this term simply as the Money GDP.

It is important to consider the implications of outside shocks on the economic system if the Money GDP is chosen as the target for the control of domestically produced incomes. We will consider two such shocks: first, an increase in the price of imported goods; and, second, a domestic shift in the relative importance of different economic activities. Both of these shocks are in fact dramatically illustrated by recent developments in connection with the supply of oil.

A rise in the price of imported goods (whether raw materials, such as imported oil, or finished goods, such as imported cars) will cause a rise in the price level and the cost of living. A dramatic example was the fourfold increase in the price of oil occasioned by the OPEC decisions of the first half of the 1970s. Such a development can best be treated as a regrettable but unavoidable reduction in output per head of the goods needed for domestic consumption, since it means that each unit of goods produced at home for export will exchange for a smaller amount of the imports needed for home consumption. A reduction in output per head of the goods needed for consumption, whether that reduction be due to reduced output per head of domestically produced goods or due to a reduced amount of imports obtainable from each unit of domestically produced exports, must be accompanied by a reduction in real wage income per head below what it could otherwise have been, except in so far as there is a sufficient erosion of profit margins to concentrate the whole of the reduction on to non-wage incomes.

Any needed reduction in the real wage could most easily take the form of a higher cost of living, due to the rise in the price of imports, without requiring any reductions in the money wage rate. For this reason a shock to the economy due to a rise in import prices does not make the choice of the Money GDP unsuitable for the money income target. This would be true even if we were to choose the gross domestic product at market price (item 8 of Table III.1) rather than at factor cost (item 6) for the target. The gross domestic product at market price is simply the sum of all money incomes generated in domestic industry (item 4), plus depreciation allowances (item 5), plus indirect taxes (item 7), and this sum is not directly affected by a rise in import prices, the term 'market price' referring only to the price of the domestic product. A shock to the economy from a rise in import prices would, therefore, not imply any need for an offsetting deflation of domestic money wages and other domestic money costs and incomes, if the gross domestic product (whether at factor cost or market price) were chosen as the target for control of domestically produced money incomes. But it would imply that money wage rates and other domestic money incomes should not be raised to offset the rise in the cost of living due to the import content of the cost of goods for consumption; and in Section 3 of Chapter II of Volume 1 we have examined the inflationary effects of a failure of money wage restraint in such circumstances.

Paradoxically, the choice of the Money GDP as the target for control of domestically produced money incomes could give rise to trouble by requiring a deflation and reduction of *money* wage incomes, if the shock to the economy took the form of the discovery and exploitation of domestically produced North Sea oil (which should raise the *real* standard of living in the UK) rather than a rise in the OPEC price of imported oil before the exploitation of North Sea oil (which would inevitably reduce the *real* standard of living in the UK). The production of North Sea oil is the opposite of a labour-intensive activity; it produces a large rise in profits, royalties and direct tax revenue with little cost in wages. When (after deduction of proper depletion allowances) all this net income is added to the Money GDP, it represents an appreciable shift of the shares of the Money GDP from wage income to non-wage income; and if the total is stabilised, wage income must be reduced. It is true that the increased government revenue could be used to reduce other taxation; and to this extent post-tax wage incomes could be restored (if direct taxes on wages were reduced) or the cost of living could be reduced (if VAT or other indirect taxes were lowered). But in both cases the need for a reduction in money wage rates as set by contractual wage bargaining would remain.

This suggests that there would be a case for raising the Money GDP target by the amount of the income from North Sea oil to offset the shock or, what comes to the same thing, to exclude from the Money GDP for income-control purposes all activities, such as North Sea oil, that were exceptionally capital intensive or lacking in labour content. The extreme form of this latter proposal would be to abandon the Money GDP as the target for the control of domestically produced money incomes and to replace it simply with total wage earnings.

If this were done, it would be necessary to decide whether or not the income of the self-employed (item 2 of Table III.1) as well as the total of wages and salaries (item 1) should be included in the target. The income of the self-employed in fact includes much that must be regarded as a profit made on capital rather than as earnings on labour; but it would be impossible to divide item 2 between items 1 and 3 of the table. Moreover, the incomes of the self-employed, even in so far as they represent a recompense for their labour, are not contractual incomes set by collective bargaining with employers; they are simply the residue which is left to them from the sale of their products after meeting their costs. If, therefore, the object is to stabilise the total fund from which contractual wage and salary incomes can be financed, it would be more suitable to confine the target to item 1 of the table. In any case, item 1 is in fact so large relative to item 2 that the choice between item 1 alone or items 1 and 2 combined is not a very important one.

The choice of the total wage and salary bill (item 1 of Table III.1) as the target for the control of domestically produced money incomes would have important advantages. It would remove the danger of shocks due to shifts in the shares of earned incomes and of incomes from property in the total, although disturbance might occur if there were in the future any dramatic movement of workers as between employed work and self-employment. It might serve as the best accompaniment for any reform of wage-fixing institutions designed to promote employment; if, for example, it were known that the total wage and salary bill were going to rise by, say, 5 per cent, it would be clear that any group that obtained a rise in pay greater than 5 per cent would mean either that some other group must receive a smaller rise in pay or else that employment would be reduced. On the other hand, the choice of a target that set a financial restraint on total wage incomes without setting any similar restraint on profits, while it would avoid disturbances due to shifts between profits and wages of the kind examined in the case of North Sea oil, would presumably present greater political difficulty for its acceptance, unless it were accompanied by strong alternative measures for the restraint of profit margins, such as are enumerated in Section 8 of Chapter I of Volume 1.

We have in the technical analysis and the exercises that follow in later parts of this volume confined ourselves to an examination of the case in which the Money GDP is the target for control of domestically produced money incomes. It would be interesting to supplement the analysis and exercises by taking the total wage and salary bill as an alternative target; this is but one of the many ways in which the present study could usefully be extended.

3. The Money Income Target: Rate versus Path of Growth

There remains a very important question about the meaning of keeping the chosen target, whether it be the Money GDP or the total wage and salary bill, on its growth path. Suppose that the choice is to preserve a 5 per cent per annum growth for the Money GDP. Does this mean that the controllers should map out for future years a growth path that shows for each future year what the Money GDP would be at each future date if it grew each year by precisely 5 per cent, and that they should continually take steps to bring the Money GDP back on to this growth path if it should at any time stray from it? Or does it mean simply that each year the controllers should aim at ensuring that over the coming year the Money GDP should grow by 5 per cent, no more and no less, from whatever value it may currently happen to have? If there were never any failure to ensure a 5 per cent growth from one year to the next, this latter interpretation of the control would give the same result as the former; the Money GDP would in fact move on its predetermined growth path.

But the economy is inevitably subject to unforeseen shocks, which will affect the Money GDP, however efficient the controllers may be. In this case the two interpretations of the control target differ widely in their implications. This is illustrated in Figure III.1. The solid line in Figure III.1(a) shows what would happen to the level of the Money GDP if, starting at 100 in year 1, it grew each year by precisely 5 per cent; and the

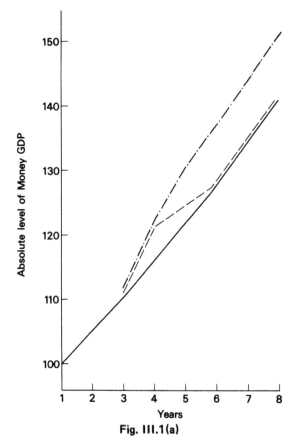

Fig. III.1(a)

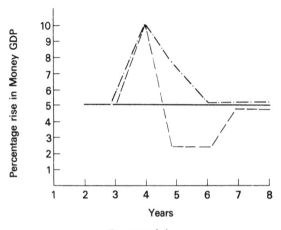

Fig. III.1(b)

solid line in Figure III.1(b) shows simply this constant 5 per cent growth rate. We suppose that between years 2 and 3 the Money GDP suffers an unexpected inflationary shock and grows by 10 per cent instead of 5 per cent; this path is shown by the dashed and the crossed lines between years 3 and 4 in the figure. The dashed lines show what will happen to the Money GDP and its growth rate if the controllers are successful in bringing the target back on to its predetermined solid-line growth path within two years. The crossed lines thereafter show what will happen to the Money GDP and its growth path if the controllers take action merely to bring the rate of growth back within two years to its predetermined 5 per cent level.

The control problem is clearly immensely more difficult in the former than in the latter case. The former course involves slashing the rate of growth from 10 per cent to 2.5 per cent at year 4, holding it to this depressed level for a second year, and only then allowing the rate of growth to recover to 5 per cent. The latter course involves cutting the rate of growth only from 10 per cent to 7.5 per cent at year 4 and then to 5 per cent for the next and all subsequent years.

Which interpretation of the target mechanism should one adopt? The former and more austere interpretation has two advantages over the latter, more relaxed interpretation. In the first place, it is better calculated to deter the authorities from giving in to the temptation of adopting an easy financial policy in order to cope with a particular politically difficult situation, knowing that it is likely to lead to an excessive growth in the Money GDP but persuading themselves that this is a once-for-all slippage that will not make their future problems any more difficult. Such a situation could lead to a gradual discrediting of the whole control mechanism, whereas a knowledge that today's slackness would call for a double dose of austerity tomorrow could have a sobering political effect.

In the second place, an important purpose of inflation control is to provide the background for the formation of firm and well-founded expectations about what is likely to happen to the value of money, so that money contracts can be made without uncertainty about their real implications. To realise that the Money GDP will over the years move on the predetermined solid line of Figure III.1 rather than on some dotted line, the level of which cannot be known in advance, provides a much more reliable base for the formation of expectations about the real implications of money contracts.

These dangers might be largely met if it were possible to ensure that the controllers would always take the most effective measures that they could to ensure a 5 per cent growth in the Money GDP. As a result, in so far as the outside shocks to the system are as likely to be deflationary as inflationary, the future would be as likely to show errors that produced rates of growth below 5 per cent as it would be to lead to rates of growth above 5 per cent; and in this case much of the uncertainty about the future value of money might be removed.* We do not discuss in this volume any of the political, institutional or constitutional arrangements whereby the control of the rate of growth of the Money GDP might be removed from day-to-day political influences — as the price of gold was removed from such influences during the maintenance of the fixed-parity gold standard. If, however, it could be done, the stabilisation of the rate of growth rather than of the level of the Money GDP might be preferred on the grounds of the greater simplicity of its operation.

In the analysis and exercises that follow, we have taken the more austere and difficult target, namely the level of the Money GDP as illustrated by the dashed lines in Figure III.1. There can be no doubt that the control problems that we discuss later would be much simplified if we had taken as the target the rate of growth of the Money GDP as illustrated by the dotted lines of Figure III.1. It would be of great interest if our analysis and exercises were to be reworked on this alternative interpretation of the target.

4. The Money Income Target: Choice of Growth Rate

There remains the choice of level for the planned rate of growth of the domestically produced money income. Should it be 10 per cent, 5 per cent or 1 per cent per annum? And should it necessarily remain the same from year to year?

A high rate of growth of domestically produced money incomes implies

---

*But if the shocks to the system were more often inflationary than deflationary, one would see growth rates above 5 per cent more often than not, so that there would be a gradual and unpredictable upward drift.

a high rate of inflation of money prices. The first question to be considered is, therefore, whether there is any advantage to be gained from bringing the rate of price inflation down from a high (say 10 per cent) level to a low (say 4 per cent) level. Suppose that in each case the rate of inflation were constant and were correctly and certainly anticipated. Many of the familiar costs of inflation would disappear because they in fact depend on the rate of inflation being variable, uncertain and incorrectly anticipated. If everyone is confident that the price level will rise at 10 per cent and if these expectations are always perfectly realised, it is possible to make arrangements that avoid most of the undesirable effects of inflation on economic injustices and inefficiencies. Many contracts can be made that allow for the inflation of money prices; thus a money wage contract could be set so that the money payment went up automatically by 10 per cent each year; and the rate of interest at which money was lent could be raised by an extra 10 per cent to allow for the fall in the real value of the capital sum. Tax arrangements could be made that allowed for the changes in the real value of capital assets and that automatically raised personal tax allowances by 10 per cent a year. Similarly social benefits, pensions, and so on could be automatically raised each year.

Nevertheless there would remain certain costs due to the high rate of inflation. In the first place, the adjustments of money prices could involve extra book-keeping and extra calculations to be made for the application of indexing of the various kinds discussed above, and in some cases these could be considerable. In the modern developed economy, most prices are set and kept unchanged for a time, providing information and convenience for buyers and sellers. In such cases, there is always some cost involved in changing the price tags, in adjusting the issue of postage stamps to new rates, in adjusting the mechanisms of slot machines and the automatic recording of charges at petrol pumps, in changing computer programs, in altering the prices marked on goods in a retail store, and in issuing new and up-to-date catalogues and price lists. Prices cannot be changed every minute; but the higher the rate of inflation the more frequently they must be changed or the greater will be the inefficiencies and injustices that arise from infrequent but very large and sudden jumps in price.

In the second place, with a high rate of inflation there is some loss involved in holding cash since it will constantly be losing its real value. But it is inevitable that some cash should be held for the finance of transactions that cannot be covered by other means. There would be an incentive to hold as little of one's wealth in the form of cash, and such an economising in the holding of cash balances could lead to inconvenience, if the rate of inflation was very high. During the hyperinflations in Germany and Austria after the First World War, wage earners on the receipt of their pay literally ran to the shops to buy goods before prices went up still further.

The costs of an inflation that is constant and is correctly and certainly anticipated need not be very great unless the rate of inflation is very high indeed. But the case is very different when the rate of inflation is variable and not correctly or certainly anticipated. The problem can no longer be met simply by making money contracts that allow for the future reduction in the real value of money. Since that reduction is not known, there will be a very real uncertainty attached to money contracts, which will in itself impose a cost on business. There will result a number of injustices and inefficiencies owing to contracts that are based on a wrong anticipation of future inflation rates. Business plans will go wrong. Pensioners and those who have lent or borrowed money will find that the distribution of income and wealth depends upon the luck of the draw in the guessing game about future inflation.

Some of these costs can be mitigated by processes of indexing. Thus a contract can be made in terms of money, subject to that amount of money being adjusted from time to time according to an index of whatever has in fact turned out to have been the rate of price inflation since the signing of the contract. But it is not possible to avoid all inflationary losses by indexation. There is always inevitably some time lag involved in indexation. It takes some time both for the statisticians to collect the necessary information about individual price changes and to construct the relevant price index and also for the users of the price index to apply it to the particular money payment involved, particularly in those cases in which, for the reasons given above, there are real costs involved in making frequent changes in money price tags. The indexed price is never quite up to date and thus there is necessarily an uncorrected element of inefficiency and injustice that will be the greater, the more variable, the more uncertain and the higher the inflation rate.

Such an inflationary situation may be inevitable whenever conditions are such that economic agents are attempting to obtain incompatible real results out of the economy. In such circumstances expectations are bound to be disappointed and in a monetary economy this may well take the form of an explosive inflation of prices, in which the inflation rate will always exceed the expected rate. In such conditions indexation may only help to stoke up the flames of inflation.

To take the simplest possible case, suppose there to be only two goods, A and B, with prices set at P_{at} and P_{bt} for period t. If each good has an equal weight in the general price index we can express the general price level as $P_t = P_{at} + P_{bt}$. Suppose that the sellers of A wish to set the price of A at a level that commands a real income of α in terms of general purchasing power so that they set a price $P_{at} = \alpha \hat{P}_t$ where $\hat{P}_t$ is what they expect the general price level to be during period t. Suppose they expect the general level of prices to rise at the rate at which it rose in the last period, then

$$\hat{P}_t = P_{t-1} \frac{P_{t-1}}{P_{t-2}} \; ;$$

that is to say, the expected price level $\hat{P}_t$ is equal to the general level of prices in the last period (P_{t-1}) multiplied by 1 plus the rate of price inflation in the previous period P_{t-1}/P_{t-2}. We then have

$$P_{at} = \alpha P_{t-1} \frac{P_{t-1}}{P_{t-2}}$$

and similarly

$$P_{bt} = \beta P_{t-1} \frac{P_{t-1}}{P_{t-2}},$$

where β is the real purchasing power that the sellers of β aim at achieving from their selling price P_{bt}. With $P_t = P_{at} + P_{bt}$, we have

$$\frac{P_t}{P_{t-1}} = (\alpha + \beta) \frac{P_{t-1}}{P_{t-2}}$$

so that if $\alpha + \beta > 1$, the inflation will be explosive and will increase indefinitely from period to period. In fact the intentions of the sellers of A and B are incompatible since they are together trying to obtain more in real purchasing power than they are together producing in real supplies.

Indexing by the sellers of A and B in these circumstances may make the inflationary explosion more certain and more rapid than it would otherwise have been. The rate of such an explosive inflation is bound sooner or later to reach the hyperinflationary heights at which the mere costs of high inflation become intolerable quite apart from the inefficiencies and injustices owing to the fact that the rate of inflation cannot in these circumstances be correctly anticipated.

We may summarise by saying: that while there are real costs in having a higher rather than a lower rate of inflation, these costs are not intolerable provided that the inflation rate is not excessively high and, above all, provided that it is constant and capable of being correctly and certainly anticipated; but that there are very serious costs involved in an inflationary situation where the rate is incapable of correct and certain anticipation and in particular where excess demands on resources may lead to an explosive inflation.

This leaves unanswered the question whether it may not be desirable in some circumstances to attempt to reduce the uncertainty about the future rates of inflation so that they can be anticipated more correctly without necessarily holding the future planned rates at a constant level. Should the announced target rate of growth of domestically produced money incomes necessarily be the same from one year to the next?

This question is particularly relevant if one is starting from a markedly stagflationary position of heavy unemployment combined with a high rate of inflation and is planning a transition to a more satisfactory state of

Table III.2

Years	Unemployment percentage	Growth rates (% p.a.) of money									
		Domestic product	Wage rate	Domestic product	Wage rate	Domestic product	Wage rate	Domestic product	Wage rate	Domestic product	Wage rate
		1		2		*Along transitional paths* 3		4		5	
0	12	10	10	10	10	10	10	10	10	10	10
1	10	7½	5½	9	7	11	9	10	8	12	10
2	8	5	3	8	6	10	8	10	8	12	10
3	6	5	3	7	5	9	7	10	8	12	10
4	4	5	3	6	4	8	6	10	8	12	10
5	4	5	5	5	5	5	5	10	10	10	10
6	4	5	5	5	5	5	5	10	10	10	10
.	.	.	.	.	.	.	.	.	.	.	.
.	.	.	.	.	.	.	.	.	.	.	.
.	.	.	.	.	.	.	.	.	.	.	.

affairs. Table III.2 is devised to illustrate the implications of different choices for such a transitional period.

We assume that we start from a position in which the total of domestically produced money incomes is rising at 10 per cent a year and in which the unemployment percentage is constant at 12 per cent. All the various transitional paths shown in the table are based on the assumption that the unemployment percentage is to be reduced by 2 percentage points in each of the next four years (i.e. by 8 percentage points) until it reaches 4 per cent in the fourth year. The various transitional paths then show how the rate of rise of the money wage rate would have to behave in order to allow for the 2 per cent rise in employment in each year, given the planned path for the rate of growth of the total domestically produced money incomes.

There is a very simple numerical relationship between the rates of inflation of the total of domestically produced money incomes and of the money wage rate. If total wage earnings make up a constant proportion of domestically produced income, then the rate of inflation of the money wage rate will be equal to the rate of inflation of the total of domestically produced money incomes in all the years when the volume of employment is constant (i.e. in years 0, 5 and 6 in the table). But, in order to allow for an (approximately) 2 per cent rise in the volume of employment in each of the years 1, 2, 3 and 4, the rate of rise of the money wage per head must be (approximately) 2 percentage points lower than the rate of rise of the total of domestically produced money incomes and so of the total of money earnings available to be distributed among an (approximately) 2 per cent larger labour force.

Transitional path 1 shows how very sharply the rise of the wage rate would have to be constrained to allow not only for an 8 per cent growth of employment over the first four years, but also for a rapid reduction over the first two years of the target rate of growth of the total of domestically produced money incomes from a 10 per cent to a steady 5 per cent level.

Transitional path 2 shows how the restraint on wage increases would be mitigated if the transition from a 10 per cent to a 5 per cent target rate of growth of total of domestically produced money incomes were spread over five years instead of two.

Transitional path 3 shows what would have to happen to the target rates of growth of the domestically produced money income to enable the necessary reduction in the rate of inflation of the wage rate to be spread evenly over five years, while at the same time the unemployment percentage was brought down from 12 per cent to 4 per cent over 4 years. The interesting feature of this path is that the target rate of growth of the domestically produced money income would have to be raised initially in order to help to absorb the unemployed.

Transitional paths 4 and 5 illustrate cases in which there is no attempt to bring the inflation down from the high 10 per cent rate to the low 5 per cent rate, but only an attempt by appropriate wage restraint to achieve the low level of unemployment without an inflationary explosion. In path 4 the target rate of inflation of the domestically produced money income is kept constant at its initial 10 per cent level and wage restraint takes the form of reducing wage inflation temporarily for four years from 10 per cent to 8 per cent to absorb the unemployed. In path 5 wage restraint takes the even more modest form of requiring workers to accept the same constant rate of wage inflation of 10 per cent in spite of the improved employment situation, the whole adjustment taking the form of raising the target for domestically produced money income by 2 percentage points temporarily for the first four years.

The transitional paths shown in Table III.2 are, of course, greatly simplified accounts of a single basic relationship between reducing the rates of inflation and the rates of unemployment, starting from a serious stagflationary situation. Which type of path should in fact be chosen would depend essentially upon the political background at the time the effort was made and in particular upon what type and degree of reform of wage-fixing arrangements could be achieved. It is not perhaps very useful to go further than to point out the underlying numerical implications of the different types of transitional strategy.

5. The Balance of Payments Target

We turn next to a discussion of what is meant by a balance of payments target.

A country's balance of payments on current account measures the excess of the value of the country's exports of goods and services to foreigners over the value of its imports of goods and services from foreigners. A surplus on the balance of payments on current account so defined is the same as the country's foreign investment in the sense that it measures the net amount of the country's exports that are being used to build up the country's net holding of foreign assets abroad rather than to pay for the import of additional goods and services. In what follows, therefore, we shall talk of a country's total investment as being the sum of its domestic investment (i.e. the value of the addition to its real capital equipment at home) plus its foreign investment (i.e. the value of the increase in its overseas assets, which is necessarily equal to its balance of payments on current account). The country's total investment thus measures the value of the amount of its current output of real goods and services that it is using to build up capital resources for future use at home and abroad rather than for current use and consumption.

The balance of payments on current account, being the excess of what foreigners are spending on the country's products over that part of the country's total expenditure which it is devoting to the purchase of foreign rather than of domestic products, thus also measures one element of net additional expenditure on the country's products, the total of which it is the object of demand-management policies to keep on a moderate, steady growth path. An increase in foreign investment (i.e. in balance of payments on current account), just like an increase in domestic investment (i.e. an increase in the domestic expenditure on new machinery, etc.), represents an increase in money expenditures on the products of domestic industry.*

We cannot, however, simply define the balance of payments target as being the absence of a deficit or of a surplus on the balance of payments on current account. A country that is relatively rich in capital resources

---

*The above analysis is not strictly accurate because the balance of payments on current account includes not only the excess of the country's exports of domestically produced goods and services over its imports of foreign products but also the excess of any net income received from operations overseas (item 9 of Table III.1). The balance of payments on current account does accurately measure the amount of the *national* product (item 10 of Table III.1) that is devoted to foreign investment; but it is the balance of payments on current account less net income received from operations abroad that represents the relevant net addition to the value of the *domestic* product (item 8 of Table III.1). In what follows we neglect to make this distinction. To do so would much complicate the exposition without adding anything of substance.

may quite naturally be investing part of its current income abroad in countries that are poor in capital resources and in which, therefore, the yield on capital is relatively high. The overall balance of payments may be said to be in equilibrium when the balance of payments on current account is just sufficient to provide the foreign funds needed to finance any net outflow of private capital funds for investment abroad. The balance of payments is thus in deficit when the balance of payments on current account is less than the net outflow of funds on private capital account; and any such deficit must be met by official funds from the foreign-exchange reserves of the central bank or the government or by some form of official borrowing of foreign funds undertaken for the purpose of financing the deficit.

We may summarise the argument so far by means of the formulae:

Foreign investment = Balance of payments on current account
= Outflow of private capital funds − loss of official foreign-exchange reserves.

and

Balance of payments deficit = Loss of official foreign-exchange reserves
= Outflow of private capital funds − the balance of payments on current account.

A country's balance of payments on current account will be determined by such factors as the country's level of money incomes, money prices and money costs relative to foreign money incomes, money prices and money costs, adjusted for the foreign-exchange rate. The international flow of capital funds will be determined by other factors such as the expected yields on different forms of assets at home and abroad, the yields being determined among other things by the rates of interest at home and abroad and by expected changes in the foreign-exchange rates, which will affect the future value in home currency of assets denominated in terms of foreign currencies. The problem of maintaining equilibrium in a country's balance of payments is the problem of matching a country's balance of payments on current account (which is determined by one set of factors) with the international flow of capital funds (which is determined by another set of factors).

6.   The Investment Ratio Target

Consider an economy in which the targets that we have discussed so far have all been successfully achieved: (1) there is full employment; (2) the total of domestically produced money incomes is on its planned growth path; and (3) the international flow of capital funds matches the balance of payments on current account. But suppose that this happy state of affairs has been achieved in conditions that result in a very low level of domestic investment (i.e. of expenditures on new capital development at home) and of foreign investment (i.e. of the net foreign demand for our products), these low investment expenditures being offset by high expenditures on private or governmental consumption of goods and services for current enjoyment. In other words, suppose that the total of domestically produced money income is at the correct planned level but is being distributed between investment to provide for future growth (whether at home or abroad) and the current consumption of national resources (whether by the government or by individuals) in a way that gives too little weight to the future and too great a weight to the present in the use of resources. It would be desirable to take measures to shift expenditures from consumption to investment. We will call the desired ratio of investment expenditures to current consumption the investment ratio target.

There is a close relationship between this investment target and the level of the public sector borrowing requirement (PSBR) that is appropriate to match it. Since the PSBR has in recent years been itself treated as an important economic 'target', it may be useful at this point to consider this interconnection.

In order to do so it is necessary to anticipate the conclusions of the discussion on the relationship between 'targets' and 'control weapons' in Chapter V. We shall argue there that the appropriate controls to use to stimulate investment would be a depreciation of the foreign-exchange rate (to stimulate foreign investment by shifting demands from foreign on to domestic products) and a reduction of the interest rate (to stimulate domestic investment in new capital equipment). To prevent these increased investment demands from inflating domestically produced money incomes above their planned growth path, current consumption expenditures must be reduced. In Chapter V we shall argue that the appropriate 'control weapons' for this purpose would be fiscal, taking the form either of a reduction in the government's own current expenditures on goods and services or of a rise in tax rates to reduce demands for goods and services by personal consumers. In either case, as investment was raised to its target level, the public sector borrowing requirement would be reduced as government tax revenues rose and/or government current expenditures fell. At any given level of the total of domestically produced money incomes, a rise in investment would be accompanied by a fall in the public sector borrowing requirement.

On this analysis it is the rise in investment rather than the fall in the PSBR that is the real target. Many monetarists have recently treated the PSBR as if it were itself a target for control; they have been concerned about the danger that a need for a high level of governmental borrowing might compel the banking system to extend credit of one kind or another to the government (by the purchase of government stock of one kind or another); that this would create new money; and that this in turn would stoke up the inflation of money costs and prices. This worry is, however, totally irrelevant if the combination of the *four* weapons of wage-fixing, fiscal policy, interest-rate policy and foreign-exchange policy have been so devised as to achieve the *three* targets of full employment, balance of payments and control of domestically produced money incomes. There can then be no general inflationary threat from whatever turns out in these conditions to be the appropriate level of governmental borrowings; but it may be that, within the non-inflationary total of money expenditures, investment expenditures are too low and consumption expenditures too high.

That is, however, not quite the whole of the truth. We have argued so far that the level of investment is the target and that the level of the public sector borrowing requirement is simply a consequence of taking action to achieve the investment target. But there could be circumstances in which it would be nearer the truth to say that the PSBR was the target and that the choice of level of investment was the means whereby that target was achieved.

The size of the total national debt (i.e. of the sum of all past net borrowings by the government) is in itself a matter of some economic importance quite apart from the question whether or not an otherwise desirable balance between national consumption and national investment is being maintained. An example may help to explain the point. Suppose that the individuals in society are in a particularly miserly frame of mind and are saving an excessively large proportion of their incomes. The government may consider that investment of national resources for future use on a scale needed to mop up all these savings would be excessive. There might in these conditions result a large budget deficit that represented a borrowing by the government of the excess private savings and the use of these savings by the government for current consumption purposes, either in the form of government expenditures for current social consumptions or of payments of social benefits to those individuals who would be likely to spend them on current personal consumption. The national debt would grow without any growth in real income-bearing assets to match it. The individual holders of the national debt would become wealthier and wealthier as their savings accumulated; and such an accumulation of individual wealth would naturally reduce both incentives to save (which in the circumstances might be desirable) but also incentives to work and enterprise (which would be altogether undesirable). A millionaire may cease to work and plan to live on his capital even though there are no real income-bearing assets lying behind his millions. In brief, a high ratio of deadweight national debt to true national income may be a source of serious economic disincentives.

A growth of the money national debt that merely keeps up with the growth of the money national income, whether that growth be due to growth of real output or to an inflation of prices, will not cause any extra burden of this kind. Nor will a growth of the national debt that is incurred in order to finance real income-bearing capital assets in the public sector cause any undesirable incentive effects of the kind described above; the wealth indirectly owned by the individual owners of the debt is producing real income from which the individual citizens are in fact enjoying a real advantage in one form or another.

Moreover, any problems arising from the mere size of the national debt must in any case be regarded as a long-term structural matter. A rapid but temporary accumulation of national debt due to the fiscal implications of offsetting a temporary cyclical slump in private investment or in net exports is not, of course, an occasion for concern. What would matter is a more permanent underlying trend for the ratio of deadweight national debt to grow excessively in relation to the national income.

What would constitute an excessively high ratio of national debt to national income and what would constitute a desirable ratio between investment and consumption? These questions raise important problems concerning long-term growth and economic incentives that it is not the purpose of this volume to discuss. We must proceed simply on the assumption that there is some desirable level for investment that takes into account both the desirability of storing resources up for future use rather than consuming them for present use and also any consequential effects on the size of the national debt and so on incentives. We assume that as a result we have a planned structural ratio of investment to consumption that we wish to attain over the years. This we call the investment ratio target.

7.   Short-Term and Long-Term Targets

We have now defined what we mean by the three targets for money income, balance of payments and investment ratio. There remains an important distinction to be drawn between these targets, one that will play a basic role in our subsequent analysis. This distinction and its relevance can best be understood by comparing the money income target with the investment ratio.

It is essential for the success of a New Keynesian policy that any serious divergence of total money expenditure from its target growth should be promptly corrected. An incipient moderate inflationary movement of the total level of money expenditures, by raising spendable incomes and by leading to expectations of further inflation, can, given the dynamic positive feedback relationships in a modern economy, result in an important multiplied inflationary movement. Resulting large cyclical inflations and deflations would play havoc with the wage-fixing arrangements and with full employment in a New Keynesian set-up. Because of these rather rapid dynamic vicious spirals of inflation and deflation it is of great importance that divergences from the target for total money expenditures should be promptly nipped in the bud by rapid and effective financial policies of counter-inflation or counter-deflation. In this sense we may say that the money income target is a short-period target, since it is important to correct errors quickly in as short a period as possible.

The investment ratio target, on the other hand, may be regarded as something that can be treated rather as a longer-period structural desideratum. This does not mean that it is necessarily unimportant. What it does mean is that one should not be greatly concerned if the correction of a divergence from the target is achieved somewhat slowly by structural adjustment over a period of time. The basic reason for the distinction is that in the case of the money income target an error that is relatively unimportant in itself may well rapidly multiply itself into a very substantial and important error unless it is rapidly corrected, whereas an investment ratio error carries no such threat of rapid multiplication.

The balance of payments target lies somewhere between the other two targets. Its mere existence does not carry with it a threat of rapid dynamic multiplication. But a balance of payments deficit means that the authorities, the central bank or the government have got to find the necessary foreign-exchange funds to finance the deficit. Their foreign-exchange reserves may be limited and there may well be political or other constraints on the amount of official borrowing of foreign exchange that they are able and willing to undertake. In other words, it may be necessary to adjust a balance of payments deficit fairly rapidly.

We shall return later to this distinction between errors from targets that must be rapidly corrected and those that can be left to slower, structural correction; in the analysis of Chapter V this difference between what we shall call short-term and long-term targets will be found to play a decisively important role.

CHAPTER IV

Three Financial Weapons: Fiscal, Monetary and Foreign-Exchange Measures

1. Four Types of Time Lag

Financial measures can be divided into the three broad groups of fiscal, monetary and foreign-exchange measures. Each of these categories raises a host of important questions about their operation and their effects, and no attempt can be made in one brief chapter to cover all the issues involved. All that is attempted is a summary account of the probable importance and speed of operation of each of the main categories of financial controls in their effects on each of the three financial targets for money income, balance of payments and investment ratio.

One of the most important questions about the various financial instruments of control is the speed with which each control can be made to operate on each of the three targets. There are four important lags to be considered:

(1) What we may call the *recognition lag* is the time that it takes for the authorities to realise that there is a divergence of the actual from the desired level of any one of the targets.

(2) What we may call the *decision lag* is the time that elapses between the authorities' knowledge of a divergence between the actual and the desired level of any one of the targets and the formulation by the authorities of the appropriate corrective action to be taken.

(3) What we may call the *adjustment lag* is the time that elapses between the decision to vary one of the instruments of control and the actual variation of that control.

(4) What we may call the *effect lag* is the time that elapses between the variation of the instrument of control and its actual effect on any one of the targets.

The recognition lag is common to all the instruments of control, though it will vary for the different targets since the time it will take to assemble the relevant statistical information will vary between domestically produced money incomes, the balance of payments and expenditures on capital investment. Nor can the recognition lag for any one of the targets be regarded as a single, simple, fixed period. Rough estimates may be available fairly quickly but then be liable to subsequent revisions as more and more information becomes available. The more reliable the statistical data, the more confident and bolder can be the action taken by the controllers. Thus the problem is to choose the best combination of delay before 'recognising' the need for action and of appropriate degree of boldness for the control action then to be taken. This raises an important statistical and control problem for the technical design of policy rules but one with which we have been unable to deal systematically. To do so would have required a major investigation into measurement errors.

A first requisite for effective controls is thus to ensure as prompt and reliable a set of statistics as possible. In the Note to Chapter VII some of the issues involved are discussed in connection with the money income target, i.e. in connection with the figures for the Money GDP or for the total wages and salary bill. But we do not in this volume go at all deeply into this very important aspect of the matter, which deserves much further consideration.

The decision lag is common to all the instruments and all the targets. It raises administrative and political problems that we do not discuss at all. But it is of the greatest importance that institutional arrangements should be devised that enable decisions on these matters to be taken promptly. The administrative, political and constitutional issues involved deserve much thought and discussion.

The adjustment lag will raise problems that are specific to each instrument of control and the effect lag raises problems that are specific to each particular combination of instrument and target (e.g. how long will it take for a change in a given rate of tax to have an effect upon the Money GDP?). One of the main purposes of the rest of this chapter will be to provide a brief account of these adjustment and effect lags.

2. Fiscal Measures

For the study of demand-management problems, fiscal arrangements must be considered from two rather different aspects. In the first place, there is the question how far a given set of taxes and public expenditures will have an automatic stabilising or destabilising effect upon the total of money expenditure in the absence of any changes in the existing tax schedules and governmental expenditure programmes. In the second place, there is the question how promptly and how effectively the total of money expenditures can be raised or lowered by changes in the tax schedules and/or governmental expenditure programmes. In this volume we are concerned with both of these questions.

Consider the first of these problems. Suppose the level of total money expenditures on domestically produced goods and services and so the total of domestically earned money incomes goes up for some unspecified reason. Will the existing fiscal arrangements cause this initial inflation of expenditures to be damped down or to be stoked up? Two examples may help to explain the nature of the question. In so far as the increased demand had led to an increase in output and employment, the existence of a structure of generous benefits for the unemployed would help to stabilise the system, since the consumption expenditures of the unemployed would be reduced as the number of unemployed fell, so that the demand for additional goods and services would rise less rapidly than the wages earned by those newly employed in their production. On the other hand, in so far as the initial increase of money expenditures had resulted in increased prices rather than increased output and employment, the existence of an important structure of specific indirect taxes, the rates of which did not automatically rise with the prices of the taxed products, would exercise a destabilising effect, since those whose money incomes had risen as a result of the increased selling prices would be paying a smaller proportion of these incomes in taxes and would have that much more real purchasing power available to spend on goods and services.

Table IV.1 is devised to show these structural effects. We consider in

Table IV.1

	The net stimulating effect of an unchanged fiscal control rises (+), remains the same (0), or falls (—) as a proportion of the gross domestic product at factor cost when there is a uniform proportionate rise in all	
	Factor-cost prices	Quantities
Government expenditures on goods and services:		
Real programme	0	—
Cash programme	—	—
Taxes/subsidies:		
Indirect:		
Specific tax	+	0
Specific subsidy	—	0
Ad valorem tax	0	0
Ad valorem subsidy	0	0
Direct:		
Regressive income tax	+	+
Regressive income subsidy	—	—
Proportionate income tax	0	0
Proportionate income subsidy	0	0
Progressive income tax	—	—
Progressive income subsidy	+	+

column 1 the situation that would arise if all factor-cost prices rose in the same proportion, for example by 10 per cent. The Money GDP would as a result also rise by 10 per cent. We ask of each form of fiscal control whether, if it were maintained at an unchanged level, it would represent a larger (+), or smaller (−) or an unchanged (0) net stimulating effect. In column 2 we ask the same question of each form of control if a 10 per cent rise in the Money GDP were due to a 10 per cent increase in every quantity instead of a 10 per cent rise in every price.

The first item considered in the table is a governmental programme to purchase a given amount of goods or services (e.g. a certain number of units of a particular piece of equipment for the armed forces). If all prices, including the price of the goods purchased by the government, go up by 10 per cent, the government expenditure itself will go up by 10 per cent and will thus represent an unchanged proportionate item in total demand. But if prices remain constant and all real outputs in the economy go up by 10 per cent, the government's purchase will automatically represent a smaller proportionate stimulus to total demand. On the other hand, a governmental programme to spend a given amount of money on a certain type of good or service (the second item in the table) would represent a smaller proportionate stimulus to total demand whether the rise in total demand was due to a general rise in prices or in quantities.

The remaining items in the table represent various categories of tax or subsidy. The first of these is a specific indirect tax, e.g. a tax of a given amount on a pint of beer. If total expenditures go up by 10 per cent because of increases in factor costs with all quantities unchanged, the revenue from the specific tax will represent a smaller proportion of the Money GDP (which we measure at factor cost); the tax will, therefore, be exerting a smaller proportionate damping effect, which we represent in the table as a net increase in a stimulating effect. But if the inflation of the Money GDP had been due to a 10 per cent increase in all quantities, including the quantity of the taxed product, the proportionate effect of the tax on total expenditures would have been unchanged. Conversely, part of the proportionate stimulating effect of a specific subsidy would be lost as a result of price rises but its proportionate effect would remain unchanged as a result of an increase in every output.

A similar analysis can be applied to the other taxes and subsidies covered in the rest of the table. For example, the negative signs against regressive income subsidies (e.g. unindexed social benefits) and progressive income taxes represent the so-called 'fiscal drag' — net tax revenue rises more quickly than the total income tax base, whether the inflation of the tax base is due to price rises or to quantity increases. As a consequence the government would by its net tax revenue be extracting from private spenders a larger proportion of an increased national income, thereby damping the increase down.

These stabilising or destabilising features of the existing tax structure must be built into the dynamic model of the UK economy on the basis of which the examination of the problems of demand management proceeds; they help to determine how stable or unstable the system is that we seek to control by means of changes in tax schedules or in governmental expenditure programmes.

We turn now to the second of the two questions raised above and proceed to consider how prompt and how important will be the effects of the main categories of fiscal control when governmental expenditure programmes or rates of tax are used as regulators and are adjusted upwards or downwards in order to exercise control over one or more of the three macro-economic targets of money income, balance of payments and investment ratio.

Changes in programmes of governmental expenditure on goods and services are likely to be liable to severe adjustment lags and costs. Suppose that a decision had been taken that for control purposes it was desirable to reduce governmental expenditure on goods and services by £x million. Such a decision would involve a revision of defence, educational, industrial or other governmental policies. The revision of the relevant programmes is bound to involve real cost in disturbance of long-term policies and to take time before there can be any actual reduction in expenditure. The adjustment lag is in this case considerable. It is true that the effect lag on the demand-management target is zero, since the actual variation of governmental purchases of goods and services is simultaneously both a change in the control (government expenditure) and also a change in its effect on the target (the level of total expenditures). But on the grounds of the length and cost of the adjustment process governmental programmes of expenditure on goods and services cannot be regarded alone as providing sufficiently flexible and prompt regulators.

Changes in governmental programmes of expenditures on transfer payments, such as pensions, unemployment benefit and other social benefits, are not subject to such long adjustment delays; but, like changes in rates of direct taxation of personal incomes, they may be subject to some effect lags as the recipients take time to adjust their consumption expenditures to their changed spendable incomes. However, such effect delays are likely to be small in so far as the changes affect the poorest members of society; but for this very reason their use as control mechanisms is likely to be subject to special limitations on distributional grounds.

Some changes of tax schedules are subject to considerable adjustment lags and costs. For example, a tax like the existing income tax, liability to which is calculated on an annual basis and whose administration is designed for annual adjustment of the rate of tax, is bound to be subject to considerable adjustment lag and cost. In the case of an indirect tax, on the other hand, the base is not necessarily an annual one but is simply the amount spent on the product in any given period, whatever its length may be; as a result the problems of adjustment will be less formidable. Adjustment problems will, of course, exist in any case, but they can be much reduced if administrative arrangements are specifically designed to make prompt variation of rates as easy as possible. These issues are discussed below in Part Three in the case of the income tax, indirect taxes such as VAT, and payroll charges such as national insurance contributions or a payroll tax. The conclusion of that discussion is that the adjustment lags and costs could be reduced to very acceptable levels in the case of certain indirect taxes and payroll charges, so that they might be used as reasonably prompt regulators, and that the same could be true of the income tax if the cumulative principle of tax deduction under the present PAYE arrangements were abandoned.

The question remains whether, after adjustment, direct and indirect taxes would be quick and important in their effects on the money income, balance of payments and investment-ratio targets.

A distinction must be drawn between the effects of changes in direct and indirect taxes upon the level of money expenditures and so upon domestically produced money incomes. Properly used, changes in indirect taxes are likely to be more effective for this purpose than are changes in direct taxes. A cut in income tax that is expected to be only temporary will probably stimulate savings rather than expenditure; a cut in an indirect tax, and so a reduction in the price of the goods concerned, that is expected to be only temporary is likely to stimulate expenditure rather than savings. But against this advantage of indirect taxation must be set the danger that, unless the tax changes are in fact made promptly and without hesitation on the part of the authority concerned, they might lead to destabilising speculation on the part of consumers. Thus if consumers observe that total demand is in fact exceeding its target level they may expect the controllers to be about to raise the rates of indirect tax in order to damp down the level of demand. Consumers may, in such circumstances, increase their purchases in a speculative attempt to anticipate the rise in indirect taxation and in the price level, thus stimulating still further the excess expenditure on goods and services − a development that would need to be nipped in the bud by a prompt upward adjustment of the tax rates. Provided that the authorities are prepared to act without hesitation, it should be possible to devise tax-regulator arrangements that would in fact have a prompt and important effect in helping to keep the total money demand for goods and services on its target path.

The effect of these fiscal regulators on the balance of payments target will in general be complementary to their effect on the money income target. A reduction of tax that increases the consumers' total demand for goods and services is likely to increase their demand for domestic products (thus raising the Money GDP) and for imported products (thus reducing the balance of payments on current account and exerting a negative effect on the overall balance of payments). Particular taxes may have other distinctive effects on the balance of payments. Thus a tax that was levied exclusively on imported products and not at all on domestically produced products would be likely to induce a shift away from imported on to domestic products, with a resulting positive effect on the balance of payments. In the exercises carried out in the latter parts of this volume we confine our attention to tax regulators that do not have any such discriminatory effects as between domestic and foreign transactions. The significant effect of an expansionary change in a tax regulator may, therefore, be expected to be a prompt and important increase in the Money GDP and a prompt and important negative effect on the balance of payments, the relative magnitudes of the two effects depending upon the ratio of domestic products to imported products in the types of general expenditures that are stimulated by the tax reduction.

In so far as reductions in tax rates or increases in social benefits cause increases in personal consumption, they will result in a reduction of the ratio of investment to consumption. Moreover, they will inevitably increase the budget deficit, which (for the reasons given in Section 6 of Chapter III) may in itself justify a higher investment ratio target. For both these reasons we may conclude that reductions in tax rates are likely to lower the actual investment ratio relatively to its target level.

The general conclusions to be drawn from this very cursory examination of the fiscal weapons may be summarised in the following way. It should be possible to devise tax regulators that could have prompt and important effects on total money expenditures. This would mean that an expansionary use of such regulators (i.e. a reduction in the relevant tax rates) would lead to (1) a prompt and important increase in the Money GDP, (2) a prompt and important negative effect on the balance of payments, and (3) some reduction of the actual investment ratio relative to the investment ratio target — and vice versa in the case of an increase in the relevant tax rates.

3.   Monetary Measures

We turn next to a consideration of financial control exercised through monetary measures.

It is possible to draw a distinction between monetary controls that are exercised through control of the *quantity* of money and those that are exercised through control of the rate of interest, i.e. of the *price* charged for acquiring new amounts of money by borrowing from the banking system. This distinction corresponds to the distinction drawn for fiscal instruments in Table IV.1 between a regressive income subsidy (e.g. social security benefits fixed in terms of unindexed cash amounts) and a system of proportionate income taxes or subsidies. If the total money national income goes up, a fiscal control that takes the form of a fixed cash payment of social benefits or a monetary control that takes the form of supplying a fixed stock of money (cash) will represent a smaller proportionate stimulus to the national income. But in these circumstances a fiscal control that operates on a proportionate rate of subsidy to incomes and a monetary control that operates on the rate of interest charged for hiring money rather than on the amount of money available to be hired will exert an unchanged proportionate effect on the total national income.*

We have in this work confined our examination of fiscal controls to proportionate direct taxes on income and to *ad valorem* indirect taxes, which, so long as the rates of tax are unchanged, exert an unchanged proportionate effect on the national income. Similarly in the case of monetary controls, we shall confine our attention to controls over rates of interest that, so long as the rates are unchanged, exert an unchanged proportionate effect on the economy rather than considering controls exercised through the quantity of money. In the case of fiscal controls, our choice is purely arbitrary. In the case of monetary controls, the choice is not at all arbitrary; there are in fact very substantial reasons for it.

The problem can best be explained by considering what one means by 'the amount of money'. Money as a unit of account constitutes a precise unit: the value of anything in the market can be expressed as worth so many pounds sterling. But the quantity of money held as a stock of purchasing power at any one time is an elusive concept that is difficult to define. Strictly speaking one might define the quantity of money simply as the total amount of bank notes and cash in circulation, since payment of a debt by means of these instruments is what is legally sufficient to meet the debtor's obligation. They constitute the economy's 'legal tender'. But there are in fact many other forms of assets that are commonly used to make payments between creditors and debtors; in particular such payments are made by the use of cheques to transfer from debtor to creditor the ownership of a deposit balance with a bank, this deposit in turn being merely a legal liability on the part of the bank to supply notes or cash (legal tender) to the owner of the deposit. But should time deposits (i.e. deposits with banks on terms that require the owner of the deposit to give, say, seven days' notice before he is free to make use of the deposit — a requirement that the bank may or may not normally waive) be counted as part of the money stock? If so, should deposits of money with building societies be counted as part of the money stock? Or should the value of Treasury bills, which can be readily sold for a given amount of money, be considered as good as holding other forms of 'money' as a stock of purchasing power that can be used at short notice?

---

*In times of rapid inflation of the general level of prices of all goods and services it is the real rate of interest (i.e. the money rate of interest minus the rate of inflation of the general level of money prices) rather than the money rate of interest that is relevant. This distinction is discussed later in this section.

It is in fact impossible to draw any useful hard and fast line between assets that are to be treated as 'money' and those that are not. There is a whole spectrum of assets with different qualities that make them more or less good substitutes for cash (legal tender). Assets may be said to be more or less liquid according as they are better or worse substitutes for legal tender; and their degree of liquidity may be considered along three dimensions. An asset may be said to be more liquid, (1) the more certain is the money value at which it could at any time be sold or realised, (2) the smaller the cost and disturbance needed to sell the asset for that given value, and (3) the more customary it is for the asset to be accepted as a means of payment for discharge of a debt. A house is thus very illiquid because (1) the owner does not know what it will be worth in a year's time, (2) it will cost a lot of trouble and expense to sell it, and (3) people are not in the habit of accepting houses as a means of payment of household bills. At the other extreme, a current account deposit with one of the main banks is on all three headings very liquid. There is an almost infinite range of intermediate assets, and it is entirely arbitrary where one draws the line in any attempt to define the stock of money precisely.

Suppose, however, that the authorities do draw a precise dividing line. Suppose, for example, that they define the total of notes, coin and current account deposits with the clearing banks as 'money' and all other assets as 'non-money'. To regard this quantity as a significant control for demand-management purposes could lead to ridiculous results. There have been periods, for example, when those who are in charge of choosing investments for the very large sums accumulated by pension funds, insurance funds and similar institutions have chosen to 'go liquid' because they have expected the prices of stock exchange securities and government bonds to fall in the future. During such a period the government has had to borrow by selling its securities to the banks, which have financed these purchases by means of the moneys that the pension fund managers have accumulated and kept in the form of additional deposits with the banks. When the pension fund managers have changed their minds and have decided to reduce the liquidity of their funds by investing their bank deposits in government securities, the banks have sold government securities to them in return for cancelling the deposit liabilities of the banks to the pension funds. While the pension funds went liquid, the amount of so called 'money' increased greatly because of the increased deposit liabilities of the banks; when the pension funds invested in less liquid assets, the amount of 'money' decreased greatly. It would be ridiculous to argue (although some observers have done so) that there was a great threat of demand-management inflation when the pension funds went liquid, a threat that was removed when they invested in less liquid assets. All that had happened was that the central bank (with its control over the banking system) and the government (with its control over the forms of national debt by which it will finance its borrowings) had issued liquid assets ('money') when the pension funds chose to go liquid and less liquid assets ('non-money') when the pension funds chose less liquid investments.

If the authorities had decided at all costs to maintain constant what it had arbitrarily decided to define as the stock of money, there would have been great fluctuations in the money values of government securities, which would have been greatly destabilising from the demand-management point of view. As long as the pension fund managers refused to invest in government securities, the government would have had to sell its securities at very greatly reduced prices (i.e. at a much higher rate of interest) in order to tempt the pension fund managers or other investors to change their minds and to invest after all in government securities; and this sharp rise in interest rates might have had an undesirable restrictive effect on borrowing by private enterprise for business expenditures of one kind or another. It would in fact be a most undesirable form of monetary control to cause restrictions or stimulations to actual business expenditure simply because property owners were choosing assets of a more or a less liquid nature and thus were causing meaningless variations in the demand for a particular class of assets that by a quite arbitrary definition did or did not fall into the category of 'money'.

What the monetary authorities (i.e. the government with its control over the forms taken by the national debt and the central bank with adequate controls over the rest of the banking system) can do, and do very wisely, within wide limits is to set and control certain rates of interest. The banking system can clearly set rates of interest at which it will lend on given security to private customers. As far as government securities are concerned, the banking system together with the government can act as a giant 'buffer stock' in government securities, being willing to sell a given security to all comers in return for cash or bank deposits at a certain selling price or to buy it from all sellers at that same or a slightly lower buying price. It can set prices of this kind for a wide variety of government securities ranging from three months Treasury bills to irredeemable 2.5 per cent consols. The fact that it is possible to operate controls over rates of interest in this way does not, of course, imply that it does not matter what rates are chosen; on the contrary, as will be argued later, it is most important on other grounds to choose sensible rates. But it is sensible to choose the rates on those other grounds and then by fixing the rates at these chosen levels to allow the various owners of assets to choose the liquidity mix that pleases them rather than to depart from rates that are sensible on those other grounds simply in order to induce the public to hold a liquidity mix of assets that for some reason or another the authorities consider to be 'proper' or 'respectable'.

It is the money rates of interest on various types of government security that the authorities can control in this manner; but the money rate of interest must be distinguished from the real rate of interest. Suppose that all money prices are rising at 10 per cent per annum and that the money rate of interest to be earned on a government security is 12 per cent per annum; then the real rate of interest is (approximately) 2 per cent per annum. Thus a person who invested £100 in the security could obtain £112 at the end of the year in capital plus interest; but since the price of a commodity that cost £1.00 at the beginning of the year will cost £1.10 at the end of the year, the number of goods that he could purchase will have risen only from 100 to 112/1.1, i.e. from 100 to 101.8i8 or by approximately 2 per cent. In periods of rapid inflation wise lenders and borrowers of money will make their calculations in terms of what they expect the real rates of interest to be, i.e. in terms of the money rate of interest less the expected rate of inflation of the general level of prices. The monetary authorities can control only the money rates of interest, but they can set these monetary rates at levels that are intended to represent what they consider to be an appropriate real rate of interest by adding to the desired real rate an amount to allow for what they judge to be the generally expected rate of price inflation.

It remains to consider how promptly and how greatly changes in the rates of interest as set by the monetary authorities can affect the three macro-economic targets of money income, the balance of payments, and the investment ratio. Changes in interest rates can be made very promptly and very frequently by the monetary authorities, who have merely to change the prices at which they will deal in the various government securities or to announce a change in the rates at which they will lend or borrow. Thus what we have called the adjustment lag is very short for monetary controls. But the effect lags, i.e. the speeds at which a change in interest rates will affect the various targets, vary very considerably between one target and another. We will accordingly consider the probable effects on each of the three targets of a reduction of the money rate of interest and so, at any given level of expected price inflation, of the real rate of interest.

A reduction of the interest rate is likely to exert some stimulating effect on the borrowing of monetary funds to spend on the purchase of durable capital goods or durable consumption goods of a kind that are not liable to great risks. Thus an instrument of production that is likely to produce without great risk a real yield of, say, 5 per cent per annum will enjoy a net profit if the real rate of interest at which funds can be borrowed for its purchase is below 5 per cent and a net loss if the real rate of interest is above 5 per cent. A reduction of the rate of interest is likely in this way to stimulate the total demand for capital goods. But the effect lag would probably be a lengthy one, since the investment of funds in new additional capital goods is likely to involve a fairly prolonged process of formulation of new plans and programmes for capital development before any actual expenditure takes place.

A reduction of the rate of interest may also affect the amount that people decide to save out of their incomes. But this effect is not likely to be as marked as the effect on investment in additional durable capital goods; and in any case it is uncertain whether the effect would be to induce people to save less (i.e. to spend more on consumption goods) because the yield on their savings is reduced and is therefore less attractive or to save more because they now have to save more in order to obtain any given future income on their savings.

One may conclude that a reduction in the interest rate is likely to cause an appreciable, but delayed increase in the total level of expenditures on goods and services.

Any such delayed stimulus to the total level of expenditures on goods and services is likely to cause some complementary delayed effect on the balance of payments, since part of the increased expenditures is likely to take the form of an increased demand for imports. But there is another much more important and much more prompt effect of a reduction in interest rates in causing a negative movement in the balance of payments on capital account, if the reduction occurs in the country in question without any similar reduction in other countries.

A reduction in a country's domestic interest rate may be expected to cause a large, but temporary outflow of funds as fund holders at home and abroad adjust their existing portfolio holdings in favour of the foreign countries whose interest rates have not been reduced. Once this portfolio adjustment had taken place, the large shift of funds would cease; it would, however, be followed by a permanent but smaller outflow of funds as the continued new savings of fund holders at home and abroad were attracted in the newly adjusted proportions to the foreign countries whose interest rates had not been reduced. Thus, if a country's domestic interest rate is gradually reduced, the gradual change in existing portfolios will cause a continuing outflow of funds; when the reduction ceases to take place and a lower rate has been established, there will result a continuing increased outflow of funds financed from current savings. One may conclude that a reduction of the interest rate will have a prompt and important negative effect on the balance of payments some of which will persist indefinitely.

As we have already argued, a reduction in interest rates is likely to have an appreciable though somewhat delayed effect in stimulating expenditures on capital goods. This will also raise the investment ratio.

In this discussion of the effect of the interest rate on each of the three macro-economic targets we have spoken as if there were only one interest rate, which we have called *the* interest rate. But, as we have already made clear, there is a whole range of interest rates that depend upon the length of life of the security in question, varying from the short-term rate on Treasury bills to the long-term rate on irredeemable consols. These different rates may have different degrees of influence on the three different targets. Thus plans for investment in new long-lasting capital goods are more likely to be influenced by long-term than by short-term interest rates. On the other hand, hot money is likely to flow rapidly from one country to another according to differences in short-term interest rates. Within certain limits the monetary authorities can decide to influence one rate rather than another by purchase of the type of security whose rate of yield they wish to lower rather than the type of security whose yield they wish to maintain. In this way they can attempt to modify the relative interest-rate effects on each of the three targets.

Subject to this modification we may conclude that a reduction in interest rates is likely to have (1) a delayed stimulating effect on money income, (2) an immediate and pronounced negative effect on the balance of payments, and (3) a delayed stimulating effect on the investment ratio.

4.   Variations in the Foreign-Exchange Rate

The third weapon we have to consider is the foreign-exchange rate. The authorities can influence this rate by either of two different mechanisms.

First, the authorities can peg the foreign-exchange rate by offering to buy or sell foreign currencies at a fixed rate in terms of the domestic currency, setting probably a somewhat higher price in domestic currency for their sales of foreign currency to, than for their purchases of foreign currency from, the rest of the market. This is to operate a 'buffer stock' in foreign currencies just as we have seen in Section 3, the price of government securities and so their rates of yield can be pegged by operation of a 'buffer stock' in such securities. There is no obvious limit to the purchase at a fixed price of foreign currencies by the authorities since domestic funds can always be issued by the authorities for that purpose. But the sale of foreign currencies at a fixed price is, of course, subject to any limit set by the availability of foreign currencies to the authorities for the finance of such sales. The authorities must rely for this purpose either on their own ownership of reserves of foreign currencies or else on some form of official direct or indirect borrowing of such currencies from the monetary authorities of the foreign countries. We may call this the use of 'official finance' for the pegging of the exchange rate.

Second, the authorities can leave the price of foreign currencies in domestic currency to find its own level by the free competitive forces of supply and demand in the foreign-exchange markets, refraining themselves from any purchases or sales of foreign currencies. Even with this system of freely floating exchange rates the authorities can still influence the rate of exchange by taking measures that influence the private demand for, or supply of, foreign currencies. Our analysis in this volume is based upon the assumption that the authorities do not take any direct measures to control foreign capital movements or imports or exports. But there remains one very important influence that cannot be neglected. By changing domestic rates of interest in the way described in Section 3 of this chapter, the authorities can greatly affect the incentives to shift more or less capital funds between domestic and foreign investments. The rate of interest, and in particular the short-term rate of interest, can be regarded as a very important means of affecting the foreign-exchange rate in a regime of freely floating exchange rates.

The relative attractiveness to private capital funds of yields in the domestic and foreign capital markets depends not only upon the relationship between the rates of interest in the two markets but also upon expectations of changes in the rate of foreign exchange between the currencies concerned. Thus suppose that the rate of interest abroad is 10 per cent per annum but that the domestic currency is expected to depreciate in terms of the foreign currency by 2 per cent per annum. An investment of £100 for a year abroad will yield approximately 12 per cent in terms of sterling, since the capital fund and the 10 per cent interest on it will at the end of the year exchange for a 2 per cent greater number of pounds than they would have done at the old exchange rate. Thus the level at which the domestic interest rate must be set in order to affect the flow of private funds must take into account the expectations of changes in the exchange rate as well as the actual level of the foreign interest rates.

Both of the two methods discussed above for controlling the foreign-exchange rate involve very short adjustment lags. If the first method is chosen, the adjustment lag is negligible since all that is required is that the authorities change the buffer stock prices at which they offer to buy or sell foreign currencies. Such rates can be varied daily or even hourly. If the second method is adopted, the adjustment lag is again likely to be short. As we have seen in Section 3 of this chapter, the adjustment lag in changing the rate of interest can be very short and the effect of a change in the short-term interest rate on the demand for foreign currencies is likely to be prompt.

In the rest of our analysis we assume that the former of these two methods has been adopted. This means that the authorities at any one time offer to buy or sell foreign currency at stated prices, the price at which they will sell foreign currency for sterling being somewhat higher than the price at which they will buy foreign currency with sterling. These buying and selling prices would be subject to change from time to time; and we discuss in the following chapter the principles upon which such revisions of the exchange rate might be made.

If it were decided to maintain the exchange rates at their stated level, the authorities would have to be prepared to lose or to gain reserves of foreign currencies in so far as the market demand for foreign exchange exceeded or fell short of the market supply. They would then have to decide whether simply to rely on the use of official reserves of foreign exchange to stabilise the exchange rate or whether to adjust domestic interest rates in order to adjust the international flow of capital funds in such a way as to put a stop to the loss or gain of official reserves of foreign exchange. We discuss in the next chapter the principles on which this choice might best be made.

We have already considered the effect of a changing rate of foreign exchange, or more accurately the effect of an expectation of a change in the rate of foreign exchange, on the flow of funds between one currency and another, and thus either upon the balance of payments (if the authorities meet the flow out of official finance) or upon the rate of foreign exchange itself (if the exchange rates are allowed to float freely). It remains to consider the magnitude and the speed of the effects of a higher or lower exchange rate (as contrasted with those of a rising or falling exchange rate) upon the three macro-economic targets.

For this purpose we must distinguish between two possible sets of condition in which the change in the foreign-exchange rate takes place. First, suppose that all prices are rising at an inflation rate of 5 per cent per annum abroad but at a rate of 8 per cent per annum in the home country. A depreciation of the home currency by 3 per cent over the year will leave the real terms of trade between the home country's products and the foreign country's products unchanged.* The exchange-rate variation will have had no real effect; it will simply offset the monetary effects of a difference in the rates of inflation of money prices. Second, it is possible that the rates of general price inflation do not differ in the two countries. In this case, a depreciation of the pound by increasing the number of pounds needed to purchase a given amount of foreign currency would raise the price of foreign goods relative to the price of domestic products both at home and abroad.

The ultimate effect of an exchange-rate variation that alters the real terms of trade is likely to be very substantial; but its effect is likely to be much delayed and indeed is likely at first to be in a perverse direction. Suppose the pound is depreciated by 10 per cent. This makes foreign products 10 per cent more expensive relatively to domestic products. Ultimately this is likely to induce purchasers at home and abroad to shift their purchases on a considerable scale from foreign products on to domestic products, at least in the case of the trade of countries whose products compete with each other. But it may well take some considerable

*If the lower inflation rate in the foreign country is due not simply to a lower rate of growth of its money national income but to a higher rate of growth of its productivity and of its output per head, there will be real effects operating not through a change in relative prices but through a change in relative real incomes. The foreign country will have a higher real income relative to the home country; for this reason, even if relative prices are kept constant by a 3 per cent depreciation of the home currency, the foreign country may purchase more imports from the home country as well as more of its own products thereby exercising a positive effect on the home country's balance of payments. In any case it will, of course, also be true that with a 3 per cent higher rate of inflation in the home country the money rate of interest will have to be 3 per cent higher in order to result in a real rate of interest that corresponds to that which is ruling in the foreign country; this difference will be reflected in the rate of depreciation of the home currency in terms of the foreign currency.

time before traders change their plans and their orders and before, therefore, the flows of trade are much altered.

If the flows of trade are not immediately altered, the depreciation of the pound by 10 per cent will leave the sterling value of exports unchanged but will raise the sterling price of imports by 10 per cent, since 10 per cent more pounds are needed to purchase a given foreign currency value of imports. There will be a corresponding negative effect upon the country's balance of payments on current account. But as purchasers at home and abroad shift their purchases from foreign on to domestic suppliers, the value in sterling of the country's exports will rise and of its imports will fall. Ultimately it is likely that this substitution of domestic for foreign products will go far enough not merely to offset the initial deterioration in the balance of payments but to cause a substantial and lasting improvement in it.

These effects on the balance of payments on current account may carry with them some corresponding indirect effects on the Money GDP unless they are offset by other measures. Thus the initial necessity to meet a higher sterling expenditure on imports may mean that domestic purchasers have less income available to spend on domestic products with some immediate deflation of the Money GDP. When purchasers at home and abroad have shifted their purchases on to sterling products, there will ultimately be some tendency for the Money GDP to be inflated.

To summarise, variations in the rate of foreign exchange can be achieved with little or no adjustment lag. The effect of a depreciation of the currency that merely offsets a difference in the rates of price inflation at home and abroad will be negligible in real terms. But in so far as a depreciation of the currency does alter the real terms of trade it is likely ultimately to have an important, direct positive effect upon the balance of payments and incidentally thereby some indirect positive effects upon the Money GDP. All these effects are likely to be considerably delayed and the immediate effects are indeed likely to be perverse and in the opposite directions from the ultimate effects.

CHAPTER V

The Marriage of Weapons and Targets

1. Introduction

In Chapter II we gave reasons for preferring a New Keynesian strategy (i.e. the use of the wage rate to promote employment and the use of financial measures to control the total level of money incomes) to a Cross-Linked Keynesian strategy (i.e. the joint use of wage-rate and financial policy to obtain the best joint outcome of employment and control of inflation). But within the framework of this New Keynesian strategy we have now broken down the weapons of financial policy into the three components of tax rate, interest rate and foreign-exchange rate to cope with the three targets of money income, balance of payments, and investment ratio. The question thus arises whether each one of these three weapons should be separately linked to one and only one of these three targets or whether within this restricted field of financial policies one should adopt the Cross-Linked solution and seek for the best combined use of the three weapons that will achieve the best combined outcome for the three targets.

Discussion of this problem will be postponed until the end of this chapter. We shall start the discussion of the issues that arise in the use of the three weapons on the assumption that, for one reason or another, it is necessary to aim each weapon separately at one and only one target. We do this simply because it appears to be the best way to describe and to analyse the basic problems that underlie any attempts to achieve simultaneous success with all three *desiderata* – control of money incomes, of the balance of payments and of the investment ratio.

(i) *Prompt Adjustment of Money Income and of the Balance of Payments*

We start then with the question: If one was required to link each weapon with one and only one target, which weapon would one choose to link with which target? The answer to this question would depend very largely upon the force and the speed with which each weapon might be expected to operate on each target and upon the speed with which it was desired to correct any divergence from any one target. Commonsense suggests that if one puts great stress on the need to keep one particular variable promptly on target, one should try to control that variable with a weapon that affects it both promptly and forcibly, whereas one can be resigned to

Table V.1

Weapons	Targets		
	Money Income	Balance of Payments	Investment Ratio
	(1) *Desired speed of correction of any divergence from target:*		
	Prompt	Prompt in case of scarcity of foreign-exchange reserves	No pressing need for prompt correction
	(2) *Speed and extent of effect of each weapon on each target:*		
Tax rate	Quick and large	Quick and large	Quick and large
Interest rate	Slow and moderate	Quick and large	Slow and moderate
Foreign-exchange rate	Perverse at first then slow and large	Perverse at first then slow and large	Perverse at first then slow and large

using a weapon that acts less promptly for the control of a variable that one does not require to keep on target so promptly. For this purpose we summarise in Part 1 of Table V.1 the conclusions that we reached in Chapter III about the desirability of prompt adjustment of each target variable and in Part 2 of the table the conclusions that we reached in Chapter IV about the extent and the speed with which each weapon might be expected to affect each target variable.

A cursory examination of Table V.1 suggests that the tax rate should be used for control of domestically produced money incomes because this is a target that one desires to correct promptly and the tax rate is the only instrument with a prompt and large effect on that target. This leaves the interest rate to be used for a prompt control of the balance of payments[*] (which may need prompt adjustment in the absence of abundant foreign-exchange reserves) and the foreign-exchange rate to exert a slow structural adjustment of the investment ratio (a target that we do not require to be adjusted very promptly). The use of tax policy as a prompt regulator of domestically produced money incomes and of the short-term interest rate as a prompt regulator of the international flow of capital funds and so of the balance of payments need occasion no great surprise; but the linking of the foreign-exchange rate to the control of the investment ratio calls for some further analysis and explanation.

(ii)   *Structural Adjustment of the Investment Ratio*

The proposition is perhaps best understood by considering a particular example. Consider a country which has a successful wage policy that is

[*]See Mundell (1962).

maintaining full employment, against the background of a successful tax policy that is keeping total money expenditures and so the total of domestically produced money incomes on a steady growth path, together with a successful interest-rate policy that is matching the international flow of capital funds to the current account balance of payments. But suppose that conditions are such that this has resulted in an undesirably low investment ratio. A depreciation of the foreign-exchange rate may, as we have seen in Section 4 of Chapter IV, have perverse effects in the short run and we shall return to this later. The long-run effect of the increased competitiveness of domestic products will, however, be to increase the country's exports and reduce its imports. The resulting improvement in its balance of payments on current account represents an increase in foreign investment; it will also call for a reduction in interest rates since less capital funds need be attracted to the country to match its current account balance of payments. The reduction in interest rates will eventually help to stimulate domestic expenditures on capital development. Thus foreign investment (i.e. the balance of payments on current account) and domestic investment (i.e. the level of domestic expenditures on capital development) will both be raised. But this inflationary effect on domestically produced money incomes will have to be offset by a rise in tax rates with a consequential reduction of the public sector borrowing requirement and of personal consumption.

Thus the ultimate structural effect of a structural change in the foreign-exchange rate, if the other rules of the game are observed, will be to raise the investment ratio by raising both domestic and foreign investment and reducing consumption expenditures. In the final equilibrium so reached, full employment will be maintained; inflation will be controlled; the total resources applied to capital accumulation rather than to consumption will be at the desired level; and the distribution of investment between domestic and foreign investment will be decided by the yields on each form of investment.

2.   A First Draft of the Rules of the Game

The rules of the game can thus be summarised as: use (1) the wage rate to promote employment, (2) the rate of tax for prompt adjustment of domestically produced money incomes, (3) the rate of interest for prompt matching of international capital flows to the balance of payments on current account, and (4) adjustment of the foreign-exchange rate to achieve long-run structural change in the investment ratio. One must, however, add a number of important comments on, and qualifications of, these simple rules. This we do under four main headings.

(i) *Small Countries Specialising in Production for Export*

The analysis is relevant only for the reasonably large industrialised free-enterprise economies in which domestic production for the domestic market is a reasonably large element in total economic activity. It is not relevant for the small country that concentrates most of its domestic production on exports and satisfies its domestic consumption primarily from imports. In the case of such a country it would not be appropriate to use the tax rate to control the total level of expenditure on domestic products, since an increase in disposable income due to a tax reduction would be spent mainly on imports and its main effect would thus be on the balance of payments. Control over expenditure on its domestic products could be effectively achieved only by influencing the foreigners' demands for its exports through, for example, the longer-run effects of a variation in its foreign-exchange rate. In such a case the proposed allocation of weapons to targets would need modification. But in this book we are concerned with the problems of the United Kingdom, where domestic production for domestic use is sufficiently great to meet the requirements of the proposed rules.

(ii) *Two Aspects of Foreign-Exchange-Rate Policy*

In describing the operation of the rules of the game as outlined above, we spoke of a change in the foreign-exchange rate as if it always involved a change in the relative prices of domestic and foreign products. But this is not the case; an adjustment of the foreign-exchange rate will be necessary in order to prevent a change in the relative prices of domestic and foreign products if the general level of money prices is rising at a different rate at home than the rate of general price inflation abroad. With a New Keynesian policy, the money-price level of the country's products will be the outcome of the rate of change in the country's output per head and in the money wage rate resulting, at full employment, from the rate of growth that has been set for the total money demand for labour or for the products of labour. There is no *a priori* reason to believe that the country's money-price and cost levels will be moving exactly in line with those in the rest of the world. The structural adjustment that may be needed to control the country's balance of payments on current account and so its foreign investment is not in fact an adjustment of the exchange rate itself. What is needed is an adjustment of the country's domestic price and cost levels relative to those of the outside world after conversion at the current rate of exchange or, in other words, an adjustment of the real terms of trade between the country's own products and the competing products of the rest of the world.

This suggests that exchange-rate policy should be considered at two levels. First, the day-to-day adjustment of the foreign-exchange rate through an official exchange equalisation fund might be conducted in such a way as to keep constant an index of the price or cost of the country's tradeable products relative to the price or cost of the competing tradeable products of the rest of the world. We may call such an index a competitiveness index since it measures the ability of home products to compete in price or cost with similar foreign products. Continuous adjustment of the foreign-exchange rate so as to keep such an index constant would serve to offset divergences that would otherwise have resulted simply and solely from divergences in the different national rates of money-price and cost inflation.* Secondly, there should from time to time be further exchange-rate adjustments in order to effect structural changes in the competitiveness index of the relative prices or costs of domestic and foreign competing tradeable products, the competitiveness of domestic products being increased by such a structural depreciation of the exchange rate if greater domestic and foreign investment was needed in order to raise the country's investment ratio and to relieve an undesirable accompanying budget deficit.

(iii)   *The Reasons Against a Reversal of Roles for the Rates of Interest and of Foreign Exchange*

The rules of the game proposed above suggest that the rate of interest should be used to maintain equilibrium in the balance of payments and

---

*A better short-term arrangement might be to adjust the exchange rate so as to keep constant the ratio of the money wage of a unit of domestic labour to that of foreign labour. If price mark-ups on labour costs remained unchanged, this arrangement also would maintain a constant degree of competitiveness between home and foreign products so long as rates of increase of productivity were the same at home and abroad. But suppose that foreign prices were rising less rapidly than domestic prices because output per head was rising more rapidly abroad than at home, while money wages per unit of labour were rising at the same rates. Suppose further that, as suggested in the main text, the domestic currency were then depreciated in order to offset the divergent rates of change of product prices. The result would probably be an appreciable improvement in the home country's balance of trade. Money incomes would be rising faster abroad than at home, while the relative prices of home and foreign products remained unchanged, with the result that the foreign demand for home products would most probably be expanding more rapidly than the home demand for foreign products. To offset this inflation of the home country's foreign investment, a structural appreciation of the home currency would now be needed. Whether this secondary structural appreciation would need to restore the foreign-exchange rate to its original level before the relative increase in foreign productivity would depend upon the income elasticity of demand for imports in the foreign country and upon the elasticity of substitution between domestic and foreign products. If the income elasticity were very high and the elasticity of substitution low, the secondary structural appreciation of the home currency might have to be on a scale that did more than simply reverse the original short-term depreciation needed to equalise the product prices. It may, therefore, be better to adopt the equalisation of the prices of labour rather than that of the products of labour as the short-run starting point and to treat as structural exchange-rate adjustments those subsequent changes that were required to be made from this base.

that the foreign-exchange rate should be used to set in motion those structural changes that are needed to adjust the country's investment ratio and thus incidentally to look after undesirable budget deficits or surpluses. However, a lower rate of interest is the natural price-mechanism instrument for stimulating private domestic investment and the price of foreign currencies in terms of home currency is the natural price-mechanism instrument for equating supply and demand in the foreign-exchange market. Thus it might appear much more natural to reverse the proposed rules and use the interest rate for coping with the investment ratio and the foreign-exchange rate for coping with the balance of payments.

It is important to realise why this reversal of the proposed roles for the rates of interest and of foreign exchange is not acceptable.* Consider once more the situation described in Section 1(ii) which was used to elucidate the operation of the proposed rules of the game. We start with full employment, with the total of domestically produced money incomes on its planned growth path, and with the balance of payments in equilibrium, but with an undesirably low investment ratio. Let us suppose that the authorities react to this situation by reducing the rate of interest in order to promote domestic investment, in spite of the fact that it will discourage the flow of international capital funds and cause a balance of payments deficit. Suppose that it lets the foreign-exchange rate float freely to find its own level at which it will deal with the balance of payments deficit by equating supply and demand in the foreign-exchange market. What will happen?

The resulting depreciation of the currency, which reduces the country's money prices and costs relative to those in the rest of the world, while it will almost certainly in the long run have the desired effect of improving the country's balance of trade, is likely to do so only with considerable delay as trade is gradually diverted into the more profitable channels. Indeed the immediate effect may be perverse. Before the channels of trade are diverted, the rise in the price of imports may cause a temporary deterioration in the balance of trade.

If this happens, the exchange-rate depreciation will be intensified as the temporary worsening of the balance of trade is added to the adverse effect of low domestic interest rates on the international flow of capital funds. In fact this depreciation will have to go so far as to cause fund holders at home and abroad to consider:

(1)   that the exchange rate has become grossly undervalued;
(2)   that the exceedingly favourable rate of exchange will gradually improve the balance of trade;

*The argument that follows is similar but not identical to that put forward by Dornbusch (1976).

(3)   that the expected future improvement in the balance of trade will
       cause an appreciation of the exchange rate from its grossly under-
       valued level;
(4)   that the appreciation of the exchange rate is about to start; and,
(5)   that the rate of appreciation will be sufficiently rapid.

The expected rate of appreciation is, of course, crucial. In comparing
yields on assets at home and abroad it is the rate of interest at home plus
the rate at which the home currency will appreciate in terms of foreign
currency that must be compared with the rate of interest on foreign funds.

The use of the rate of interest for the domestic purpose of controlling
domestic investment regardless of its relationship with interest rates
abroad is in this way liable to cause violent swings in the exchange rate. If
the divergence of interest rates were substantial, if the movement of
foreign funds were sensitive to such divergences, and if the channels of
trade did not respond much and/or responded only slowly to changes in
relative prices, the swings in the exchange rate might have to be on a
totally intolerable scale; indeed extreme circumstances can be imagined in
which the currency would become virtually valueless. But even in much
less extreme cases, the swings would lead to marked temporary changes
in relative prices that would need subsequent reversal. In our example the
sharp depreciation would lead to a marked increase in the cost of living
due to temporary excessive rises in the cost of imports and to misleadingly
high temporary boosts to the country's tradeable products.

Appropriate wage-fixing and informed business planning might be
much easier if the temporary collapse of the exchange rate were avoided.
This would be the virtue of the proposed rules of the game. A moderate
structural depreciation of the exchange rate maintained until its salutary
effect on the balance of trade and so on foreign investment had worked
itself out would avoid the disturbing effect of excessive temporary swings;
and the ultimate improvement in the balance of trade would require a
smaller attraction of international capital funds to cover it, and would
thus allow a reduction in interest rates, which in turn would lead to a
stimulation of domestic as well as of foreign investment.

(iv)   *The Use of Foreign-Exchange Reserves*

But we cannot neglect the problems that would in any case arise if the
proposed rules of the game were applied without modification during the
transitional period while a structural change in the foreign-exchange rate
was in the process of working out its ultimate beneficial effects. Suppose
in the case where an undesirable low investment ratio needs to be raised
the rules were applied without modification. What would happen?

The situation calls for a structural depreciation of the home currency in
order to improve the country's foreign investment (i.e. its balance of

payments on current account), which will reduce the need to attract international capital funds to the country and will thus enable the interest rate to be somewhat reduced, which in turn will encourage domestic investment, which together with the increase in foreign investment will require tax rates to be raised to bring about a matching reduction in private consumption. But during the process of change the depreciation of the exchange rate is likely, as we have seen, to have the perverse effect of causing a negative instead of a positive movement in the country's balance of payments on current account as the price of imports rises and more is spent on imports. Some part of this increased expenditure on imports may be financed out of income that would otherwise have been saved; but for the rest it would have to be met by a reduction in expenditures that would otherwise have been made on domestic products. A strict application of the rules of the game would involve the following adjustments until the time came when this perverse movement was reversed and the ultimate positive effect on the balance of payments on current account began to reveal itself: the rate of interest would have to be raised instead of lowered, which would begin to restrict instead of stimulate domestic investment; the rate of tax would have to be lowered instead of raised and the budget deficit increased instead of decreased in order to stimulate consumption sufficiently to offset any reduction in the demand for home products due to the temporary decline in foreign and domestic investment.

It may well be impossible to avoid some temporary reduction in tax rates and worsening of the budget deficit if the deflationary effect of the temporary decline in foreign investment is to be offset. But the temporary perverse rise in the rate of interest with its perverse restriction of domestic investment would be avoided if the temporary deterioration in the balance of payments on current account were financed by the use of foreign-exchange reserves. One can accordingly properly modify the rules of the game by suggesting that, in so far as the required reserves or other forms of official financing of a balance of payments deficit are available, a temporary balance of payments deficit due to the temporary perverse effects of a structural exchange-rate depreciation should be met not by an increase in the rate of interest, but by the use of foreign-exchange reserves; and, conversely, a temporary balance of payments surplus due to the temporary effects of a structural exchange-rate appreciation should be met not by lowering the rate of interest, but by the accumulation of foreign-exchange reserves.

3.   A Revised Set of Rules of the Game

The rules of the game that were given in Section 2 can, therefore, be revised in the following way: (1) use the wage rate to promote employment; (2) use the rate of tax for the prompt adjustment of total money expenditures; (3) subject to rule (6) below, use the rate of interest for prompt matching of international capital flows to the balance of payments on current account; (4) make day-to-day adjustments in the foreign-exchange rate so as to keep constant a competitiveness index of domestic prices (either of products or of labour inputs) relative to foreign prices; (5) make occasional structural adjustments in this competitiveness index with consequential structural adjustments of the exchange rate in order to achieve a structural change in the investment ratio; and (6) rely as far as possible on the use of foreign-exchange reserves or other sources of official international finance instead of on interest-rate adjustment under (3) to meet the temporary perverse effects on the balance of payments of structural exchange-rate adjustments made under rule (5).

4. International Co-operation in Monetary and Foreign-Exchange Policies

In the preceding sections we have been dealing with a single country, which has adopted a New Keynesian strategy in a large world in which the other countries are operating a miscellany of other policies with their price levels, rates of interest, total levels of demand, etc., all given as an unalterable exogenous variable to the decision-makers in the single country under examination. The question arises whether and, if so, how best the system could be successfully generalised if every country in the free-enterprise world adopted a successful domestic New Keynesian policy, each keeping its own domestically produced money incomes on a predetermined steady growth path by tax policy and maintaining full employment by appropriate adjustments of wage rates. How could the countries concerned best co-operate in monetary and foreign-exchange-rate policies?

It is clear that some co-operative modification of the rules of the game would be called for. The need for this can be clearly seen if we imagine a world in which all countries have full employment, controlled growth of their domestically produced money incomes and equilibrium in the balance of payments, but in which all simultaneously have undesirably low investment ratios with undesirably high budget deficits. Such a state of affairs is in no way impossible; it would mean that, throughout the world, interest rates were too high to allow a sufficient level of private invest-ment, even though the rates of interest of the different countries were in appropriate relationships to each other to attract capital funds to match balances of payments on current account. The unmodified rule book given in Section 3 would require each country to make a structural depreciation of its own currency in terms of every other currency, which is an absurd impossibility.

One way of attempting to depreciate a country's currency is to reduce the domestic interest rate in order to encourage an outflow of capital funds. In so far as all the countries did reduce their interest rates in simultaneous but vain efforts to depreciate their currencies, the result would be entirely favourable, since this would encourage domestic investment in all the countries. But this result could be more sensibly and effectively achieved by direct co-operation in their monetary policies.

Appropriate principles of international monetary and foreign-exchange-rate co-operation can easily be devised. They may be outlined under the following three headings:

(a) *Interest Rates*   Subject to what is said under (c) below, the various rates of interest in the various countries should be kept in a relationship to each other such that their effects on international capital flows maintain equilibrium in the overall balances of payments of the various countries. But when throughout these countries or in the great majority of them there is a need to raise investment ratios, the whole international structure of interest rates should be lowered by co-operative central bank action – and vice versa if all countries are facing undesirably high investment ratios.

(b) *Foreign-Exchange Rates*   The day-to-day adjustment of foreign-exchange rates made in order to keep constant a competitiveness index of a country's prices relative to prices in other countries could be greatly improved and eased by international co-operation, first, in the choice of appropriate consistent indices for the various countries and, second, by the increased supply of official finance, through such bodies as the European Monetary System and the International Monetary Fund, available for the control of exchange rates.

Structural adjustments of the pegs of the competitiveness indices would be made co-operatively, but only when there were some countries that were suffering from excessively low, and others that were suffering from excessively high, investment ratios. The competitiveness pegs would then be altered so as to increase the competitiveness in foreign markets of the low investment-ratio countries and to reduce that of the high investment-ratio countries. The ultimate effect would be to increase the balance of trade and foreign investment of the former group and to reduce the foreign investment of the latter group, and to enable thereby a reduction in interest rates in the former group and a rise in the latter so as to keep the overall balances of payments in equilibrium; the change in interest rates would encourage domestic investment in the former group and discourage it in the latter, so that there would be a growth of total investment in the former group and a reduction in the latter group.

(c) *Foreign-Exchange Reserves and Official Financing of Balances of Payments*   When structural adjustments of foreign-exchange rates and of the competitiveness pegs were made as outlined in (b), there would be temporary perverse effects on the balances of trade, the foreign investment of the depreciating countries being temporarily reduced and that of the appreciating countries temporarily increased. In order to avoid the undesired effects of a temporary perverse rise in interest rates in the former and of a temporary perverse fall in the latter group of countries, it would be desirable that the former group should temporarily lose foreign-exchange reserves and that the latter should gain them. This is *par excellence* an opportunity for advantageous co-operation. Arrangements for temporary official financing should be easy to make in such circumstances: the former group of countries will wish to prevent an excessive temporary depreciation and the latter group will wish to prevent an excessive temporary appreciation of their currencies. These are the underlying circumstances in which in a well-ordered co-operative international system of New Keynesianism reliance on foreign-exchange reserves would be desirable.

5. Cross-Linkage Revisited

In the preceding sections of this chapter we have discussed the problems of financial control on the assumption that each one of the financial policy weapons (tax rate, interest rate and foreign-exchange rate) must be used exclusively to attempt to hit one and only one of the three targets (money income, balance of payments and investment ratio). But the questions arise whether or not this is a desirable principle and whether or not one could not achieve better results by adopting the more sophisticated control-engineering technique of cross-linking the three weapons and targets in such a way that the effect of each weapon on all three targets is taken into account in devising the rules for the use of each weapon.

In Chapter II we discussed the possibility of adopting what we called a Cross-Linked Keynesian strategy under which wage-fixing would take account of the control of inflation as well as the promotion of employment, while demand-management policies would take account of their effect on employment as well as on the control of inflation of money incomes. We argued in favour of what we called the New Keynesian strategy of using the wage rate exclusively for the promotion of employment and demand-management policies exclusively for control of the inflation of money incomes. We reached this conclusion primarily because of the nature of the wage-fixing problem, the solution of which calls for a decentralised system of decision-making on principles that can be readily understood and accepted as natural. In any such system it would be difficult to see how the use of the wage rate to control inflation (requiring a *reduction* in the wage rate because the cost of living had *risen*) could be readily organised or well understood.

The corpus of financial policies — tax rates, interest rates and foreign-exchange rates — can, indeed must, be centralised. There may be some merit of easier public understanding in making each part of the central financial administration responsible for one of the targets — the chancellor of the exchequer in his budget arrangements being responsible for the control of domestically produced money incomes and the governor of the Bank of England in his interest-rate policy for balance of payments equilibrium. But the gain in understanding would be limited, particularly when one takes into account such matters as the use of structural exchange-rate adjustments as an instrument for structural control of the investment ratio and the choice of use of foreign-exchange reserves rather than of interest-rate adjustment to look after the balance of payments during the first perverse effects of a structural exchange-rate adjustment. However much one may make different parts of the central financial machinery of government responsible for one of the targets, understanding of the rules of financial policy is not going to be greatly eased.

There would seem, therefore, to be no decisive advantages of this kind to be derived from linking each financial policy weapon to one and only one target. A single, centralised, sophisticated financial plan that took account of the effect of each weapon on all three of the targets is not to be ruled out. The questions, therefore, remain (1) whether or not the rules for the use of each weapon in such a sophisticated financial plan would in fact differ greatly from those outlined in Section 3 for the case in which each weapon was linked with only one target, and (2) how much would be gained from the adoption of such a sophisticated plan in the form of reduction of the divergences of incomes, balance of payments and investment from their desired target levels.

In any such cross-linking procedure due attention would have to be paid to the differences in the speed with which it is desirable to adjust the different target variables and to the differences in the speed with which each weapon affects each target. Since the direct marriages of each weapon to each target that have been suggested in this chapter have been dictated precisely by these differences of speed of reaction, it is not clear how much would be gained by the more sophisticated procedure. But there would undoubtedly be some gain and it might be substantial; it is a matter that calls for further investigation.*

6. The Procedures Actually Adopted in this Volume

In the preceding sections of this chapter we have described what we consider would be an ideal treatment of the marriage of financial controls and targets. In the rest of this volume we have had to adopt a less

---

*The factors determining the size of this possible gain are discussed in Section 4 of Chapter XII.

sophisticated treatment. In accordance with the ideal treatment, we have investigated the use of taxes as a regulator of the total of domestically produced money incomes (as measured by the Money GDP) leaving – as discussed in Volume 1 – the fixing of money wage rates as the method for promoting employment against this background of a steady rate of growth in the money demand for the products of labour. But we have had to treat the effect of interest-rate policies and foreign-exchange-rate policies on the balance of payments and the investment ratio in a much more rough-and-ready and cursory fashion.

The problem with which we have been confronted is the absence in our model of the UK economy of a satisfactory account of the capital-flow elements in the balance of payments. The ideal treatment discussed earlier in this chapter depends essentially upon the effects of variations in the rate of interest on international capital movements. In the absence of adequate information on this relationship we have had radically to simplify our treatment of the rate of interest and the rate of foreign exchange.

What we have done is as follows. As far as the rate of interest is concerned, we have assumed that the short-term money rate of interest is varied with the rate of price inflation so as to maintain a constant real rate of interest. As far as the rate of foreign exchange is concerned, we have allowed for such automatic adjustments as would be necessary to stabilise an index of the competitiveness of UK products relative to similar foreign products, and have introduced the control rule that this stabilised competitiveness index should itself be adjusted through suitable changes in the exchange rate in such a way as to aim at keeping the balance of payments on current account on a predetermined growth path.

The implications of this treatment are twofold. First, it is implicitly assumed that any difference that may arise between the balance of payments on current account (controlled as explained above through adjustments of a competitiveness index so as to be kept as far as possible on a predetermined growth path) and the flow of international funds (as influenced by a constant real rate of return in the UK) can be met by the use of foreign-exchange reserves or other official financing. Second, the treatment implies that one is not concerned with the long-run investment ratio and its accompanying budget balance that may result from the need to maintain total money expenditures on a target growth path when private domestic investment is influenced by a constant real rate of interest and foreign investment is controlled to move on a predetermined growth path.

The question arises how far this rough-and-ready treatment of the rate of interest and of the foreign-exchange rate detracts from the analysis carried out in the rest of this volume. There is no doubt of the value of the analysis as exercises in the development and application of control-engineering techniques to a dynamic economic model. But how far can these exercises be considered to teach real lessons about the application of a New Keynesian policy to the UK economy? It may, we think, be claimed that they do adequately capture many, if not all, of the problems involved.

The basic issues are (1) how promptly and effectively the use of tax rates as regulators can succeed in keeping the Money GDP on a pre-determined steady growth path, and (2) how great a change in wage-fixing arrangements would be needed in these conditions to maintain a high and stable level of employment. What we have done allows for all the internal dynamic lags and responses in the economy except only for the possible effect of changes in the real rate of interest on domestic investment. It allows also for the interconnections between the effect of demand-management control on the outcome of wage-fixing arrangements and of wage-fixing arrangements on the outcome of demand-management controls.

It would, of course, be absurd – indeed impossible – to deal with these matters in the UK without taking into account the possible repercussions through the balance of payments and the real terms of trade. What happens to the total level of money expenditures in the UK and to the actual price and cost per unit of output will greatly affect the balance of trade through their effects on imports and exports, and this will feed back in an important way on the total demand for UK products. Our simplified treatment does not neglect these factors. Suppose, for example, that there were an unexpected fall in the foreign demand for UK exports. Both the ideal treatment outlined earlier in this chapter and our present rough-and-ready treatment would then require fiscal stimulation of demand through lowered tax rates in order to keep total money demand on its steady growth path. Both treatments would also require a depreciation of the exchange rate to increase UK competitiveness and thus to improve the balance of payments on current account. But they would require the exchange-rate change on different grounds – in the case of the ideal treatment in order to restore the disturbed investment ratio and in our rough-and-ready treatment to restore the balance of payments on current account to its planned target level. The precise levels of the required restoration of the balance of payments on current account may differ in the two cases, but the dynamic problems arising from the initial perverse effects of the change in the exchange rate will occur in both treatments. Indeed, the exercises carried out in later parts of this volume provide many interesting insights into the nature of the difficulties of this kind that occur because of the balance of payments problem.

We would for these reasons claim that the analysis in this volume, in addition to its interest as an exercise in the development of the application of control theory to an actual economic dynamic system, does provide important realistic clues about the feasibility of applying a New Keynesian policy to the UK economy and about the conditions needed for the success of such a policy. But it remains greatly to be desired that further work should be done to integrate an account of the international flow of capital funds into the present dynamic model of the UK economy. It would then be possible to analyse the treatment of the rate of tax, the rate of interest and the rate of foreign exchange on the lines described earlier in this chapter, first, by linking the rate of tax to the control of domestically produced money incomes, the rate of interest and the use of foreign-exchange reserves to the balance of payments, and the exchange rate to the investment ratio (as suggested in Section 3 of this chapter) and, second, by the full Cross-Linked principle of applying each of these three weapons simultaneously to all three targets (as suggested in Section 5 of this chapter).

CHAPTER VI

Discretionary Interventions

The design of financial policies for the control of the system outlined in Section 6 of the preceding chapter involves the formulation of rules for the prompt adjustment of tax rates to keep the total of domestically produced money incomes on a target growth path and for simultaneous adjustment of the foreign-exchange rate to keep the balance of payments on current account on its target path. The practical application of this idea in the analysis and exercises that follow in this volume centres round the search for a set of automatic control rules that specify precisely how much each tax should be raised or lowered in each quarter in response to the deviations of the actual from the desired development of the total of domestically produced money incomes in the recent past; and similarly for adjustment of the exchange rate in response to deviations of the actual from the desired balance of payments on current account. This constitutes a set of fine-tuned, automatic, feedback rules for the control of the economy. The question arises whether these rules should invariably be observed with unbroken precision or whether there are circumstances in which *ad hoc* discretionary adjustments should be made outside the rule book in order to meet special and unusual developments.

1. Some Examples of Adjustment of the Policy Targets

We have already discussed three ways in which account might be taken of certain special developments.

First, in Section 3 of Chapter III, we raised the question whether the target would not better be expressed in terms of controlling the rate of growth of the money value of the domestic product rather than of keeping the money value of the domestic product on a predetermined growth path, in order to avoid having to correct for past failures in the control system that had allowed serious divergences from the growth path to develop.

Second, in Section 4 of Chapter III, we discussed the desirability of setting an exceptionally high level for the target rates of growth of the Money GDP in those years in which one started with an exceptionally high level of unemployment (because of some past failure to maintain real economic activity), in order to reduce the otherwise excessive wage restraint that would be needed to promote employment.

Third, in Section 2 of Chapter III, we suggested that if the Money GDP was taken as the money income target, it should be adjusted so as not to include the value of production of North Sea oil. This was proposed because the ultimate consideration was to stabilise the growth of demand for labour, while the production of North Sea oil represented an activity with a quite exceptionally low labour requirement.

A similar adjustment of the balance of payments target will be suggested in Section 2 of Chapter VII to allow for the effects of the sudden and drastic rise in the price of imported oil resulting from the OPEC decisions of 1973 and the following years. It would not have been sensible, even if it had been possible, to attempt to achieve an offsetting increase in the excess of other exports over other imports by means of an exchange-rate depreciation; the developed oil-importing countries had to accept and absorb the resulting balance of payments surplus of the OPEC countries.

The latter is only a particularly outstanding example of the need for a discretionary adjustment of a target that has been chosen for control. There may be other less striking instances where some discretionary disregard of automatic feedback rules is desirable.

2.   Treatment of Unspecified Shocks to the System

In order to appreciate the problem it is necessary to consider the way in which the automatic feedback rules will have been devised. The economic system comprises a network of complicated dynamic interrelationships between the various elements – between prices, outputs, imports, exports, incomes, interest rates, tax rates, foreign-exchange rates and so on. Some of these variables – in our case the rates of tax and of foreign exchange – may be called 'control' variables. Of the remainder some are called 'exogenous' variables, being determined solely by outside forces (for example, the world demand for our exports). Others are called 'endogenous' variables since they are affected also by what has happened inside the economic system. For example, the demands by consumers for consumption goods will be affected by what has happened in the recent past to the consumers' incomes, to the prices of such goods, and so on. And in turn these incomes and prices will have been affected by what producers have produced and sold to meet the past demands of 'inside' consumers for consumption goods as well as the 'outside' purchasers of our exports.

For the purpose of devising practical control rules, a set of simplified hypotheses (a simplified dynamic 'model' of the economy) must be made that state how and with what degree of force and with what type of time lag each of the main 'endogenous' variables is determined by what has happened to the relevant 'exogenous' variable, to the other relevant 'endogenous' variables, and to the relevant 'control' variables such as the rates of tax. This hypothetical set of equations will be based upon observations of the relationships that have revealed themselves over the past periods of time.

The application to this 'model' of the economy of the techniques of the control engineer can result in a set of rules for adjusting rates of tax by amounts that depend precisely upon what has happened to the relevant variables in the economy, in such a way as to make the growth of the total of domestically produced money incomes conform more closely than would otherwise be the case to some predetermined desirable growth path.*

Each quarter the controllers will have before them the most recent information about what has happened to the relevant variables in the real economy (e.g. the most recent figure for domestically produced money incomes), which will tell them how much they should adjust the control variables (e.g. raise or lower tax rates in order to bring the total of domestically produced money incomes back on to its planned growth path). But the controllers could also have before them the most recent calculations from the economic model of what those relevant variables (e.g. the total of domestically produced money incomes) would have been if the model had faithfully represented everything that was going on in the economy. But suppose that the model stated that last quarter's figure would have been 100 if the model had represented the whole of the forces operating in reality, while the statisticians reported from the real world that the actual figure was only 90. How should the controllers react?

A first and very important reaction by the controllers might well be to ask the statisticians to have another good look at the real world. But if they reported confidently that the figure was in fact only 90, then the controllers must assume that there has been some factor at work depressing domestically produced money incomes that was not expressly specified in the model on the basis of which the control rules had been devised. Should the controllers take no notice of this unspecified factor and automatically reduce tax rates according to the rule book in order to boost domestically produced money incomes back from the depressed level of 90? Or should they take notice of the fact that the model stated that normal level of domestically produced money incomes was in fact already 100, if one disregarded this quarter's exceptional unspecified shock to the system?

It would be unwise to attempt any precise answer to this question for universal application in all future cases. Future history will always produce new features, some of which may be not only unexpected but also of a quite novel character. It would, however, always be sensible for the controllers to watch out carefully for unexpected divergences between the

---

*And similarly for a set of rules adjusting the foreign-exchange rate in order to control the balance of payments. However, in the rest of this chapter we confine our illustrations of the problem of discretionary modifications of the automatic rules to the case of fiscal policies for the control of domestically produced money incomes.

'actual' performance of the economy and the 'calculated' performance of what would have occurred if the model explained everything. If the controllers could recognise the nature of any such unspecified factor, one aspect that they would be wise to take into account would be whether they expected the disturbance to be only temporary and essentially unique. If so, they might well decide to set their controls on the basis not of the 'actual' value but of the 'calculated' value of the model.

An example may help to explain the reason for this choice. In the spring of 1974 there was an unspecified dip in domestically produced money incomes due to the miners' strike and the imposition of a three-day working week. There was a similar unspecified dip in the Winter of Discontent (1979—80) due to widespread strikes and industrial action. The reasons for such dips could be readily understood and could be expected to be temporary and to recur infrequently. If tax rates had been automatically reduced in order to restimulate the total of domestically produced money incomes from their abnormally low level, they would have had their effect somewhat later at a period when the temporary dip had been restored and when they would have served only to destabilise the economy by boosting it above its restored normal level.

Conversely, if the controllers understood the nature of the unspecified shock but expected it to represent a continuing or frequently recurring change in the underlying relationships in the economy so that undesired dip would have lasting effects unless it were corrected, it would be better to base the setting of the controls on the 'actual' rather than the 'calculated' values of the relevant variables.

But suppose that the controllers had no idea whether the unspecified shock would be temporary or permanent, either because they could not understand what it was that had disturbed the economy or because, while they realised what had happened, they did not know whether the change in relationships would be temporary or permanent. Should they set their controls on the basis of the 'actual' or of the 'calculated' values of the variables? A sensible course might be to use some intermediate value, the closer to the 'actual' value the smaller the weight that they placed on the possibility that the unexplained shock would turn out to have been temporary and unique. As time passed they could shift closer and closer to the use of the actual value, since if it continued to diverge from the calculated value this would increase the probability of the unspecified shock proving to represent a permanent change. Even if the unspecified shock proved to be explainable and temporary, the controllers would have to be on their guard for its reappearance, since a recurring temporary shock has much the same effect as a less severe permanent shock.

3.   Structural Forward Planning

There is another kind of discretionary intervention that may be desirable.

The Money GDP is made up of a number of elements – government expenditure on goods and services, expenditures on investment in capital goods by domestic producers, and the net demand by foreigners for the country's exports, as well as the expenditures by consumers on consumption goods and services. The fiscal controls that have been chosen for the control of total expenditures take the form of certain direct and indirect taxes whose effect will be to influence directly the level of the consumers' demands for goods and services, but not the level of the other elements, enumerated above, that make up the total demand for the country's products. These particular instruments of control have been chosen because they can be used in such a way as to have a prompt as well as a powerful effect on the total demand for the country's products.

Suppose then that for one reason or another (it makes no difference to the analysis what this reason may be) there is a marked increase in one of the other elements of demand for the country's products, which for one reason or another (again it makes no difference to the analysis what this reason may be) is likely to be maintained for some appreciable time into the future. This change will have an inflationary effect upon the total of domestically produced money incomes. If reliance is placed solely on the rule book for the automatic feedback controls, this inflationary rise in the total of domestically produced money incomes will be offset by rises in taxation, which will cause an offsetting reduction in personal consumption expenditures. But may it not be undesirable that the whole of the offsetting adjustment should fall on consumption expenditures? Might it not be better for the original lasting increase in the non-consumption element of expenditures on domestic products to be offset by a planned offsetting decrease in other elements as well as in personal consumption?

Once more an example may usefully illustrate the point. Suppose there to be a large increase in the foreign demand for the country's exports and thus a large increase in the balance of payments on current account, that is to say in the country's foreign investment. The rule book may say that this should be corrected by an appreciation of the foreign-exchange rate which, by making domestic products more expensive relative to foreign products, will shift demand back again away from the country's products. But, as we have already argued, this process is a slow one and at the outset may well even have the effect of perversely increasing the balance of payments on current account. Thus the expectation may be that for an appreciable future period the country will be faced with an exceptionally large foreign investment.* To offset this solely by a reduction in personal

---

*The improved balance-of-trade surplus, before its correction by a change in the exchange rate, could be financed by an accumulation of foreign-exchange reserves; alternatively it might be met by a reduction of domestic interest rates to encourage an offsetting movement of international capital funds (see Section 2(iv) of Chapter V). In this latter case the problem of excess demand for the country's products might be intensified by an increase of domestic as well as of foreign investment.

consumption could well call for a very substantial reduction in the real standard of living; and it might well be preferable to prepare, at least in part, for the future exceptionally high levels of foreign investment by a planned forward-looking reduction in, say, government expenditures or in some form of public domestic investment rather than to maintain stability wholly through the heavy cuts in personal consumption that sole reliance on the automatic feedback controls would require.

Considerations of this kind suggest that the best method of devising fiscal policies for the control of domestically produced money incomes may well consist of a combination of discretionary forward-looking planning and of automatic feedback adjustments. Such a system might be operated on the following lines. Once a year there would be a forward planning of both sides of the annual budget, i.e. the levels and structure of government expenditures and the levels and structure of the tax system, in such a way as to aim at the control of expenditures on domestic products over the coming quarters in the light of what were expected to be the main developments in the economy over those coming quarters. But combined with this, between the annual budgets there could be frequent and prompt changes in certain tax rates made on the appropriate automatic feedback rules (subject to the treatment suggested in Section 2 above for unspecified shocks to the system) in order to help to correct promptly any developing divergences of the Money GDP from its planned path.

The analysis of the UK economy and the control exercises that result from that analysis in Chapters VII and VIII of this volume rely basically on automatic feedback control by the prompt variation of tax rates. This should in no way inhibit their use and interpretation in a setting in which these automatic feedback controls are combined with discretionary forward-looking planning. In the analysis and control exercises that follow, the amount of fiscal intervention needed for the control of domestically produced money incomes will be represented by the changes in the revenue raised by the direct and indirect taxes as they are varied for control purposes; but this can readily be interpreted as a representation of the amount of stabilising fiscal intervention needed in one form or another, however that may be distributed between intervention resulting from annual forward-looking planning of, for example, government expenditures or from quarterly automatic feedback adjustments of the variable tax rates.

Part Two

Rerunning History

CHAPTER VII

The Formulation and Historical Application of the Control Rules

1. The Nature of the Exercise

Part Two of this book describes our attempts to 'try out' the policies that we have advocated in the previous chapters, using a macro-economic simulation model of the UK over the period 1972–85. The present chapter details the procedures that are used, and the results are presented in Chapter VIII.

Since the period 1972–85 covers a number of future years as well as past years, it is necessary to explain what is meant by rerunning history over a number of future years. As is explained in detail in Section 4 of this chapter, our procedure consists in constructing a Base Run for our dynamic model of the economy, which corresponds with the actual development of the economy before the application of our proposed control rules. We then use the same dynamic model of the economy to produce a Control Run, which shows what would have happened to the economy if, in otherwise similar conditions, our control rules had replaced the policies that were in fact applied.

This procedure was carried out at a time when reliable past data existed only up to the second quarter of 1980; for the period from 1980-85 we used a forecast produced on the Treasury model. This was based on assumptions about external economic conditions (e.g. the state of world trade) and on the assumption that the policies of the Conservative government remained unchanged. We used the forecast as if it represented what had actually happened in order to extend the period covered by our Base Run.

In short, in what follows a comparison between the Base Run and a Control Run of the economy is (1) for the period 1972–80 a comparison between what actually happened and what would have happened with our policy rules and (2) for the period 1980–85 a comparison between a Treasury forecast of what would happen on certain conditions with a continuation of present policies and what would happen in the same conditions but with the application of our policy rules. The whole exercise is thus basically an exercise in the effect that our policies would have had in the actual conditions of 1972–80 and in the conditions forecast for 1980–85.

In this exercise the structure of policy rules that we have used for the calculation of our Control Runs has been simplified in the way discussed in Section 6 of Chapter V. This simplified structure can be summarised as follows:

(1)   Tax policy is used for short-term control of total money incomes around some predetermined steady growth path. The two tax instruments used in our present exercise are indirect taxes and employees' national insurance contributions, the latter being used as representative of direct taxation.

(2)   Wage flexibility is relied upon to correct divergences from a specified level of unemployment.

(3)   The real exchange rate (defined as the money exchange rate adjusted for changes in relative wage costs) is managed to affect the competitiveness of UK products in such a way as to correct gradually any serious divergence of the current account balance from some desired level.

(4)   The authorities maintain a constant real rate of interest, allowing the money rate of interest to fluctuate with the actual rate of price inflation.[*]

It has been our task to design control rules to be followed by the policy-making institutions described in (1), (2) and (3) above. Each control variable will be used to regulate the target variable to which it is linked — subject to constraints on the degree to which the control variable may be moved — to achieve as closely as possible the objective assigned to it. Clearly, this decoupled method of control is less efficient than the cross-linked methods, which relate movements in all the control variables to all of the target variables (see Section 5 of Chapter V and also Section 4 of Chapter XII). We have further limited the control methods examined in this study by confining them to finely tuned, automatic, feedback controls, making no use of possible structural, feedforward planning of policies (see Section 3 of Chapter VI). Our work sets out to test how feasible it is to control an economy by this method.

In order to carry out this investigation, we have constructed a small model of the UK economy using equations and parameter values taken from the Treasury Macroeconomic Model. The model, which is described in Appendix A, is dynamic, quarterly, discrete-time and non-linear. It is broadly a Keynesian model with a foreign sector. It could be extended to possess monetarist features if the exchange rate were allowed to float, if the money supply were controlled on a given growth path, and if the existing factors determining wage settlements were continued in operation.

---

[*]The path of these fluctuations was somewhat smoothed in the manner and for the reasons described in Section 6 of Appendix A.

But in what follows, wage settlements are assumed to take place through suitably reformed institutions; and since the exchange rate and the rate of interest are used as policy instruments and are assumed to be fixed at appropriate rates by the authorities, we are not directly concerned with the further implications of such policies on other developments in the foreign-exchange and money markets.

2. Policy Targets for the Rerun of History

The small model of Appendix A is to be used to devise rules for the adjustment of the policy variables (rates of tax, foreign exchange and wages) in order to maintain as far as possible the target variables (Money GDP, balance of payments on current account and unemployment) on predetermined target paths. A first requirement for a rerun of history is to specify precisely what those target paths should be.

The desired value for Money GDP is supposed to start at its initial value in the second quarter of 1972 and to grow at a constant 13 per cent per annum throughout the whole period of investigation. This rate of 13 per cent per annum is almost identical to that which ruled in the quarters immediately prior to the beginning of our experiments. Its assumed continuation, without being pushed steadily downwards, enables us to investigate the effects of New Keynesian macro-economic policies designed to *stabilise*, as distinct from restrictive policies designed to *bring down*, the rate of growth of money incomes, and in the present volume we confine ourself to such investigations. Some amendments to this target path have however been introduced for reasons discussed in Section 6 of this chapter.

The target path for the current account of the balance of payments needed choosing with care. It would have been quite wrong to attempt to hold the current account balance to a fixed number (such as zero) during the period of rise in the price of oil and of other primary commodities. How much of the resulting deficit should the UK have aimed to accept and finance by borrowing? In our analysis we assume that in the 1970s the UK aimed to accept *all* of the extra deficit caused by the rise in the price of oil over and above that ruling before the fourth quarter of 1972, but *none* of that caused by the rise in the price of other raw materials. This is a compromise outcome, but at the time it would have been well understood that the non-oil developed countries would have to accept, at least for a time, the OPEC surplus. As time went on it would have become clear that the UK would soon be an oil producer; this would have provided the basis for further borrowing. We also suppose that in the 1980s the UK aimed for a surplus on the balance of payments on current account equal to 30 per cent of the projected net exports of oil and gas, as the means of paying back this borrowing.

In the wage equation used in the reruns of history to represent the needed reform of wage-fixing situations, it is assumed that money wage settlements are not directly affected by the rate of price inflation. But it is assumed that there is a critical unemployment percentage, at which there would be an upward pressure on money wage rates equal to the announced target rate of increase of total Money GDP of 13 per cent per annum. It is assumed that this critical rate remains constant throughout the period at 3.76 per cent (namely, the percentage unemployment inherited at the beginning of the exercise period). There is in fact no policy target for the unemployment percentage; but this critical rate of 3.76 per cent may take the place of such a target, since it represents what is assumed to be the level of frictional unemployment that, with our reformed wage-fixing institutions, would not exercise any downward pressure on money wage rates relative to the total expected national income.

The question may well be asked whether or not it is legitimate to assume that this critical level of the unemployment percentage remained constant at 3.76 per cent over the whole period. May not the speed and nature of technical and structural change in the UK, with the repercussions of North Sea oil and of the industrial effects of new technologies of automation, data processing, transfer of information, control processes, etc., have inevitably brought with them a rise in frictional and structural unemployment? It is possible that on these grounds we should have allowed some rise over this period in the critical level for the unemployment percentage. But these structural considerations cannot have operated so suddenly over so short a period as four years to account for more than a very small part of the rise in the unemployment percentage from 4 per cent to 12 per cent; and it is with these large short-run fluctuations of total effective demand that our New Keynesian policies are concerned.

3.   Feedback Rules for the Control Variables

The next step is to use the small model to devise feedback rules for each control variable as a means of keeping the target variable on its specified target path for the period 1972–85. These rules will be of the following kind. The tax rule will state in what way the rate of tax set to operate for any quarter will depend upon the extent to which the Money GDP has strayed from its target path in previous quarters; and the rate of foreign exchange will be similarly related to past deviations of the balance of payments on current account, and the wage rate to past deviations of unemployment, from their target paths.

The technical procedures necessary to devise satisfactory rules of this kind are explained at length in Part Four of this volume. In essence, to take the tax rule as an example, the process consists of using all the dynamic relationships assumed in the small dynamic model to operate between all the variables in the model, in order to calculate what would be the effect of, say, an immediate 1 per cent rise in the rate of tax on the values of the Money GDP, on the balance of payments on current account and on unemployment over the subsequent periods of time. On the basis of these future time responses of the three target variables to a given change in the rate of tax, a rule would be sought for the setting of the tax rate in response to deviations of the Money GDP from its target path, of a kind that would have a reasonably effective and speedy effect in bringing the Money GDP back onto its specified target path without too great a disturbance of the balance of payments or of unemployment. When preliminary rules for rates of tax, of foreign exchange and of wages have been devised separately and independently of each other on these lines, the next technical step is to make adjustments to them to enable them to operate more effectively simultaneously.

In fact the control rules that resulted from these procedures were in some cases further modified when they had been tried out in their original form on a rerun of history of the kind described in the chapter which follows. In order to improve their performance when actually applied to the events of this period, the strengths of the effect of the tax-rate rule on the Money GDP and of the foreign-exchange-rate rule on the balance of payments were considerably reduced, in order to obtain a smoother and less disturbed development of the economy. Before their strengths were modified in this way, they were found to cause unacceptably large fluctuations in the economy. The implications of these strength reductions are examined in some detail in Chapter XIV.*

The application to the history of the economy over the years 1972–85 of control rules obtained in this way clearly does not provide any decisive test of the degree to which it would have been possible to control the economy in reality during these years. In the first place, for the period 1980–5 our test is of control over a forecast of events rather than over historical events that actually happened. But there is a much more fundamental consideration, which applies to the test of control over the actual historical events of the years 1972–80. The control rules applied during this period will have been based on the dynamic relationship assumed in the model, which, in turn, will have been based on observations of the behaviour of the economy during the years 1972–80; in addition, these control rules will have been revised in the light of their effects when applied to the conditions ruling in the period 1972–80. Of course, in the real control of the real-world economy, the rules applied in 1972, 1973, 1974 could not have been based on events occurring in the period 1972–80, but only on observations of, and experiments on, the relationships in, say, the period 1962–72.

---

*The adjustment of the money exchange rate to changes in relative wage costs was also slightly smoothed for reasons explained in Section 6 of Appendix A.

This does not imply that our exercise is a futile one. It can serve two purposes. In the first place it does provide a test of the degree to which suitable, finely tuned, feedback control rules, if they could somehow or other have been devised, would have been capable of keeping the target variables on their planned growth path — a test that, as will be shown in the next chapter, they pass very adequately. In the second place, the exercise may be regarded as an example of how to use the dynamic relationships and actual conditions of the period 1972–80 to devise rules for the control of the economy in subsequent years. Of course the rules so found would remain valid for future years only in so far as the underlying relationships in the economy remained similar to those assumed in the model for 1972–80. One may hope that they would remain reasonably valid for a few years at least; as far as the more distant future years are concerned, the controllers in the real world would naturally be continually revising and bringing up to date their dynamic model and the rules derived from it, so that the rules actually applied in any one year would always rest on the relationships and conditions ruling over the immediately preceding years.

The actual control rules devised for the rates of indirect and direct tax and for the foreign-exchange rate are given in equations (4), (14) and (64) of the model of Appendix A (see Section 6), and are also described and discussed in Section 5 of Chapter XIV. They constitute straight-forward instructions to the controllers as to the rates of tax and foreign exchange that should be set in any one quarter.

Similarly the control rule for setting the wage rate is given in equation (10) of the model of Appendix A (see Section 6). It too is discussed in Section 5 of Chapter XIV. But the status of this rule is, of course, quite different. It is in no way an instruction to a central controller as to what money wage should be fixed for any one quarter, but only an expression of the way in which it would be desirable for wage settlements to react to recent levels of unemployment if a high and stable level of employment is to be attained. Whether or not the effective implementation of the reforms of wage-fixing institutions on the lines discussed in Volume 1 would result in settlements that corresponded closely enough to the desirable pattern indicated in the present volume is an open question. We return to the matter in Section 1 of the next chapter where we give reasons for suggesting that the situation is perhaps not quite so disturbing as may at first sight appear to be the case.

The control rules given in equations (4), (14) and (64) of our model for the rates of tax and of foreign exchange assume that a control variable can be set to operate in any one quarter on the basis of the values of its target variable in the preceding quarters up to and including the immediately preceding quarter — which we call a one-quarter implementation delay. If, as at present, statistics on Money GDP and the current balance of payments are released by the Central Statistical Office for quarterly periods and if tax rates and the exchange rate are to be set only four times a year at values that last for a quarter, then the assumption on which the policy rules are based implies that statistics must be made available immediately at the end of a quarter and that policy for the next quarter must be implemented instantly. This is clearly impossible. But if instead monthly statistics were available for Money GDP and the current balance and if instead tax rates and the exchange rate were liable to be altered every month (according, say, to monthly policy rules interpolated from our quarterly model), then policy rules with a one-quarter delay would allow two months for release of the statistics and for implementation of policy based upon them. For example, rates of tax for the month of April would be set on the performance of the economy up to and including the month of January, leaving February and March to cover the assembly of the statistics and the implementation of the policy.

This might well be feasible if steps were taken to speed up the collection of the necessary statistics. But in order to guard against the charge of over-optimism we have performed a more pessimistic rerunning of history, with an additional quarter's delay in the implementation of the tax and exchange-rate policies. On a fixed quarterly basis for change of tax rates this would mean a full three months for release of statistics and implementation of policy, the performance of the economy in the quarter January, February, March being used to set the controls to operate during the quarter July, August, September. On a monthly basis it would allow five months, since the performance of the economy up to the end of January would be relevant for the setting of the rates of tax and of foreign exchange to operate from the beginning of July. Of course the outcome with the longer delay is worse; for this reason it is important that the necessary statistics should be available more frequently and more promptly than at present (see the Note on the Statistical Series at the end of this chapter).

4. The Base Run: Derivation of Unspecified Shocks

In order to see how effective the proposed rules for setting the control variables would have been in keeping the target variables on their prescribed target paths during the historical period 1972–80 it is necessary first to make sure that the model will take account of all the external perturbations and shocks to which the economy was in reality exposed during the years 1972–80. Any model, and particularly a small model, is bound to represent a serious simplification of reality. It can attempt to incorporate the effects of a number of obvious, large, external developments; for example, it can expressly make allowance for the effects of an outside change in the level of world trade on the demand for a country's exports. Such elements we may call 'specified exogenous variables'. But there will be a number of other small unexplained shocks to the system — what we may call 'unspecified exogenous variables' — which will cause aberrations from the main, simplified underlying structure of relationships that are covered by the model. An important question is how well the proposed control rules would have coped with disturbances due to the unexplained shocks represented by these 'unspecified exogenous variables' in addition to the influences exerted by the 'specified exogenous variables'.

For this purpose we proceed by constructing a Base Run for the model for the years 1972–80 in the following way.

We first run the model over the relevant period of time: in our case from the third quarter of 1972 to the first quarter of 1980 given the actual values of the specified exogenous variables, for this purpose including in this category the rates of interest, of tax and of foreign exchange that were actually operative over that period. For each equation at each point of time we observe the differences between the actual value of the dependent variable and the value given by the model. This residual difference we add as an additional 'explanatory' element to the equation for that period. For example, equation (27) of our model in Section 4 of Appendix A explains the volume of United Kingdom exports in any quarter as being the combined result of (1) United Kingdom costs relative to foreign costs and (2) the level of world trade in previous quarters. Both foreign costs and the level of world trade are 'specified exogenous variables'. But in any one quarter the actual level of exports is likely to differ by a greater or smaller amount from the volume of exports that the equation says that there 'ought' to have been in view of the past values of United Kingdom costs, foreign costs and the volume of world trade. To this extent there is some additional shock to the system in that quarter, which causes this deviation of the actual volume from the volume that the equation would account for. We add this deviation or residual to the other factors determining the export volume in that quarter as representing an unexplained shock or 'unspecified exogenous variable'. The running of the model over this period of time with the addition of these residual explanatory shocks to each equation will then result in the calculated value of each variable at each point in time coinciding with the actual value of that variable at that point in time.

We also wish to rerun history into the future, to enable us to investigate the proposed policies over a longer time horizon. For this rerunning of future history, from the second quarter of 1980 to the first quarter of 1985 we take: (1) forecast values of the specified exogenous variables for the years 1980–5, and (2) the values of the other variables derived by applying these exogenous variables to the Treasury model. We then apply the present model to the same projected period, using the same specified exogenous variables. But at each point of time in each of our equations we add a residual or unspecified exogenous variable so that the calculated values of each of the variables in our present model, using the projected specified exogenous variables, coincide with the projections of that variable in the forecast based on the Treasury model.

The run of the model created from 1972 to 1985 in the manner described above we entitle the Base Run.

5. Modification of the Exogenous Variables in the Base Run

The next step is to apply the control rules to the model that includes for the period 1972–85 all the specified and unspecified exogenous variables that have been found to exist in the Base Run. But if we do this without any modification of those exogenous variables, the result is very unsatisfactory.

The reason for this is not far to seek. There are a number of situations in this period in which, if a government had been in power that was committed to a New Keynesian policy, the exogenous variables would have been quite different from those derived from the Base Run.

A first outstanding example of this occurs during the Heath–Barber boom of 1972–4. Amongst the specified exogenous variables in that period there is evidence of a planned fiscal expansion that would certainly not have been planned by any government wedded to a New Keynesian control of the Money GDP. It would not be fair on our simple automatic feedback tax rules for the containment of an inflation of the Money GDP to pit them against a deliberately contrived inflationary expansion by a determined and powerful prime minister and chancellor of the exchequer. To set a background more nearly like that which a New Keynesian government would have set for the operation of the tax rules we adjusted the specified exogenous variables of the Base Run by flattening the path of government procurement and public employment and by removing the temporary cut in the basic rate of income tax that occurred in the fourth quarter of 1972. Amongst the unspecified exogenous shocks there is one that is remarkable during the time of the Heath–Barber boom; namely, that for stocks. This shows a rapid upsurge in stock holdings beyond the rise predicted by the equation (associated perhaps with expectational effects of the 'dash for growth' and perhaps also with the very expansionary monetary policy of the time). To eliminate this increase we adjusted down the residuals in the stocks equation. The effect of all the above adjustments taken together was to eliminate some but not all of the movements away from target of Money GDP in the model Base Run during the Heath–Barber period. (Measured according to the peak to trough changes in unemployment, about half of the boom would thereby have been removed from the model Base Run.)

A second example concerns the fiscal expansion carried out by the Labour government in its first two years in office. The purpose of these measures was (partially at least) fiscally to reflate through the world slump in 1975; this objective is already pursued by our policy by other means. To eliminate or slow down these effects we removed the peaks in government procurement and investment in 1975, slowed the very remarkable increase in government employment in 1975 out over 1976 and 1977 and delayed any cut in the basic rate of direct taxation until the fourth quarter of 1976.

The third situation that caused us to revise the exogenous variables derived from the Base Run is the extreme currency appreciation experienced under Mrs Thatcher's government in 1979 and 1980. This appears to have caused a number of remarkable changes to the unspecified exogenous shocks of the model. Exports appear to have held up better to the extreme reduction in competitiveness than would have been predicted by the model's export equation (by an amount equal to between 10 and 15 per cent). This improvement was supposed to continue up to 1985 in the projection used to extend the initial Base Run, and appears in that Base Run as a string of very large positive residuals. Export prices too behaved unusually in 1979 and 1980, rising (in sterling) by more than would have been expected in the face of the extreme discipline of currency appreciation, probably in order partly to protect reduced profit margins. This higher than expected export price was also supposed to continue up to 1985 in the projection used to extend the initial Base Run, and appears too as a string of positive residuals (increasing export prices by 4–6 per cent).

This extreme currency appreciation is not consistent with New Keynesian policies, and its apparent consequences (the large residuals in the two above equations) were deemed unlikely to have occurred if New Keynesian policies had been implemented. They were removed from the model before we applied our control rules. (These changes cause the outcome in the absence of our policies to be more depressed and to have a worse current balance than that in the initial Base Run.) Before applying our control rules we also altered the Base Run's projection for wholesale and consumer prices. These supposed an implausible projection of the recovery of profit margins, which occurred in 1979 on into the 1980s. Finally, we observed in the initial Base Run for the first quarter of 1980 a very large fall in stockholdings beyond that predicted by the equation. We argued that this was also a consequence of the Thatcher experiment and eliminated it by adjusting the residuals of the stocks equation that were shown in the Base Run. (This was necessary only for the first quarter of 1980, the last period in which our model uses real historical data, since the subsequent massive fall in stockholdings was not forecast at that time to continue and so was not present in our Base Run.)

6.   Discretionary Modification of the Economic Targets

In the course of an economy's historical development, situations may well arise in which the controllers would be tempted and indeed justified in not adhering strictly to the target paths that had been laid down for the target variables. This question has been discussed in general terms in the previous chapter; here we describe the procedures adopted in our reruns of history.

In the first place, while the maintenance of the Money GDP on a 13 per cent per annum growth path was the target chosen for fiscal control, we have in fact, for the reasons given in Section 2 of Chapter III, modified this objective to imply a 13 per cent per annum growth of the Money GDP exclusive of the value of the production of North Sea oil. Since in a New Keynesian economic policy the reason for stabilising the growth of the Money GDP is indirectly to stabilise the money demand for the products of labour and since oil is markedly a non-labour-intensive product, it would have been wise and natural for the controllers to have made this modification of the Money GDP target as North Sea oil came on stream.

A second case is our adjustment of the balance-of-trade target for the OPEC oil-price increase in 1972, which has already been described in Section 2 of this chapter. At the time it would have been understood that the non-oil developed countries would have to accept, at least for a time, the OPEC surpluses and the controllers may well be assumed to have modified any pre-existing balance-of-trade target accordingly.

The third kind of discretionary modification of the control action that we have carried out is described in Section 2 of Chapter VI: reaction to an unspecified shock expected to be temporary and more or less unique. We have made such modifications only in the two cases already mentioned there as examples: the three-day week of 1974 and the Winter of Discontent of 1978–9. We operated the control rules on the principle that one should accept a temporary drop in Money GDP on such occasions, and reduced the target levels for Money GDP by 3.2 per cent, 1.7 per cent and 3.6 per cent in the first quarter of 1974, the fourth quarter of 1978 and the first quarter of 1979 respectively.

7.   Structural 'Feedforward' Planning

There is another kind of discretionary intervention which may be desirable. Because of lags in the adjustment of exports and imports to relative price changes (the famous 'J-curve' effect) there are bound to be considerable changes in the real trade balance that cannot be immediately corrected. Since we are stabilising the Money GDP by means of tax changes that quickly and powerfully affect personal consumption, there will be (as indeed all our exercises have shown) a very strong negative correlation between the real trade balance and real spendable incomes (represented by the real wage): to offset the effects of these fluctuations in the balance of trade on the Money GDP by controls over personal consumption implies very marked and probably unacceptable variations of the real wage. In the face of a deficit on the balance of trade that requires time to correct, it might thus be best not to rely entirely upon stimulus to consumption (whilst the deficit remains), followed by a restriction of consumption (when the deficit is corrected), as the means of controlling Money GDP.

For this reason we have in Section 3 of Chapter VI proposed the combination of structural feedforward planning with our automatic feedback adjustments. This is a big change in the policy proposals compared with those investigated below, *which use no planned feedforward controls.* But it does not mean that the reruns of history reported on below are meaningless. What it does mean is that, where they show a marked reduction in the real wage because of a large positive persistent balance-of-trade surplus, some part of the reduction in the real wage must be interpreted not as an actual change in the real wage but as a planned postponement of public expenditure – and vice versa in those years in which they show a marked rise in the real wage accompanying a large negative balance of trade.

Note to Chapter VII on the Statistical Series

If the policies advocated in this chapter were to be seriously applied, it would be essential to ensure that the statistical measurement of the money income target should be sufficiently reliable and frequently and promptly available.

There are three statistical measures of the gross domestic product: (1) an expenditure measure (e.g. the sum of expenditures on domestic products by consumers, investors, government authorities, foreigners, etc.); (2) an income measure (e.g. the sum of wages, profits, rents, etc., earned in domestic production); and (3) an output measure (e.g. the sum of the net outputs of agriculture, industry, services, etc.). Of these three the output measure is probably the most reliable. At present, however, it is constructed not in terms of current prices but only at constant base-date prices. But even in this form it could be used for a measure of the Money GDP if it were grossed up by an index of total home costs, which could be derived from a comparison of current-price and constant-price versions of the expenditure and income measures of the GDP. As things stand, this might well be the best measure of the Money GDP to use. It would be available on a quarterly basis; but at present there would be a delay of up to twelve weeks before it was ready for use by policy-makers.

A quarterly series of total pre-tax money wage and salary earnings could be available, the absolute level of earnings being based largely on Inland Revenue sources and the Family Expenditure Survey, but period to period movements on the Index of Average Earnings. There are problems with this series (for example, distortions due to payments of large bonuses or back pay, concentration of annual pay settlements, strikes, etc.). But this would probably be a relatively reliable index; and with the use of the Earnings Index it might be easier to produce prompt and frequent (e.g. monthly) figures than would be the case with figures for the Money GDP.

The situation calls for an enquiry covering the following five questions:

(1)   How reliable and accurate are the various existing series? For example, how frequently and to what degree has each series been liable to revision in the past?

(2)   How frequently can each series be produced? Quarterly? Monthly?

(3)   With what minimum delay after the close of the period to which it refers could each series be made available for the use of policy-makers? How far would a shortening of the delay reduce the reliability of the figures?

(4)   How important in each series are regular seasonal or other less regular disturbances? How difficult would it be to cope with them?

(5)   What would be the problems and costs involved in obtaining more relevant, more reliable, more frequent and more up-to-date data?

CHAPTER VIII

Results of the Rerun

1. Keeping to the Target Paths

Figures VIII.1–VIII.8 show how the economy might have developed over the years after 1972 if the control policies discussed in the previous chapter had been adopted instead of the policies that were in fact applied. Figures VIII.1, VIII.2 and VIII.3 show movements in the three target variables: namely the money value of the gross domestic product at factor cost (Money GDP), the unemployment percentage and the balance of payments on current account respectively, while Figures VIII.4–VIII.8 show movements in the various instruments of control: namely, the rate of indirect tax, the rate of employees' national insurance contributions, the rate of money earnings per man, the foreign-exchange rate and the index of competitiveness respectively.

All the figures show two different runs for the economy under our proposed control rules, the difference being due to the different assumptions, which are discussed in Section 3 of Chapter VII, about the delays that are inevitable between the observation of what has happened in the economy and the adjustment of the instruments of control to correct any divergences from target. What in the figures is called the optimistic Control Run is based on what in Section 3 of the previous chapter was called a one-quarter implementation delay. The pessimistic Control Run allows an additional quarter's delay in the implementation of the tax and foreign-exchange-rate policies.

For the Money GDP and the balance of payments on current account the figures show the desired target values of these variables as well as the calculated values of these variables under the optimistic and pessimistic Control Runs. In the case of the unemployment percentage, as already explained in Section 2 of the previous chapter, we have assumed that throughout the period the money wage rate would rise at the same rate as the target for money GDP excluding North Sea oil (i.e. 13 per cent p.a.) if the unemployment percentage were held at 3.76 per cent. In Figure VIII.2 this 3.76 rate takes the place of a target level for the unemployment percentage. The comparison of the Control Run values with these target values indicates the degree of success or failure of the control policies.

All the figures also show the path of the variables in the Base Run as described in Section 4 of Chapter VII. This means that the values in the Base Run for the years 1970–80 show the actual historical development of the economy, so that for this period a comparison of the two Control

Runs with the Base Run indicates what we calculate would have been the effect of our control policies on what actually happened in these years. But, as explained in Section 1 of Chapter VII, for the period from the second quarter of 1980 to the first quarter of 1985 the Base Run does not exactly reproduce what in fact happened to the economy, but rather what in 1980 a forecast indicated would happen to the economy during the years 1981–5 on certain assumptions about the future of the specified exogenous variables (e.g. the state of the world economy) and on the assumption of the continuation of the policies of the Conservative government. For these quarters, therefore, the comparison of the Control Runs with the Base Run shows the difference that our policies rather than the Conservative government's policies would have made to the economy, if the specified exogenous variables had in both cases been as were then in the forecast.

Figure VIII.1 shows the target level, the Base Run level, and the two Control Run levels for the money value of the gross domestic product at factor cost, which was set as the target variable to be controlled by variations in tax rates. The target path for this variable, as described in Section 2 of the previous chapter, was that, in the absence of North Sea oil output, it should rise at a steady rate of 13 per cent per annum from its initial value in the second quarter of 1972 (henceforth 1972Q2*). Figure VIII.1 sets this target path up to 1976Q1 at a constant level of 100, so that the movements of the Base Run and the Control Run variables above or below this line represent the extent to which they diverged at any time from the target path. For example, the value of Money GDP in the optimistic Control Run in 1975Q4 is shown at 98.3 on the figure, which means that at that time it was 1.7 per cent below the desired target path. After 1976Q1, Figure VIII.1 shows that the target path for Money GDP rises by more than 13 per cent per annum by an amount equal to the money value of oil production, since we have chosen to display the target path of the Money GDP *including* North Sea oil. (The target for Money GDP *excluding* North Sea oil after 1976Q1 of course continues along the constant 100 line.) There are two other adjustments made to the target path for Money GDP to take account of, first, the three-day week of 1974 and, second the Winter of Discontent of 1978–9. These adjustments are made because at the time these shocks would have been thought to be temporary (see Section 6 of Chapter VII).

Both the optimistic and the pessimistic Control Runs avoid the huge inflation of the Base Run value of the Money GDP from 1974 onwards. But it is a marked feature of the figure that the optimistic Control Run keeps much closer to the target level than does the pessimistic Control Run, which emphasises the great importance of reducing the

---

*Throughout this chapter we use this form of expression to indicate the year and the quarter of the year to which the analysis relates.

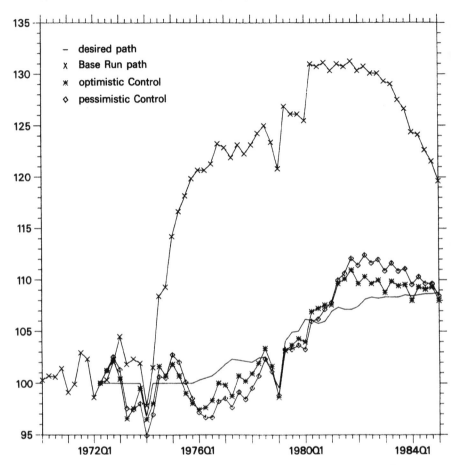

Fig. VIII.1   The Money Value of the Gross Domestic Product at Factor Cost (Money GDP). The figure shows an index, detrended at 13 per cent per annum, with an initial value of 100 in 1972Q2. (For further explanation, see text.)

implementation delays as much as possible. One would naturally expect the greater delay of the pessimistic Control to worsen the outcome. But the deterioration in the performance is due not only to the direct effect of the greater delay in adjusting rates of tax to control expenditure, but also to the fact that with the pessimistic Control it is necessary not only to change a tax rate less promptly but also to change the rate by a smaller amount in response to any given divergence of the actual Money GDP from its target level. This is a result of the arbitrary constraint that we have imposed on the extent to which a tax rate can be varied (see Chapters

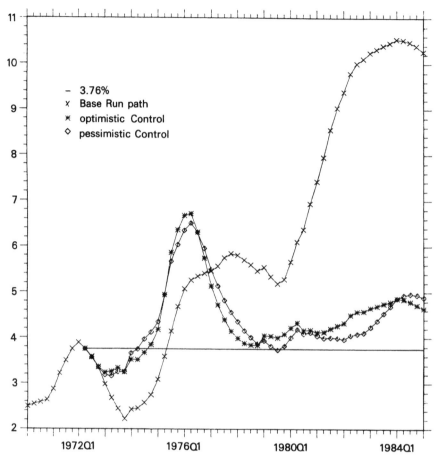

Fig. VIII.2   Unemployment Percentage

IX and XI, and Section 3(i) of Chapter XIV). A delayed response calls for
a larger change in the control variable since the error that needs adjustment
will have grown larger, so that a constraint on the size of the permissible
swings of the tax rate makes a delayed control less effective in achieving a
needed correction.*

Figure VIII.2 shows the movements in the unemployment percentage.
The outstanding feature is the fact that both the optimistic and the
pessimistic Control Runs avoid the huge increase in unemployment from

---

*If you are driving a car that is veering towards the side, the longer you delay
your adjustment of the steering wheel the more violently you will need to yank it to
avoid ditching your car. You will thus be in extra trouble if there is an arbitrary limit
to the amount of yanking.

the last years of the 1970s onwards without there being any very marked difference between the performance of the two Control Runs. The unemployment percentage remains somewhat above the target level of 3.76 per cent after 1977 in both cases. This is to be expected for the following reason. In so far as the Money GDP excluding North Sea oil is successfully kept on its target growth path of 13 per cent per annum and in so far as the proportion of the national income going to wages remains unchanged, there would be a 13 per cent per annum growth in the total wage bill. But with a growing working population seeking work the wage per head must rise by less than 13 per cent per annum in order to absorb the increased numbers into employment. The unemployment percentage must therefore be kept by the pressure of new entrants into the labour market somewhat above the critical level of 3.76 per cent to induce wage earners to demand a rise in the rate of pay of less than 13 per cent, thus making room for a growth in the numbers employed.

Both the Control Runs can be judged to have kept the unemployment percentage at acceptable levels with the exceptions of the relatively high levels of unemployment in 1975—6. These occurred because of a temporary increase in the profit markup in 1974. Thus, as Figure VIII.1 shows, Money GDP rose above target at the end of 1974, calling for fiscal restriction even when unemployment was rising. It is possible that if New Keynesian policies had been in operation this shift to profit would not have occurred. (See note † at end of chapter.) Otherwise the unamended operation of these policies in this period would have had undesirable consequences.

Figure VIII.3 shows movements in the balance of payments on current account, the size of the surplus (or deficit) in any one quarter being expressed as a percentage of the Base Run Money GDP (inclusive of the value of North Sea oil) during that quarter. The target value of the balance of payments starts at zero but, as explained in Section 2 of the previous chapter, it falls below zero after the acceptance of the need to absorb some of the OPEC oil surpluses resulting from the dramatic OPEC increases in the price of oil in the early 1970s.* After the development of the North Sea oil resources, it rises in the 1980s to a positive figure to represent some repayment of the finance needed to cover the intervening deficits.

The outstanding feature of this figure is the frightening size of the deficits that would have had to be financed between 1976 and 1982 in the case of both the Control Runs. The reason for this phenomenon is straightforward. In our Control Runs the New Keynesian policy has successfully maintained domestic output and employment during these years of world recession with a resulting high demand for imports. But at the same time there was a low world demand for UK exports together with an adverse

*There is also an adjustment of the target path due to the effect of the Winter of Discontent on exports in 1979Q1.

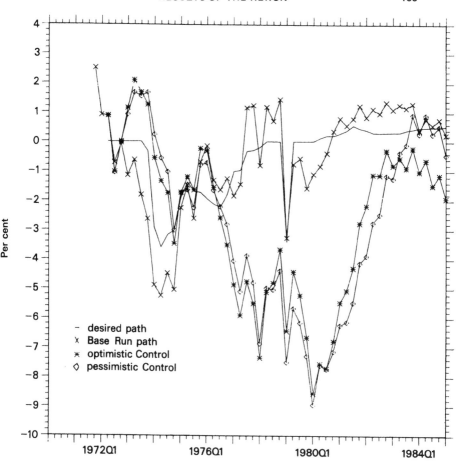

Fig. VIII.3 Balance of Payments on Current Account as a Percentage of Base Run Money GDP

movement in the prices of the sort of things that the UK imports (primary products) relative to the prices of the sort of things that the UK exports (manufactures). The reaction of our policy to this deficit, as can be seen from Figures VIII.7 and VIII.8, was with both Control Runs to depreciate the exchange rate sufficiently to improve the competitiveness of our manufactures relative to foreign products in order to improve the balance of trade. The reaction of the balance of trade to this change is, however, very slow with the result that, while the balance of payments on current account is practically restored by 1982, there remains a heavy deficit during the five years of adjustment to the world slump.

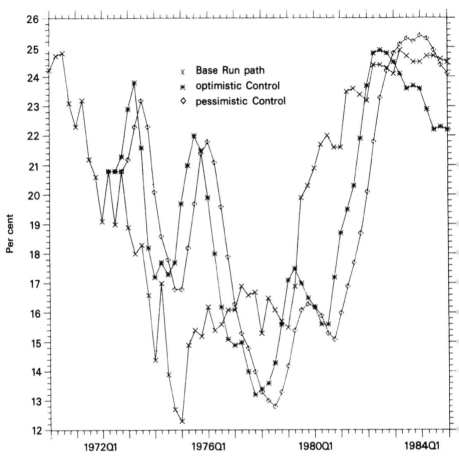

Fig. VIII.4   Rate of Indirect Taxation

A double moral can be drawn from this story: first, it is of extreme importance to a country that is so exposed as is the UK to world trading conditions that there should be international co-operation in the formulation of New Keynesian or other equally effective policies for the avoidance of slump conditions; and second, in the absence of such co-operation, effective action by one country such as the UK to avoid its own domestic slump depends upon the ability to finance a temporary but large balance of payments deficit if open trading relations with the rest of the world are to be preserved.

Figures VIII.4 and VIII.5 show the variations in indirect tax and employees' national insurance contributions (our representative of a direct tax). The two Control Runs display the variations of tax rates needed for

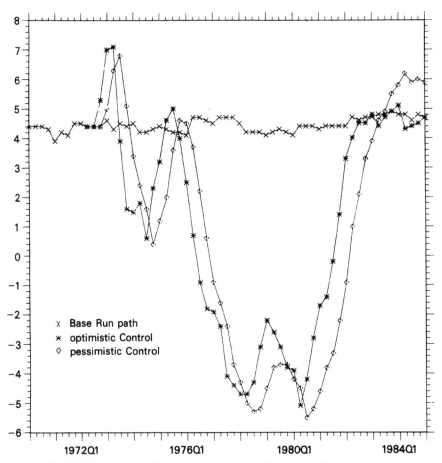

Fig. VIII.5   Rate of Employees' National Insurance Contributions

the control of total money expenditures, i.e. of the Money GDP shown in
Figure VIII.1. The range and degree of the swings in tax rates are very
similar in the two Control Runs. This is because, as explained in the
discussion of Figure VIII.1, with the pessimistic Control the response of
the tax rates to needed corrections of the Money GDP has been reduced to
ensure that changes in tax rates under the pessimistic Control Run will be
subject to the same constrained limits as with the optimistic Control Run.

The swings of the tax rates in both Control Runs are more violent than
in the Base Run. Moreover, although the range of variation is not greater
in the Control Runs than in the Base Run in the case of the indirect tax
rate, it is much greater for the employees' national insurance contribution,
which in the Base Run is to all intents and purposes constant. Taking both

taxes together, the combined tax change has displayed much sharper swings over a much greater range with the Control Runs than with the Base Run. To a large extent this is one of the costs that must be faced in designing an effective control policy; one must be prepared to make prompt changes on an adequate scale and to reverse those changes promptly as circumstances demand.

However, there is one special disturbing feature of the picture. Comparison of the Control Runs in Figure VIII.3 with Figures VIII.4 and VIII.5 shows a very close correlation between movements in the balance of payments and in the tax rates. The reason for this has been discussed in Section 3 of Chapter VI. When there is a deficit in the balance of payments (i.e. when the net world demand for UK products is low) our control policy calls for a reduction in tax rates in order to stimulate domestic expenditures so that the Money GDP can be maintained at its target level by replacing the low foreign demand with a high domestic demand. The large balance of payments changes that were discussed above in connection with Figure VIII.3 have been the dominant factor over these years in determining the tax-rate changes needed to maintain the Money GDP on its target path. But the tax changes in the Control Runs operate more or less exclusively on real consumption, so that in fact the great fall in the tax rates from 1976 to 1980 (needed to offset the large balance of payments deficits of those years) meant that over that period there was a very great rise in real disposable incomes and so in the standard of living, far outstripping any rise in real productivity. On the other hand, the very rapid rise in tax rates between 1980 and 1982 (needed to counterbalance the great and rapid improvement of the balance of payments over that short period) meant that with the Control Runs there would have been a sharp and marked absolute reduction in real disposable incomes and real standards of living over these years.

Such sharp and, in a sense, unnatural rises and falls in the real standard of living should be avoided. This factor underlines the suggestion made in Section 3 of Chapter VI that in cases of this kind at least part of the adjustment of total domestic expenditures needed to balance protracted changes in foreign demand should be made by forward planned changes in domestic expenditures other than consumption expenditures.

Figure VIII.6 displays movements in the rate of money earnings per man, which in New Keynesianism is the 'weapon' used to keep unemployment at its 'target' level. In fact, of course, the rate of earnings is not put up or down like the rate of indirect tax by some wage-controlling authority. The Control Run movements of the rate of money earnings in Figure VIII.6 represent what would happen to money earnings if wage-fixing institutions were suitably reformed, which in this case means a system in which money earnings per man have an underlying tendency to rise at a steady rate of 13 per cent per annum but will rise more (or less) quickly according as the unemployment percentage falls below (or rises above) the

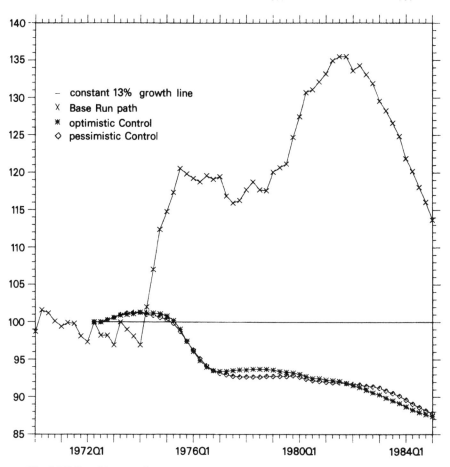

Fig. VIII.6 Money Earnings per Man. The figure shows an index, detrended at 13 per cent per annum, with an initial value of 100 in 1972Q2.

critical level of 3.76 per cent. As in the case of Figure VIII.1 for the Money GDP up until the advent of North Sea oil, we have drawn a constant horizontal line at 100 to represent the level that rate of money earnings would have had at any point if it had started at an initial value of 100 at 1972Q2 and had thereafter grown at a constant rate of 13 per cent per annum. A divergence of the rate of money earnings from this 100 base line shows the degree to which the rate of money earnings in the Base Run or in a Control Run diverge from this steady growth path.

An outstanding feature of the movements in the Control Runs is the avoidance of the huge inflation of rates of money earnings in the Base Run after 1974. From 1972 to 1974 the Control Run values of the rate of money earnings are slightly above the steady 13 per cent per annum growth because unemployment is below 3.76 per cent, as shown in Figure VIII.2. But from 1976 they are continuously falling (that is to say, the rate of money earnings is continually growing at something less than 13 per cent per annum). This is a representation of the phenomenon that we noted in discussing the unemployment percentage in Figure VIII.2, namely, the need for the rate of money earnings to grow less rapidly than the money earnings bill (and thus less rapidly than the total Money GDP) in order to make room for the employment of a larger number of workers. Much of the slow growth of the rate of money earnings relative to the money earnings bill occurs in 1975 and 1976, because of the restrictive fiscal policy in 1975 and resulting high unemployment. The reason for this we also explained when discussing the unemployment percentage.

There is one aspect in which Figure VIII.6 oversimplifies the movements of the rate of money earnings. In reality wage settlements are normally made only once a year, whilst our model supposes quarterly adjustments. If dates of annual settlements were spread evenly over the year, these settlements would correspond to our adjustments, but with bigger, less frequent jumps in response to a given employment situation in any sector. Such a spreading of settlements might be preferred in so far as it would lead to a smoother adjustment of the total wage cost of domestic production and thus, if profit margins were constant, to a smoother adjustment of the total Money GDP, and thus to less complication for the application of the fiscal controls. But even without it the annual movements in the rate of money earnings that are displayed in Figure VIII.6 are sufficiently small as to mean that it is not wholly misleading to replace annual jumps by quarterly adjustments one quarter as large.

In the design of our control policies fundamental importance must be attached to the nature of the assumed reform of wage-fixing arrangements. The basic feature must be that the wage movements respond fairly sensitively to variations in the unemployment percentage (i.e. to supply–demand conditions in the labour market) and that while they may be influenced in an important way by a steady expectation of a wage–price inflation (in our case, of no less than 13 per cent per annum), they must not be sensitive to actual price movements. If they are very sensitive to actual price movements, then there can be great fluctuations, indeed possibly explosive fluctuations, in a wage–price spiral. Thus if a rise in the level of prices caused a corresponding extra rise in wage rates, which in turn raised costs and prices and so raised still further the level of prices, there could be a marked upward spiral of inflation.

This danger is especially great if, as in our Control Run cases, the rate of indirect tax is a main instrument of control. Suppose some rise in the indirect tax rate is required for control purposes. This will raise prices (although not Money GDP which we measure at factor cost). But if this leads to a rise in wage claims, Money GDP will now tend to rise further above its target level unless there is a corresponding reduction of employment. But in so far as the Money GDP is raised, the rate of indirect tax will need to be raised still further to bring the Money GDP back on to its target path. The result could be a very vicious spiral of rising prices and money wage rates combined with rising unemployment.

The Treasury Model of 1980 contained a wage equation that purports to represent the effects of present wage-fixing institutions and that makes wage claims respond (1) to recent increases in the cost of living so as completely to compensate for such losses of purchasing power and (2) to the level of unemployment but with less sensitivity to such demand—supply conditions as in the wage equation used for our Control Runs. This equation is reproduced as equation (10) in Section 4 of Appendix A.

In the light of this, we carried out certain exercises. Each of these involved a further rerun of history, each with a different wage equation, but always with our control rules otherwise unchanged from the optimistic Control Run. First, if we modify our wage equation simply by assuming that there is a zero response of wage claims to changes in the unemployment percentage, the level of unemployment climbs drastically through the 1970s and 1980s, approaching levels currently observed. Second, if we then assume some sensitivity to unemployment, but a sensitivity only as great as that assumed in the Treasury model, unemployment grows less markedly but remains on average some 0.75 percentage points higher than in our two Control Runs. Third and most significantly, if we use the full response of wage claims to past changes in the cost of living from the Treasury equation, even if wage claims are as sensitive to unemployment as in our Control Runs, the outcome hovers on the verge of a full explosive instability of rising prices and rising unemployment. This instability is displayed and further examined in a Note at the end of this chapter. These exercises confirm the crucial importance to the whole of our control policy of achieving reform of wage-fixing institutions, so that they put a sufficiently large weight on responses of wage settlements to demand—supply conditions in the labour market and a sufficiently low weight on responses to actual changes in the cost of living.

Finally Figures VIII.7 and VIII.8 show the movements in the foreign-exchange rate* with its consequential effect on the competitiveness index of UK products *vis-à-vis* foreign products, which represent the weapons by which control is sought over the balance of payments on current account.

---

*The ratio between the exchange rate against a basket of currencies (displayed in Figure VIII.7) and the dollar exchange rate (which appears in the equation listing in Appendix A) has been treated as exogenous (i.e. the same for the Base Run path and all control paths); it is equal to the actual ratio up to 1980Q2, and equal to that projected on the Model from then onwards.

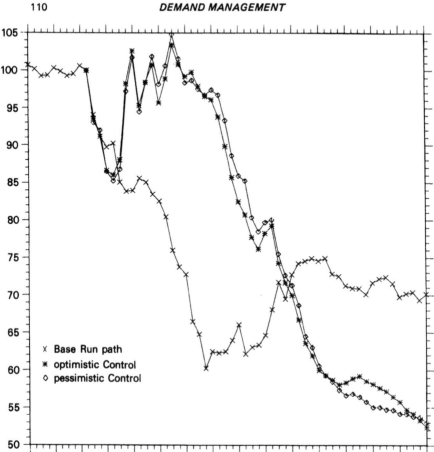

Fig. VIII.7 Effective Exchange Rate (against a basket of currencies). The figure shows an index, with an initial value of 100 in 1972Q2. A fall denotes a depreciation.

An outstanding feature of these figures is the enormous deterioration in the competitiveness of UK products in the Base Run since 1977, as domestic costs were inflated more rapidly than foreign costs, while the foreign-exchange value of the pound failed to depreciate to offset these domestic events and in fact appreciated. In contrast with this outcome, in the case of both the Control Runs, although domestic cost inflation was much less than with the Base Run, the foreign-exchange rate was consistently depreciated with the result that instead of a huge loss of competitiveness there was a consistent gain of competitiveness after 1975. As was discussed in connection with Figure VIII.3, this increase in

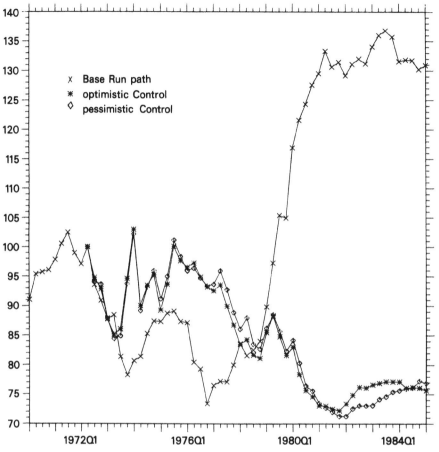

Fig. VIII.8   Index of Competitiveness (home wage costs expressed in foreign currency as a percentage of foreign wage costs with an initial value of 100 in 1972Q2).

competitiveness under the two Control Runs was the instrument whose delayed and protracted effect was to restore the balance of payments on current account from the great deficit experienced during the early years of the world recession.

Indeed, the contrasting movements of the foreign-exchange rate and of the competitiveness index under the Base Run and under the two Control Runs underlines the two contrasting methods of dealing with the balance of payments in the course of the world recession. With the Base Run, domestic economic activity has been brutally restricted with an unemployment percentage of 12 per cent or more, and the consequential great restriction of the domestic demand for imports has avoided strain on the balance of payments in spite of a huge loss of competitiveness. With the Control Runs, domestic activity has been maintained with an unemployment percentage of some 4 per cent but at the cost initially of having to finance a large balance of payments deficit, ultimate removal of which rested upon a big improvement in the competitiveness of UK manufactures.

We may perhaps summarise by saying that the policy controls seem to have worked reasonably well in keeping the Money GDP on target and in maintaining employment and economic activity, but at the cost of (1) a very large, albeit temporary, deficit on the balance of payments and (2) large swings in the rates of tax and so in real disposable incomes, the success of the whole operation depending essentially upon the implementation of a suitable reform of wage-fixing institutions.

2. Some Structural Implications

The main purpose of the present study is to examine the possibility of using finely tuned fiscal, foreign-exchange and wage-fixing instruments of control to keep the Money GDP, the balance of payments on current account and the unemployment percentage on some predetermined target paths. Section 1 of this chapter provided an exercise in this pattern of control by applying this policy to a given set of conditions: namely, to a model of the UK economy (as described in Appendix A) as it operated in the actual conditions of 1972–80 and in a forecast of conditions for the years 1980–5.

We have in fact applied the controls over a troubled and interesting period of history, and this raises a basic structural economic issue, separate from the details of the performance of our particular controls. How far can a single country that is very open to world conditions, such as the UK, maintain its domestic economic activity during a period of serious world depression? As explained in connection with Figures VIII.3 and VIII.8, the maintenance of balance of payments equilibrium in conditions in which the UK's real spendable income is maintained and developed, while foreign demand for UK exports is depressed, necessitates a very large adverse movement of the terms of trade. Is the game worth the candle? In particular, does the country gain more from maintaining its domestic production of goods and services at a full-employment level than it loses from the consequential deterioration in the terms at which it can exchange its output for imported goods? And if so, how much does it gain, and how is the net gain distributed among the main groups in the economy?

It is to be emphasised that the answers to these structural questions do not depend essentially upon the choice of a finely tuned New Keynesian strategy. Any set of controls that successfully maintained full employment and balance of payments equilibrium in the same open world conditions would be presented with these same structural questions. The particular merits or demerits of finely tuned New Keynesianism are to be judged on the grounds discussed in Section 1: how successful was it in keeping the target variables on their target paths from quarter to quarter? The present section digresses to see what indications this exercise can provide about answers to the structural questions raised above.

It so happens (see Figures VIII.1–VIII.8) that the target variables (Money GDP, balance of payments and unemployment percentage) were all more or less on their desired target levels both in 1972Q1 (just before the starting point of the control action) and also ten years later with the optimistic Control Run in 1982Q1. One can thus look at the structural implications of maintaining employment in the face of world depression by comparing the optimistic Control Run position in 1982Q1 with the position in 1972Q1. One can also at the same time compare the Base Run position with the optimistic Control Run position in 1982Q1. It should be remembered that the Base Run position in 1982Q1 does not exactly reproduce the actual position in 1982Q1 but rather a forecast in 1980 of what would be the position in 1982Q1 on the unchanged policies of the conservative government. Comparison between Base Run and optimistic Control Run at that time can nevertheless be used to give a general indication of the difference that in the assumed conditions can be ascribed to the different choice of policies. Any differences between the optimistic and pessimistic Control Runs are of no real importance for what follows. We shall therefore discuss the former only, but omit the word 'optimistic'.

Table VIII.1 shows the increase in total output (i.e. real GDP) between

Table VIII.1

	Base Run	Control Run
Increase in total non-oil output due to:		
Increase in employment	-3.0^1	4.8
Increase in productivity	11.4^1	19.6
Increase in North Sea output (4.2% of 1972Q1 GDP)	4.2	4.2
Increase in real GDP, 1972Q1–1982Q1 (quantities measured in £m. at 1975 prices)	12.6	28.6

[1] These figures, based on a forecast made in 1980, suggest a net increase in non-oil production in Base Run conditions of 8.4 per cent. Equation (37) in Appendix A, which is derived from past experience, suggested that when demand fell off employers would to a large extent maintain their labour force, allowing output per head to suffer. In fact, between 1980 and 1982 employers shed unwanted labour much more readily. The result is a similar reduction in total production, but one that is marked by higher unemployment and higher productivity than the figures in the table indicate.

1972Q1 and 1982Q1 in Base Run and in Control Run conditions. Both the Base Run and the Control Run are assumed to enjoy the same increase in real GDP resulting from the development of North Sea oil between 1972 and 1982, an addition to output that at 1975 prices represents 4.2 per cent of the level of real GDP in 1972Q1. The Control Run also has the benefit of a 24.4 per cent increase due to increased non-oil production, of which 4.8 per cent is due to an increase in the employed population and 19.6 per cent to increased output per head (representing an annual increase in productivity of approximately 2 per cent per annum over the decade). In contrast, owing to the great recession in UK economic activity, the Base Run enjoys a net increase in non-oil production of only 8.4 per cent (i.e. 11.4% – 3.0%).

Clearly there is a very large gain in total production due to the Control Run's maintenance of a high level of economic activity. But how much of this gain had to be sacrificed in order to maintain equilibrium in the balance of payments at very much worse terms of trade? This is illustrated in Table VIII.2, which shows the uses to which the increases in production were put in the case of the Base Run and of the Control Run. In the table these uses are divided between domestic consumption, domestic investment (both on private and on governmental account) and the balance of trade.* Our first and basic interest is in the proportion of the total increase in production that was absorbed in looking after the balance of trade.

In the case of the Control Run, out of the total increase of production of 28.6 per cent, an amount equal to 7.8 per cent had to be devoted to maintaining equilibrium in the balance of trade, leaving an increase equal to 20.8 per cent of the 1972Q1 GDP to be devoted to the improvement of domestic conditions.

It is important to realise what this 7.8 per cent measures. It does not indicate a need to get rid of a balance of payments deficit or to incur a positive balance of payments surplus as between 1972 and 1982. In fact, both in 1972Q1 and in the Base Run outcome for 1982Q1, the balance of trade is more or less on target (in both cases slightly below target as shown in Figure VIII.3). But because of the large deterioration in the terms of international trade between 1972 and 1982 (as discussed in Section 1 in connection with Figures VIII.3 and VIII.8), the *volume* of exported home products had to be increased by 76.6 per cent although the *volume* of imported products needing to be financed had increased by only 40.5

---

*These quantities are all measured in £m. of goods valued at 1975 market prices (including VAT and other indirect taxes). These values therefore exceed the value of the incomes going to the factors of production (wages, salaries, profits, etc.) by the amount of the revenue from indirect taxes. In order to convert these market-price values into the factor-cost value of the GDP (which is shown in the bottom line of Table VIII.2) it is necessary to deduct a factor-cost adjustment that represents the revenue from indirect taxes.

Table VIII.2 Real Gross Domestic Product (Including North Sea Oil), 1972Q1 and 1982Q1 (Quantities Measured in £m. at 1975 Prices)

	Actual 1972Q1 Real GDP	Base Run 1982Q1			Control Run 1982Q1		
		Real GDP	% increase on 1972Q1	Increase 1972–82 as % of 1972 Real GDP	Real GDP	% increase on 1972Q1	Increase 1972–82 as % of 1972Q1 Real GDP
Private:							
Consumption[1]	15,432	17,247	11.8	8.3	18,535	20.1	14.2
Investment[1]	2,693	3,117	15.7	2.0	4,271	58.6	7.2
Government:							
Consumption	5,097	6,052	18.7	4.4	6,052	18.7	4.4
Investment	2,169	1,395	−35.7	−3.6	1,395	−35.7	−3.6
Exports	5,737	8,441	47.1⎫	1.9	10,130	76.6⎫	7.8
Imports	−6,662	−8,943	34.2⎭		−9,361	40.5⎭	
Factor-cost adjustment + residual error	−2,620	−2,717	3.7	−0.4	−2,932	11.9	−1.4
Total real GDP at factor cost[2]	21,846	24,592	12.6	12.6	28,091	28.6	28.6

[1] Includes corporate investment, stock building, and private residential investment.
[2] Different prices indices are of course used for the different elements of this table – consumption, imports, exports, etc. – so that the figures represent the quantities of 'real stuff' imported, exported, etc., reckoning units of real stuff at their relative values in 1975. Since the same 'quantities' of imports that are thus included in, say, consumption are deducted under imports, the final total gives the quantities of home produced 'stuff'.

per cent between the two dates. This put a strain on real resources equal to 7.8 per cent of the 1972Q1 GDP.

In two respects both the Base Run and the Control Run are assumed to be facing the same balance of payments problem. In the first place, both are assumed to enjoy the same relief from the same output of North Sea oil, representing an increase of 4.2 per cent in resources as indicated in Table VIII.1. In the second place, as already discussed in Section 1, both are assumed to be faced with the same deterioration, some 12 per cent, in the world prices of products of the kind that the UK exports, largely manufactures, relative to the price of products of the kind that the UK imports, including primary products.*

But the marked difference, as discussed in Section 1, is the need in the Control Run for a large reduction in the price of UK manufactures relative to foreign manufactures in order to preserve the balance of trade in the world recession. This means that in the Control Run the UK terms of trade worsens (the price of UK exports relative to UK imports falls) by a further 10 per cent on top of the 12 per cent mentioned above. By contrast, in the Base Run (with its massive currency appreciation) the price of UK manufactures is greatly increased relative to foreign manufactures and the UK terms of trade actually improved by about 3 per cent.† Of course this severely curtails the demand for UK manufactures, and the balance of trade is only preserved in the Base Run by a greater restriction of total demand in the UK than in the rest of the world. But the fact that UK exports are not cheapened relative to UK imports in the Base Run means that resources equal to only 1.9 per cent instead of 7.8 per cent of GDP in 1972Q1 are needed to keep the balance of trade in equilibrium.

In brief, the Control Run indicates an increase over 1972 in total resources available for domestic use equal to $28.6 - 7.8 = 20.8$ per cent of the 1972 GDP, whereas with the Base Run the corresponding figure is only $12.6 - 1.9 = 10.7$ per cent. The Control Run thus has approximately twice as much as the Base Run available for improvement of the domestic situation.

Table VIII.2 also shows how these two amounts were used to raise private consumption, private investment, government consumption of goods and services, and government investment. The Control Run results,

---

*The deterioration in the world price of manufactures relative to that of primary products assumed in the forecast for 1982 was greater than has turned out to be the case in reality. Thus Base Run and Control Run are calculated on an over-pessimistic assumption.

†As shown in Figure VIII.8, the competitiveness index deteriorates by no less than 34 per cent in the Base Run. This could be expected from the equations in Appendix A to improve the UK's terms of trade by 11 per cent. In addition there is the unexplained shock of a rise of some 4 per cent in UK export prices discussed in Section 5 of Chapter VII, which adds about another 4 per cent improvement. These effects outweigh the assumed 12 per cent deterioration due to external factors to give an improvement of about 3 per cent.

being derived in the way explained in the previous chapter, are based upon the assumption that the real levels of the governmental demand for goods and services, both on consumption account and on investment account, remain the same in the Control Run as they were in the Base Run; in other words, these items are treated as unchanged 'specified exogenous variables'. As a result Table VIII.2 shows the same changes for these items in both Base Run and Control Run, representing an 18.7 per cent increase in government consumption and a 35.7 per cent decrease in government investment.

In both the Base Run and the Control Run the greater part of the increase in resources available for domestic use is devoted to private consumption and private investment. The greater total available in the Control Run case allows private consumption to be increased by 20.1 per cent and private investment by no less than 58.6 per cent, the corresponding percentages in the case of the Base Run being only 8.3 per cent and 2.0 per cent respectively.

It must be remembered that in the case of the Control Run the level of private consumption is a residual figure in the sense that rates of direct and indirect tax are adjusted to keep the total demand for goods and services on their target path, and the main, if not exclusive, effects of these tax changes are on consumption expenditures. Thus, in equilibrium, the level of consumption as controlled by these fiscal instruments will simply be equal to the total available national product less what is needed as a result of other structural policies and developments to satisfy the needs of the balance of payments, of governmental demands and of private investment. But these other structural policies affecting government demands and private investment might well have been different in Control Run conditions. For example, in the depressed conditions of the Base Run there is an actual cut of more than one-third in government investment. It is most unlikely that this would have happened in the full-employment conditions of the Control Run; and merely to have maintained government investment at the 1972 level would have absorbed resources on a scale necessitating a reduction in the increase of private consumption from the 20.1 per cent shown in the table to 15.2 per cent. On the other hand, the huge increase of 58.6 per cent in private investment probably exaggerates the extent to which the maintenance of economic activity by the Control Run policies would have stimulated the capital developments undertaken by private enterprise,* and to this extent private consumption could have

---

*It does this for two reasons. First investment falls less in the Base Run than equation (41) of Appendix A projects would happen with the small growth in output over the period and there is thus an 'unspecified shock' in the investment equation, which is carried over to cause an increase in investment in the Control Run. Second, in the Control Run there is a higher output, a higher capital stock and thus more replacement investment; and the term relating replacement investment to the capital stock in equation (41) is perhaps too large.

risen by more than the indicated 20.1 per cent. Furthermore we may have overestimated the amount of resources needed to satisfy the balance of payments, since the estimates of the elasticities of response of exports and imports to changes in competitiveness may well have been on the low side.* To this extent also private consumption could have risen yet further.

The precise figures in Table VIII.2, which result from our exercise in finely tuned fiscal controls, should be taken with a grain, perhaps even with a small spoonful, of salt; they are nevertheless of such an order of magnitude that one can probably deduce with some confidence that with the Control Run policies as contrasted with the Base Run policies there could be substantial improvements in private consumption, after making allowance for the maintenance of equilibrium in the balance of payments and for the development of domestic investment.

There remains, however, a further question, which concerns the distribution of this improved standard of living. This is illustrated in Table VIII.3. The last line of this table simply repeats the figures for real private consumption from the top line of Table VIII.2. The rest of the table analyses the post-tax private disposable incomes, derived (1) from employment, (2) from social benefits, (3) from interest on government debt, and (4) from other sources of income from property; it is from the sum of these disposable incomes that the levels of real consumption of the bottom line are financed. The last three lines of the table indicate that the proportion of private disposable incomes that are saved was somewhat lower in the Control Run than in the Base Run. (This is because inflation is lower in the Control Run; see equation (67) in Appendix A.) This has the consequence that the superiority of the Control Run over the Base Run in the standard of living as measured by their consumption levels was somewhat less marked than if it is measured by their real disposable incomes, being 23.9 per cent against 17.0 per cent in the case of post-tax disposable income instead of the 20.1 per cent against 11.8 per cent in the case of consumption. There are in addition some very marked differences in the make-up of the totals of disposable income in the two cases, of which the following four features deserve special notice.

First, while the *post-tax* real disposable income from employment increases by 13.6 per cent in Control Run as contrasted with an increase of 9.8 per cent in Base Run conditions, the *pre-tax* real earnings increase by less in the Control Run conditions (namely, by 4.8 per cent) than in the Base Run conditions (namely, by 14.1 per cent). The reason for this is that the *money* levels of the personal allowances for income tax have been treated as a specified exogenous variable and have thus been kept at the same level in the Control Run as they were in the Base Run. As money price inflation was much greater in the Base Run than in the Control Run,

*See the comments following equation (27) in Appendix A.

Table VIII.3 Personal Sector Disposable Income and Consumption, 1972Q1–1982Q1[1]

	1972Q1 £m. 1975	Base Run 1982Q1 £m. 1975	Base Run % increase from 1972Q1	Base Run Increase from 1972Q1 as % of 1972Q1 Real GDP at f.c.	Control Run 1982Q1 £m. 1975	Control Run % increase from 1972Q1	Control Run Increase from 1972Q1 as % of 1972Q1 Real GDP at f.c.
Employment income[2]	14,971	17,077	14.1	9.6	15,697	4.8	3.3
− income taxes on employment[3] income	−1,652	−2,428	47.0	−3.5	−790	−52.2	3.9
− employees' national insurance contributions	−632	−723	14.4	−0.4	−489	−22.6	0.7
= post-tax employment income	12,687	13,925	9.8	5.7	14,418	13.6	7.9
+ social grants	2,237	3,558	59.1	6.0	3,310	48.0	4.9
+ debt interest receipts from government, net of tax[4]	386	615	59.3	1.0	1,173	203.9	3.6
+ other[5]	1,435	1,492	4.0	0.3	1,853	29.1	2.0
= disposable income	16,745	19,591	17.0	13.0	20,754	23.9	18.4
× ratio of consumption to disposable income	0.9216	0.8804	−4.5	....	0.8931	−3.1	....
= consumption	15,432	17,247	11.8	8.3	18,535	20.1	14.2

[1] All entries are money values deflated by the price of consumers' expenditure.

[2] Wages and salaries plus self-employment income.

[3] In the model, income taxes on employment income are not explicitly identified. So in this table income taxes are allocated *pro rata* according to the ratio of employment income minus tax allowances to the total taxable income on which income taxes are calculated (see equation (65) of the model in Appendix A). Our assumption that *all* tax allowances are credited against employment income is an over-simplification, which however counteracts the neglect in the model of higher than basic rates of tax, which fall primarily on non-employment income.

[4] In the model, personal sector receipts of government debt interest are not separately identified, but it is assumed both in the present calculation and in the model that 80% of government debt interest goes to the personal sector. Income tax is deducted at the standard rate.

[5] Dividend receipts, rent receipts, employers' other pension contributions plus a small residual unidentified in the model, minus the balance of income taxes.

this results in the real level of personal tax allowances being much higher in the Control Run than in the Base Run, with the consequence that direct tax deductions are much lower in the Control Run than in the Base Run. But since consumption is the residual to be controlled by fiscal policy in the Control Run, any laxity in direct taxation must be counterbalanced by severity in indirect taxation, leading to a higher cost of living and so to a lower pre-direct-tax real wage. It may be that the Control Run would have been more realistically calculated on the assumption that it was the *real* rather than the *money* values of the personal tax allowances that should have been treated as the unchanged specified exogenous variable, in which case the 13.6 per cent increase in post-tax disposable income from employment would have been distributed between a real pre-direct-tax wage income (shown in the first line of the table) and the direct tax deductions (shown in the next two lines of the table) in a way more like the distributions in 1972 and in the 1982 Base Run. But it is the post-direct-tax employment income and not its distribution between pre-direct-tax income and amount of direct tax deduction that is relevant both for our New Keynesian fiscal control policies and also for the workers' real standard of living, so that this marked difference in the make-up of disposable employment incomes as between the Base Run and the Control Run is of quite secondary importance for our present purpose.[*]

The second notable feature of Table VIII.3 is the marked rise in social grants between 1972 and the 1982 Base Run, which is to be explained by the large rise in the payments of unemployment benefit and supplementary benefit due to the large rise in unemployment. But an unexpected feature of the table is the fact that social grants in the Control Run are not much lower than those in the Base Run in 1982, even though the level of unemployment in the Control Run remains close to the relatively low 1972 level. The economic model on which these calculations are based almost certainly underestimates the reduction in social grants that would in fact result from keeping unemployment down to the 1972 level.[†] In

---

[*]It is interesting to note that as a fluke coincidence the increase of 4.8 per cent in the total pre-tax real employment income between 1972 and the 1982 Control Run exactly corresponds to the increase of 4.8 per cent in the employed labour force over this period. In other words, the real earnings per head before deduction of income tax remain the same between 1972 and the 1982 Control Run. More or less the whole of the available improvement in real employment income per head is taken out in the greatly improved personal allowances under the income tax. The difference between the zero growth in real earnings per head and the 19.6 per cent growth in product per worker shown in Table VIII.1 is arithmetically accounted for as follows (a minus sign lowers real earnings per man): (1) shift to profit, −5 per cent, (2) fall in the price of consumption goods relative to the price of domestic output, + 3.1 per cent, (3) terms of trade loss as percentage of Money GDP, −7.9 per cent, (4) increased payments to the oil sector for oil purchases, −6 per cent of Money GDP, (5) increased indirect tax burden, −3.8 per cent; total, −19.6 per cent.

[†]The adjustment made to the coefficient on unemployment in equation (86) in the model in Appendix A caused it to take too low a value.

fact social grants in the Control Run conditions would be less than those shown in Table VIII.3 unless there had been a substantial change in other social policies (e.g. in raising the real value of child benefits) to absorb much of the saving on the costs of unemployment relief. But once again for our present purposes this is of secondary importance. Since consumption is the residual in the control mechanism, it follows that if social grants had been less than as shown in the table for the Control Run, then taxation would have been correspondingly reduced and post-tax employment incomes correspondingly increased to maintain the same level of total consumption expenditure. If we combine post-tax employment income with social grants (i.e. take the 'private' wage and the 'social' wage together) the figure in the 1982 Control Run is 18.8 per cent up on the corresponding 1972 figure.*

This 18.8 per cent increase available in the Control Run to raise the post-tax real disposable incomes from employment and social grants may be compared with the 23.9 per cent increase that the table shows to be available for disposable incomes as a whole. Indeed, while disposable incomes from earnings and social grants together rose by 18.8 per cent, disposable incomes from interest on government debt rose by no less than 203.9 per cent and from other property incomes by 29.1 per cent. These two last rises were markedly greater than in the Base Run where the two corresponding increases in 1972 were 59.3 per cent and 4.0 per cent respectively. The Control Run is thus marked by an appreciable increase in the ratio of incomes from property to incomes from work and social grants.

This shift towards incomes from interest on government debt in the case of the Control Run is the third notable feature of Table VIII.3. It may be explained on the following lines. As was explained in Section 1, because of the world recession there was a heavy deficit in the balance of payments between 1976 and 1981, a deficit that, because of the delays in the responses of trade channels to price changes, was only slowly removed by the necessary exchange-rate adjustments (see Figure VIII.3). With a New Keynesian policy this depression in the external world's net demand for UK products was balanced by a reduction in tax rates to stimulate consumption expenditures. These tax reductions implied a budget deficit, so that by the time that equilibrium was restored to the balance of payments the national debt and the interest payable on it had

---

*The 1982 Control Run figures show (1) high personal tax allowances with (2) high social grants, which are two of the basic conditions necessary to remove the poverty trap. But they do so at the cost of no increase at all between 1972 and 1982 in the real wage rate before deduction of direct tax. We might thus describe the Control Run outcome as a combination of a New Keynesian policy to maintain full employment and a tax policy to remove the poverty trap, the latter being a feature that is quite irrelevant for the purpose of this study.

grown to a markedly higher level than would otherwise have been the case.*

Fourth, there is a shift towards other property incomes in the Control Run. The reduction in the foreign-exchange rate and the consequential deterioration in the terms of trade needed to make UK manufactures cheap relative to foreign manufactures, which we have discussed above, will in fact cause some shift to profit. Thus if profit margins on home production of goods for use at home remain unchanged, profit margins on goods that compete with foreign goods in export or in domestic markets are likely to rise because the depreciation of the exchange rate will raise the sterling price of foreign manufactures. This increase in the profitability of industries engaged in competition with foreign suppliers causes an appreciable shift of income in favour of the owners of business enterprises. In the Control Run the share of profit in Money GDP increases by some 5 per cent, largely for this reason.

We may summarise the conclusions of this section in the following way.

The Control Run policies, if successful, will certainly lead to a considerably higher real output than will the Base Run policies. This will be sufficient to leave a considerably higher amount of real resources to be used for domestic purposes, even when allowance has been made for the considerably greater amount of domestic resources needed to keep the balance of payments in equilibrium, so long as the UK is maintaining a full-employment level of activity in the teeth of a world slump.

Control Run policies would without much doubt result in a higher level of capital development and investment activity at home under the stimulus of expanding markets due to the maintenance of economic activity, but there is every reason to believe that there would still remain a sufficient amount of increased product to enable standards of consumption to be promoted to higher levels with Control Run policies than with Base Run policies.

The distribution of disposable income would, however, be more favourable to incomes from property relative to earned incomes in Control Run conditions than it would be in Base Run conditions. First, the financing of a greater budget deficit due to the maintenance of domestic economic activity by reduced taxation during the first years of world recession would lead to a higher national debt and thus to increased

*As explained at length in Chapter V, the longer-term structural changes that would be appropriate under a New Keynesian policy, if it were designed to improve the budgetary balance and reduce the national debt, would be as follows. Reduce the exchange rate in order to encourage a balance-of-trade surplus and reduce interest rates in so far as this balance-of-trade surplus allowed foreign lending to rise without a strain on the overall balance of payments. The reduction in interest rates would serve also to encourage domestic private investment. Taxes would then be raised to hold down consumption in order to balance the increased expenditures on UK products due to the increased foreign and domestic investments; and the consequential budget surplus would serve to reduce the national debt.

payments of interest to national-debt holders. Second, the maintenance and stimulation of profit margins resulting from the maintenance and stimulation of the demand for UK products, particularly through the stimulus to the demand for products that competed with foreign products, would result in some shift to profits relative to wage incomes in UK businesses. Because of this, the absolute level of wage earnings and social grants would be much the same in the Central Run as in the Base Run. But a considerable part of the higher property incomes would of course accrue to the wage earners as a result of their savings.

Finally, it cannot be too often repeated that the success of these New Keynesian policies (and indeed, as far as one can see, of any alternative policies for the maintenance of effective demand for domestic products) depends above all on a successful and appropriate reform of arrangements for setting rates of money pay.

Note to Chapter VIII on the Effect of Price Compensation in Wage Bargaining on the Stability of New Keynesian Policies

In Section 1 of this chapter we mentioned exercises in which we carried out further reruns of history, each with a different variation in the wage equation, but with all our control rules otherwise unchanged from the optimistic Control Run. The line marked variant 1 in Figure VIII.9 displays the outcome for unemployment if we use the full response of wage claims to past changes in the cost of living from the Treasury equation (see equation (10) in Appendix A), whilst assuming that wages are just as sensitive to unemployment as in our Control Runs. As stated in Section 1, the fluctuations in unemployment verge on instability.*

Part of the problem, as explained in Section 1, is that the rate of indirect tax is a main instrument of control, with increases in indirect taxes for control purposes leading to increases in prices, thence to increases in the rate of money earnings, prices, Money GDP, and again taxes. Suppose instead that wage bargainers could be dissuaded from seeking compensation for the effects of control movements in the rate of indirect tax but that otherwise there was full response of wage claims to past changes in the cost of living caused by other factors, and that every other aspect of history was as in variant 1. The outcome in this case is displayed as variant 2 in Figure VIII.9. The outcome is oscillations that are perhaps more damped and of smaller magnitude (which we would expect), but with a shorter period (because the response of taxes to higher Money GDP in the chain of reaction in variant 1 set out above is sufficiently

---

*In this Note we confine ourselves to showing the effect of various wage equations only on unemployment.

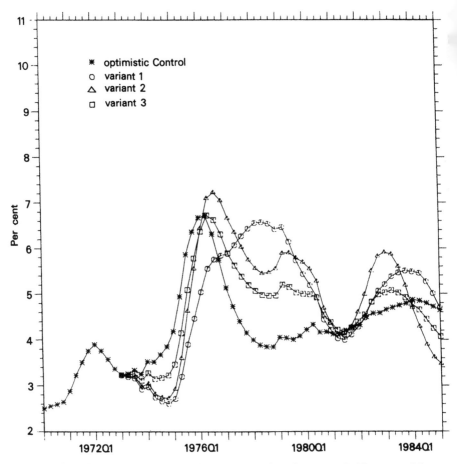

Fig. VIII.9   Unemployment Percentages for Reruns of History with Different Wage Equations.

lagged to introduce a smoothing effect that is not present in variant 2). Such oscillations are clearly still not acceptable.

Now suppose that, as in variant 2, there is no compensation for the effects of control movements in the rate of indirect tax, that there is only a 50 per cent response of wage claims to past changes in the cost of living caused by other factors, and that every other aspect of history is as in variant 2. The outcome in this case is displayed as variant 3 in Figure VIII.9. The oscillations appear only on the edge of what might be acceptable.

One might be able to *design* a system of control that would adequately reduce the oscillations of the economy in the circumstances of variants

1, 2 or 3, using the methods of policy design described in Chapters XII–XIV. We have already done some work along these lines, which we do not discuss in this book. However, even without detailed study, it is obvious that in order to reduce the oscillations it would be necessary to reduce some or all of the strength of fiscal control, the speed of competitiveness adjustment in the face of balance of payments difficulties, and the effect of unemployment on wages. (Our preliminary work confirms this statement.) The cost to be paid for these reductions in control activism would be that the economy would be even more sluggish in response to shocks such as the reduction in the world demand for British products that occurred in the world slump of the 1970s. A detailed design exercise of this kind would thus be unlikely to alter our conclusion of this chapter (which was reinforced by examination of variants 1, 2 and 3) that there needs to be a reform of wage-bargaining procedures that places a low weight on responses to actual changes in the cost of living.

We note in passing that the problem of instability in variants 1, 2 and 3 is *not* due to the absence of rational expectations in wage bargaining, or to wage sluggishness caused by staggered fixed wage contracts. Under rational expectations, and wage contracts lasting for only a quarter of a year, wages would respond one-for-one to *current* price increases (apart from forecasting errors, which we cannot accurately describe with our model) rather than, as in variants 1, 2 and 3, to changes in prices in the recent past. In a fourth variant we investigated the effect if everything were as in variant 2 except that there was a one-for-one response of wage claims to that part of *current* changes in prices not due to changes in the rate of indirect tax. The outcome displayed wild instability and is not shown here.

This result is in profound contrast with what is suggested by simple models of the natural rate of unemployment. In these simple models the existence of rational expectations and the absence of multi-period wage contracts together imply a 'vertical short-run Phillips curve'. This means that (apart from forecasting errors on the part of wage bargainers) unemployment always remains at a constant level equal to its non-accelerating inflation rate, which in this case would be 3.76 per cent. The instability in our case occurs because of important lags elsewhere in the model that cause a delay in the response of unemployment to increases in prices. The principal lags are that

(1) the fall in consumption in response to an increase in prices takes time (see the lagged real income terms in equation (67) in Appendix A);

(2) the fiscal control of Money GDP in face of an increase in prices is not instantaneous;

(3) unemployment takes time to respond to changes in real activity (see equation (76) in Appendix A).

To remove the lag in wage bargaining if these other lags remain appears simply to speed up the wage—price spiral in response to shocks; but because this wage—price spiral does not exercise the immediate influence over unemployment that would discipline wage claims and destroy its operation, the result of an increase in prices is an 'overshoot' of wages and prices in the present, which causes an overshooting of unemployment in the future.

†In reality in 1974 the profit markup fell: there appears to have been some increase in the ratio of prices to historic labour costs (perhaps caused by higher import costs) but an increase insufficient to keep up with accelerating wage increases. In our rerun of history the acceleration of wage increases is of course removed, but no adjustment is made for the higher ratio of prices to current labour costs which therefore remains.

Part Three

**Some Administrative Problems
of Fiscal Control**

CHAPTER IX

The Use of Indirect Taxes as a Regulator

In this and the two following chapters we consider some of the practical problems that would arise if rates of tax were to be varied frequently and promptly in order to control the flow of total money expenditures on goods and services. In Chapter X we consider the problems that would arise in the use of income tax, and in Chapter XI those that would arise in the use of taxes or other levies on wages, as regulators of demand. We start in this chapter with the problems involved in making frequent changes in the rates of indirect taxes.

1. Quantitative Effects

The indirect taxes which are relevant for this purpose are VAT and those excise duties that are enumerated in Section 3 below. In 1980/1 the yield of these indirect taxes was as follows:

VAT	£10,967m.
Excise duties	£ 9,951m.
Total	£20,918m.

In 1980/1 the gross domestic product at factor cost was £231,082m., so that the revenue from VAT represented some 4.8 per cent and the excise duties some 4.3 per cent of the Money GDP. Variations in these indirect taxes could thus constitute a very significant regulator of demand. A 10 per cent variation of all these rates of duty above or below their ruling levels would thus have represented a variation of plus or minus some 1 per cent of Money GDP; and there is no reason why variations in the rates of duty should be so strictly limited. In the case of VAT, for example, a 10 per cent change would represent a change of only 1.5 percentage points on a VAT rate of 15 per cent (i.e. a variation between the limits of 16.5 per cent and 13.5 per cent). Indeed, as is explained in Section 3 below, there are already existing powers for the use of VAT as a regulator that allow a 25 per cent variation of the existing rate (i.e. a variation between 18.75 per cent and 11.25 per cent).

The quantitative impact effect of a tax change depends also upon the extent to which the taxpayers adjust their consumption or their savings to meet the change. Hence the effects of changes in indirect taxes are likely to differ considerably from those resulting from changes in direct taxation or in the receipt of transfer payments (e.g. a social dividend). In so far as a change in a direct tax or a transfer payment and so in disposable income is expected to be temporary (which is likely to be so in the case of a stabilising surcharge or subsidy), then on the 'permanent-income' principle the temporary change is likely to affect mainly the taxpayer's savings. In so far, however, as a rise in an indirect tax and so in the money price of consumption goods and services is expected to be temporary, there will be a strong incentive to postpone consumption until prices fall again. This could, however, lead to a perverse speculative effect if, in anticipation of an expected rise in an indirect tax in a period when damping down of money expenditures is needed, consumers spent heavily in order to purchase before prices were raised. The moral is that if indirect taxes are to be used successfully as a fine-tuning regulator the authorities must be able and willing to change the rate quickly and, if necessary, frequently. By speed of change is meant a short time lag between the realisation by the authorities that the economy needs a boost or a restraint and the actual application of the new rate of tax.

The basic question is, therefore, whether quick and frequent changes in rates of indirect tax would be administratively feasible.

2. The Distinction between the 'Destination' Principle and the 'Origin' Principle

Indirect taxes can be levied in principle either on what is produced or on what is consumed. In a closed economy, in which what is produced at home is consumed at home, the distinction may have administrative implications but is of little economic importance. If the goods in question enter into trade with other countries, the choice of principle is important.

VAT and the excise duties are at present levied on domestic consumption, i.e. on what is called the destination principle, imports being subject to tax and exports being untaxed. A rise in the rate of tax at any given exchange rate may, therefore, be expected to have a favourable effect on the balance of trade in that it would discourage the domestic purchase of imports as much as the purchase of home-produced goods and would encourage the sale of home-produced goods in the untaxed export markets in preference to the taxed home market. In so far as this occurred the balance of trade would be improved, but simultaneously *pro tanto* the effect of the rise in the rate of tax in restraining the growth of expenditure on domestic production, which is the major objective of the change, would be damped down. These effects could, of course, be offset by some simultaneous appreciation of the exchange rate.

If, however, indirect taxes were levied on domestic production, i.e. on what is called the origin principle, with exports taxed and imports untaxed, the position would be different. A general rise in the tax rate, by reducing consumers' real incomes, would in both cases have some favourable effect on the balance of trade in reducing the demand for all goods (including imports) and releasing home resources for the production of exports. But with imports untaxed and exports taxed, any favourable effect on the balance of trade from a general reduction in domestic spending power would be likely to be swamped by a switch of spending from taxed home produce to untaxed imports, while production for exports was discouraged by the tax just as much as was production for the home market. In so far as this worsened the balance of trade it would *pro tanto* increase the effect of its main objective in damping down home activity. These effects could be offset by some depreciation of the exchange rate.

3. Existing Powers to Vary Indirect Taxes for the Regulation of Demand

The authorities already possess powers to make limited changes in rates of duty for the purpose of regulating the economy.

The excise duties with existing regulator powers attached to them are the following:

(1) Tobacco products duties:
    (i) Cigarettes
    (ii) Cigars
    (iii) Hand-rolling tobacco
    (iv) Other smoking tobacco and chewing tobacco;
(2) Duties on hydrocarbon oils, petrol substitutes and power methylated spirits;
(3) Duties on alcoholic drinks (beer, wine, spirits, cider);
(4) Car tax;
(5) Betting and gaming duties (except licence duties);
(6) Duties on matches and mechanical lighters.

The regulator power covering group 1 is in section 6 of the Tobacco Products Duty Act 1979, and the regulator power covering all the other groups is in the Excise Duties (Surcharges or Rebates) Act 1979.

Indirect taxes that are not subject to regulator powers are the protective duties, the EEC agricultural levies, vehicle excise duties (not collected by Customs and Excise), various minor licence duties that are in the nature of registration fees, and the Northern Ireland elements of what were 'transferred taxes' between 1920 and 1973. There seem to be good reasons for leaving all of these out of consideration in the present context.

For all of the duties mentioned in groups 1–6 above, the maximum regulator change allowed is 10 per cent on either side of the existing rate. The power relating to the tobacco products duties may be used separately for each separate rate of duty. The power relating to the other duties may be used separately for group 2, for group 3 and for groups 4, 5 and 6 together, but may not otherwise differentiate.

The regulator power was first introduced in section 9 of the Finance Act 1961, and at the time it covered purchase tax also. The original concept was that it must apply uniformly over its whole field, and indeed that was claimed by the then government as one of its major virtues – its scope was so wide that it would be capable of producing significant economic effects without weighing too heavily upon any single sector of industry. In 1964, however, the same government decided that a measure of flexibility was desirable, and the Finance Act of that year contained a provision for applying the regulator separately to tobacco, drinks, oils, purchase tax, and the rest. The reason was that the duties on drink and tobacco had been substantially increased in the 1964 budget, and it was thought that it would be inexpedient to raise them again if a regulator surcharge should seem necessary during that summer.

VAT was given a separate regulator of its own when it was introduced in the Finance Act 1972, with a limit not of 10 per cent but of 20 per cent, later increased to 25 per cent. The tobacco products duties were given their own regulator in 1976, when they were introduced to replace the old tobacco leaf duty.

The regulator was used in July 1961 to put a surcharge on all of the taxes within its scope. In 1966 there was a surcharge for tobacco, drink and purchase tax, and in 1968 there was a surcharge for tobacco, drink, oil and purchase tax. The regulator has never been used for excise duties alone in the narrow sense, i.e. omitting purchase tax, and there has never been a regulator rebate for any of the excise duties.

Most of the excise duties involved are affected by changes in VAT, since VAT is charged on duty-inclusive values. Betting and gaming, however, are (broadly speaking) exempt from VAT, and fuel oil and lubricating oil are zero rated.

4.   The Administration of Variations in the Rates of Excise Duties

Unlike VAT, the excise duties are single stage. The point of charge varies from duty to duty, but generally speaking it is well before the point of sale to the final consumer (e.g. delivery from manufacturer's premises, or delivery out of bonded warehouse). Rate changes thus do not apply to goods that have already 'passed the duty point' before they come into operation; hence the common phenomenon of retail sales at 'pre-budget prices' after a budget increase in one or other of the duties concerned. The period that normally elapses between the duty point and the retail sale varies, of course, from commodity to commodity, as also do the facilities for storage pending retail sale. In any case the public usually expect a duty *reduction* to be passed on to them immediately, even though it has not applied to the goods they are actually buying. Customs and Excise have power in section 128 of the Customs and Excise Management Act 1979 to restrict deliveries of goods out of bond for periods not exceeding three months when there is reason to fear forestalling, but the use of the power has its disadvantages as well as its advantages and is avoided as far as possible.

Administrative difficulties arising from changes in excise-duty rates are fewer and less intractable than those arising from changes in VAT rates, which we discuss in Section 5 below. There are fewer taxpayers to notify, no rentals or continuous services to cope with, no retail re-pricing to be done. If the government undertook to confine itself to a limited range of possible rate changes, on the lines suggested for VAT in Section 5(i), the big manufacturers and producers of excise-duty goods would no doubt work out all the corresponding price changes for themselves, and keep them up to date, as part of their own contingency planning.

It seems questionable, however, whether it would make sense to require the excise-duty industries, and their customers, to carry the whole burden of regulating the economy, given that nowadays the excise duties affect only pretty narrow sectors of consumption. There might, however, be expected to be non-fiscal objections to any *decreases* in either oil duties or tobacco duties — even small decreases within a generally rising trend: energy policy objections in the case of oil, health objections in the case of tobacco. But if those two groups had to be excluded from the full potentialities of a regulator provision, rather little would be left in the excise-duty field. It would not appear unreasonable to rely on the general level and trend of oil and tobacco duties to meet the lasting structural problems of energy and health, but at the same time to allow some variations around the trend levels in order to achieve temporary absorption or release of general spending power.

5.   The Administration of Variations in the Rate of VAT

(i)   *Some General Problems*

The administration of VAT involves collecting tax from a very large number of taxpayers. The basic procedure for the normal producer or wholesale dealer is that on the occasion of the issue of an invoice from a seller to a purchaser, the seller adds to the price of the goods an amount equal to the current VAT rate on that price. The producer or wholesaler then periodically, i.e. at the close of a period known as his 'tax period', pays to the Customs and Excise a net amount equal to the VAT that he has charged on his sales during that period, less the VAT that he has been charged on his business purchases during that period.

The standard tax period is three months. Taxpayers who regularly receive net repayments of VAT may opt for monthly tax periods, but are not encouraged to do so. There is a good case for abolishing monthly tax periods altogether in order to save staff in Customs and Excise. The quarterly tax periods are, however, staggered in the sense that for some taxpayers they end in March, June, September and December, for others in April, July, October and January, and for others in May, August, November and February. Thus the work of the Customs and Excise in dealing with tax returns is spread evenly over the months while the taxpayer enjoys a quarterly tax period.

There are certain transactions – notably retail trade and rental or similar continuous contracts for services – for which variations in VAT rates would present special problems. These are discussed in Section 5(ii) below. But there are a number of difficulties of a more general kind. There are a very large number of persons who are liable to VAT and a very large number of different goods and services on which VAT must be charged. With a change in the VAT rate a large number of persons must be notified of the new rate; they must acquire new ready reckoners for the adjustment of their VAT-inclusive selling prices; and they must adjust a very large number of prices. This means that, unlike the case of excise duties, some advance notice must be given of a change of rate, but at the same time the period of advance notice should be as short as possible in order to avoid opportunities for large-scale forestalling.

Because of these difficulties it would probably be impossible to envisage unlimited flexibility for changes in the rate of VAT. Certain constraints on such changes would probably be necessary. It should, however, be recognised that these constraints relate only to regulatory changes in VAT, and do not affect the 'normal' budgetary changes. A possible system may, therefore, be viewed as one in which the 'norm' rate of VAT is determined in the annual budget, as at present, and in which regulatory variations around this rate may occur subject to the following suggested constraints:

(1) The number of rates that could be levied might be limited by restricting them to full percentage point rates, e.g. VAT might be levied at 15 per cent or 16 per cent, but not 15.5 per cent. This restriction would have the advantages of not only ensuring relative ease of calculation in most cases, but also, by limiting the set of possible rates, allowing a similarly limited set of ready reckoners to be produced for the use of VAT payers.

(2) The magnitude of rate changes might also be limited in such a way that the rate could never be changed by more than some fixed amount, e.g. 2 percentage points on any one occasion.

(3) It is clearly important that there should be some limitations on the frequency with which rate changes occur. For example, the restriction might be specified in such a way that rate changes could only occur on specific dates at three-monthly intervals. This raises problems of avoiding moveable holidays such as Easter. Perhaps a better alternative might be to allow rate changes to occur only on the first day of any calendar month, and only three or more months after the last regulatory change. This latter method would have the advantage of increasing flexibility without increasing frequency of change, and might help to avoid some of the perverse speculative effect that might accompany fixed-date change.

Constraints 2 and 3 taken together would, therefore, impose a maximum range in which the rate might change in any twelve-month period. If rate changes were restricted to 2 percentage points on any occasion, the maximum rate change in any year would be 8 percentage points around the 'norm' set in the budget. This, of course, would not exclude the possibility of larger changes resulting from changes in the 'norm' rate itself.

(4) Flexibility of the VAT rate would operate more smoothly in a system that, as at present, has only a single positive rate of VAT. The reintroduction of a multiple-rate scheme would obviously create additional difficulties for the use of the VAT regulator.

(5) In addition, the minimum period of notice that precedes any rate change might be specified. A six-day interval, including a weekend, has been allowed for three of the four major rate changes that have occurred since the introduction of VAT; a fortnight was allowed for the fourth (the introduction of the 25 per cent rate in 1975). The problem would be eased by the fact that constraints 1, 2 and 3 above would mean that at any one time there would be only a limited number of possible new VAT rates.

With the computer, this might make it possible for Customs and Excise to have ready in advance, for all possible new rates, a complete set of notifications and new ready reckoners, which could immediately be sent out on the announcement of any change of rate. With a limited number of possible new rates an alternative procedure might be as follows. On the announcement of the 'norm' VAT rate on the occasion of the annual budget, all VAT payers might be issued with a set of ready reckoners covering all VAT rates which were possible within constraints 1, 2 and 3 before the next annual budget. If a new VAT rate could come into operation only on the first day of a calendar month, the rule could be that one week before the beginning of each month an announcement was made of the rate that would rule during the coming month, regardless of whether there was going to be a rate change or not. If this became the recognised routine, it might well be possible to avoid informing each registered VAT payer by post of a change in the rate. Announcement by wireless, in the press and at all post offices a week before the end of each month might suffice.

With either of these arrangements a minimum specified period of notice of a week might suffice, though it would, of course, always be possible to make special arrangements for a longer period of notice if on any occasion there were special reasons to make this desirable.

(ii)   *Some Special Cases*

There are certain types of transactions for which changes in the rate of VAT raise more difficult problems. The main problems arise in three cases:

(a)   retail trade;
(b)   rental dealers and contracts for continuing services;
(c)   the Post Office.

(a)   *Retail Trade*   The special problem of the retail trade arises for the following reason. Retailers sell in the main to personal consumers. It is impractical for retailers as a general rule to issue invoices to their customers most of whom, being final consumers, do not need them, since they cannot reclaim the VAT charged on their purchases. For this and other reasons retailers sell goods over the counter for prices that include VAT; the daily gross takings of the shop from sales will be recorded but no record will normally exist of the receipts from sales of particular categories of goods − nor would it be feasible in most cases to introduce a system that did keep such records. This would present no special difficulty if all categories of goods sold were liable to VAT at one and the same rate. VAT would be payable by the retailer at a given rate on the total of his gross takings from sales during any period at which any one rate of VAT was operative. Since VAT is included in the retail selling price the ruling rate of VAT, which for normal purposes is expressed as a tax-exclusive rate, would have to be converted to a tax-inclusive rate (known as a 'VAT fraction') for application to retail sales. Thus a VAT rate of 15 per cent would be converted into a VAT fraction of 15/115 or 3/23 for application to receipts from retail sales.

The difficult problem arises because not all goods are liable to the same rate of VAT. At present there are only two rates: a 15 per cent standard rate and a zero rate of tax on a class of zero-rated goods. Takings from retail sales are not normally recorded according to categories of goods sold, but the VAT fraction of 3/23 must be levied only on that part of takings from retail sales that arises from sales of categories of goods that are not zero-rated.

There are at present no less than nine special schemes for retail traders to resolve this problem. These schemes may be arranged under the following four headings:

Schemes A, B and F. These are broadly speaking the schemes which cover those cases in which the problem does not arise because either (Scheme A) the retailer is selling exclusively goods that fall into a single tax category, *or* (Scheme B) the greater part of his sales are at the positive rate of tax so that a simple, if not strictly accurate, rule of thumb can be devised for deducting from his takings a figure to allow for sales of zero-rated goods, *or* (Scheme F) the business is one in which the takings from the sales of the various categories of goods can be, and are, separately recorded.

Schemes C and E. When the retailer purchases his goods from the manufacturer or wholesaler, the distinction between the categories of goods can readily be made since the VAT will have been charged at the appropriate rate on the supplier's invoice. Schemes C and E are basically ones in which the retailer calculates his VAT liability in advance when he purchases the goods. In both cases, the prices at which the retailer will probably sell those goods is calculated (in the case of Scheme C, which is confined to small businesses, this is done on conventional mark-ups and in the case of Scheme E, which is available also for large businesses, it is done on more accurate estimations). The retailer's future VAT liability is calculated as these prospective sale values multiplied by the appropriate VAT fractions, less the VAT that he has been charged on the purchase of the goods.

The snag with these schemes (which might otherwise be the simplest and most appropriate ways of dealing with all retail trade) is that the retailer may be unfairly hurt or unfairly advantaged on the occasion of a change of tax rate. He will have incurred his VAT liability when he buys the supplies; if he has to sell them later when VAT is at a higher rate, he stands to make a windfall profit by selling at a higher price or, if the VAT rate has been reduced, he stands to bear a loss in being forced to sell at a lower price stocks on which he has paid VAT at the higher rate. Under Scheme C there is no adjustment for loss or gain on stocks. Under Scheme E stock must be taken on the occasion of any change of rate in order that the retailer may obtain on his existing stocks the appropriate repayment of tax if the VAT rate has gone down or be charged the appropriate extra tax if the rate of VAT has gone up.

Schemes G and H. Under these schemes, on the occasion of calculating his net tax liability at the close of his tax period (i.e. at the close of any given three-month period or at the close of any month, as the case may be), the retailer must calculate what proportion of the values of his total purchases of goods over the year ending at the close of his tax period fell into the various tax categories. (Under Scheme G the values of these purchases are the VAT-inclusive amounts paid for their purchase; under Scheme H they are reckoned as the values at which at the time of purchase they were calculated to be likely to be sold to the final consumers). The retailer's total sales during the tax period for which the tax liability is being reckoned will be split between the various tax categories in proportions equal to these proportions of goods purchased over the year ending with the tax period. The relevant VAT fractions will then be applied. This system of apportioning sales between the various tax categories can be continued unchanged when the VAT rate of tax is varied. The additional information that is necessary is to have recorded the total value of the retail sales (and so the values of the retail sales in the different categories) that occurred during the days covered by the one rate of tax and those that occurred during the days covered by the other rate of tax.

Schemes D and J.   These schemes are very different from each other except that for different reasons they both involve annual adjustments of tax liabilities.

Scheme D starts by simply apportioning the sales of any tax period according to the cost of purchases during that same period. But since a trader may buy his highly taxed goods during a period of low total sales and his zero-rated goods during a period of exceptionally high total sales (or vice versa) he may stand to pay much too much (or much too little) in tax. These possibilities are avoided under Scheme D by requiring an adjustment once a year under which the year's sales are apportioned according to the year's purchases of the various categories of goods; and a tax surcharge or rebate is made to adjust the tax actually paid during the year to the adjusted year's liability. This works so long as there are no changes of tax rates during the year. If there are any such changes, a special adjustment is made covering less than a year, i.e. covering the period between the last adjustment and the day of the tax change. This may well be an acceptable compromise if tax-rate changes occur infrequently. But if there were frequent changes, the situation would be very different. To take the extreme case, if there were a tax-rate change every tax period, this would be equivalent to having Scheme D without the annual adjustment.

Scheme J depends upon an annual adjustment that involves stocktaking. It results in splitting a year's sales between the various tax categories according to the categories of supplies bought by the retailer in the course of the year (as in the case of Scheme D) but also (unlike Scheme D) with an adjustment for the change in the stocks of the various categories as between the beginning and the end of the year. By means of the extra device of taking stock in the course of the year whenever there is a change of tax rate, this method also enables the sales to be apportioned accurately not only for the year as a whole, but also for any sub-periods of the year that have been liable at changed rates of tax. This is thus perhaps the most accurate method of all for apportioning total sales between the various categories. But like Scheme E, it involves taking stock whenever there is a tax change.

To summarise, all the retail schemes would involve keeping records in such a way that when there is a tax change the total sales revenue received during the period of operation of the earlier rate of tax could be distinguished from the total sales revenue received during the period of operation of the later rate of tax. Apart from this there would be no additional complications for Schemes A, B, F, G and H, except the inevitable nuisance of applying different tax rates to the sales in the different periods. Schemes E and J require in addition the taking of stock whenever the rate of tax is changed. They would remain appropriate, therefore, only to businesses that were able and willing to take stock frequently. If not, presumably such businesses could turn to Scheme H. The small business under Scheme C might be in difficulties in having either to bear the risk of gains and losses on the occasion of tax changes or to move to a scheme like G, which requires keeping records of purchases for up to a year for the purpose of apportioning current sales.

The nine existing schemes have been explained at some length in order to illustrate the sort of problems that more frequent changes in VAT would present for retail traders. These schemes have in fact been designed in response to successive situations and requirements that have arisen since VAT was first introduced; if more frequent changes in VAT rates were to be seriously contemplated, it might be wise to review the whole pattern of retail schemes in the light of this new situation.

(b) *Rental Dealers and Contracts for Continuing Services* Special problems due to changes in the rate of tax arise in the case of dealers who hire out durable equipment on contract to users for a predetermined periodic (weekly, monthly, quarterly) money rent. For example, a business that purchases a TV set and then hires it out at a fixed weekly rent to Mr Smith, will be able to claim repayment of any VAT charged to it on the purchase of the TV set, but will have to charge Mr Smith VAT on the weekly rent payable by him. Although the contract can be made in terms that make Mr Smith liable for a predetermined rent (exclusive of VAT) plus whatever rate of VAT is in operation at the time of any given weekly payment of rent, there are obvious inconveniences in a total weekly rent that is liable to change from month to month. Mr Smith must be made aware of the new amount and in turn must make arrangements to vary his payment.

It would be conceivable to design an alternative scheme for such rental dealers rather on the lines of Scheme C for retailers. That is to say, conventional mark-ups on the value of the purchase of a TV set by the business concerned might be agreed that represented the present value of the future rentals that were likely to be received on such a set; and the business concerned might pay VAT on the occasion of the purchase of the set on the VAT-exclusive cost of the TV set, multiplied by the appropriate conventional mark-up. The business would then be free to hire out the set at any rent it pleased without further liability to VAT. This would in effect amount to paying VAT at the rate ruling at the time of the purchase of the TV set in advance on the rental to be received from it. It would have the advantage of avoiding changes in the predetermined rental. It would have the disadvantage of risking windfall losses or gains to the rental dealer, if during subsequent weeks of the rentals on existing sets a change of VAT rates meant that new competing rentals by other businesses on newly purchased sets obliged the business to reduce, or enabled it to raise, its rentals on old sets purchased at the old rates of VAT.

However, there would be difficulties in any such arrangement. There are a large number of different durable goods of different types and qualities that are hired out to consumers, and the setting of conventional mark-ups would therefore either have to be very rough and ready or else would involve a lot of detailed negotiation and administration.

Moreover, this solution would not be relevant for contracts for continuing services, such as a contract at a fixed periodic payment for the periodic window cleaning of a particular building, since in such cases there is no durable good that is being rented to the consumer. The variation in the VAT rate in such cases means that either the contracted charge to the consumer must be varied or else the provider of the service must be prepared to absorb the change of VAT rate in his own net revenue from the service.

A possible solution would be to allow rental charges and fixed service contracts to be exempt from regulatory variations in the VAT rate, but not from changes in the basic 'norm' VAT rate. That is to say, such contracts would be fixed to charge VAT on the rent or service at the basic 'norm' rate ruling at the time of the contract and would be changed during the period of the contract only if the basic 'norm' rate was itself changed. Such an arrangement would to that limited extent weaken the effect of the regulator; but if the regulatory changes of rate were likely to be as frequently in one direction as in the other, it would not involve any appreciable unfair burden on, or relief to, transactions of this nature.

(c)   *The Post Office*   The Post Office computer is apparently not sufficiently flexible to charge different rates of VAT on calls made during different periods during which different rates of tax were ruling. Either the Post Office should improve its computer facilities (indeed one might have hoped that one of the main advantages of computerisation should be that changes of this kind could be made without too much trouble), or else it would be necessary to devise some special *ad hoc* arrangements for the Post Office. But clearly the computing inadequacies of our great telecommunications corporation should not be allowed to stand in the way of the stabilisation of the UK economy.

CHAPTER X

The Use of Income Tax
as a Regulator

In the period 1973–80 income tax revenue varied between 12 per cent and 18 per cent of net national income at factor cost; in the same period it constituted 32–42 per cent of total tax revenue (including national insurance contributions). Even the substantial shift from direct to indirect taxation in the 1979 budget did not undermine the dominance of income tax as the single largest element of government revenue. Consequently income taxation holds a widely acknowledged position of power as an instrument of economic policy. However, there are at present limitations on the flexibility with which this policy instrument is applied. Within the existing system a single tax schedule, announced in the annual budget, applies throughout the tax year, and for Schedule E taxpayers this tax schedule is applied to earnings in a cumulative manner, in accordance with the PAYE system. In this chapter we raise the question of the difficulties involved in changing the tax schedule, in terms of the burdens thereby imposed on taxpayers, employers and the Inland Revenue, with a view to assessing the possibility of making more frequent changes in the schedule than occur at present.

1.   Some General Costs of a Change of Tax Schedules

To a certain extent some of these imposed costs are already apparent in a system that regularly introduces a new tax schedule after the fiscal year is in progress. These costs include those borne by the Inland Revenue in altering individuals' codings and producing and distributing revised tax tables. Likewise employers must absorb the costs of putting the new tax schedule into effect, in accordance with the revised tax tables. Companies also have to modify their payments of Advance Corporation Tax in line with the change in the basic rate of income tax, and withholding from interest payments requires subsequent correction. Taxpayers themselves are subject to the costs of the delay with which the changes are implemented. All these factors will in turn have implications for the government via the impact on its revenue flows and the consequent implications for the financing of government expenditure.

2. The Difference between Cumulative and Non-Cumulative PAYE
Systems

When considering the possibility of implementing more frequent changes
in the tax schedule, the duplication of these costs would have to be offset
against any additional benefits that might accrue. However, it is to be
expected that additional costs would arise, which must also be taken into
account. The major impact would, of course, fall on Schedule E, since it
is only in the context of a pay-as-you-earn (PAYE) system that mid-year
changes in the tax schedule would have any special implications over and
above those already experienced as a result of the annual budgetary
changes. In order to identify these additional costs it might be useful to
examine the experience of other countries that operate a PAYE system
subject to mid-year changes in the tax schedule.

   In Australia, for example, there have on occasions been two, or even
three, different tax schedules applying at different stages in the year.
However the Australian PAYE system is non-cumulative, which means that
the tax schedule currently in force is applied to current incomes without
reference to previous incomes or tax payments; when a new tax schedule is
introduced it is applied to incomes in subsequent tax periods, again in
isolation from all other periods. The government then produces an 'annual
equivalent' tax schedule, which is applied retrospectively to total annual
income to determine tax liability. Any discrepancies between this liability
and the amount of tax actually paid during the tax year, which might arise
when income payments are not spread evenly through the year, are then
eliminated by the appropriate year-end adjustments. It should be noted
that this need for year-end adjustments does not arise primarily from the
flexibility of the tax system, but is a consequence of non-cumulative
withholding irrespective of whether changes in the tax schedule occur. In
any event the Australian system of personal allowances operates in such a
way that the likelihood of any individual taxpayer having a large outstanding tax liability is small: the system produces a bias towards rebates. The
flexibility of the Australian income tax system is, therefore, heavily
dependent on the non-cumulative nature of their PAYE system; and the
additional costs imposed by mid-year changes in the tax schedule would be
expected to be equivalent to those resulting from the normal annual
change, plus the (presumably minimal) costs of producing an 'annual
equivalent' tax schedule and distributing it to taxpayers.

   This does not allow us to infer, however, that a similar degree of
flexibility could be introduced into the UK system equally costlessly, the
major factor that militates against so doing being the cumulative nature of
the UK PAYE system. Rather than treating each tax period independently
as the Australian system does, a cumulative tax system operates on
aggregates of income, allowances and tax payments throughout the tax
year up to the present period. Adjustments are therefore made continuously

throughout the year, so that in the normal course of events, no year-end discrepancies need to be eliminated. This advantage, however, is offset by the costs of the much larger informational requirement of a cumulative system, since employers need to know each employee's earnings and tax history for the current tax year. This cost is especially burdensome where employees frequently change their place of employment. In addition, exceptional cases have to be treated non-cumulatively, introducing a further complication into the operation of the system.

For the purposes of assessing the possibility of introducing flexibility into the UK PAYE system, however, the most important feature of the system is that marginal tax rates in force apply retrospectively to total taxable income to date. Any change in the tax schedule would therefore give rise to an instantaneous, discrete change in tax liability for the year to date. While decreases in the rate of tax would give rise to rebates, which would have substantial consequences for the flow of government finance, increases in the tax rate would give rise to liabilities that do not relate to any current income receipts, and that are potentially large relative to income received in the subsequent tax period. For an individual whose income is spread evenly over the tax year, this can be seen in Figure X.1.

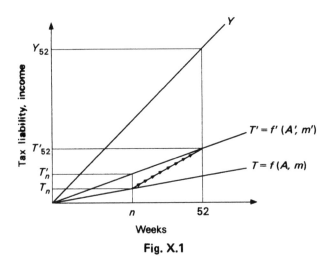

Fig. X.1

If the original tax schedule is $T = f(A, m)$, where A denotes the individual's allowances and m the marginal tax rate(s), then at week $(n + 1)$ a new tax schedule $T' = f'(A', m')$ is introduced, which has lower personal allowances and/or higher marginal rates, there is an immediate increase in the individual's liability of $(T'n - Tn)$. Such discrete changes in liability obviously raise considerable problems, which any proposal to introduce flexibility must overcome.

3.   One Solution of the Problems due to the Cumulative System

A promising starting point seems to be that of finding some way of spreading this immediate change in liability over the remainder of the year. One way of doing this would be to make continuous estimates of the individual's annual income, Y_{52}, using this as a basis for determining annual tax liability (given the new tax schedule), T_{52}, then spreading this estimated liability evenly over the remaining tax periods, so that a smooth continuous transition is made from present tax paid, T_n, to final tax liability T'_{52} (moving along the arrowed line in the diagram). In terms of the administration of such a system, this would obviously require major changes in the accounting procedures used. A set of three tax tables would be required: one to estimate income for the remainder of the tax year, a second to estimate annual tax liability, and a third to determine tax due this period. The mechanics of such a system are outlined in Note 1 at the end of this chapter.

This system introduces flexibility into the cumulative PAYE system, while ensuring that tax due is not subject to immediate and potentially large changes, but without necessitating year-end adjustments. Apart from the costs of introducing a completely new PAYE accounting system such as this, the additional costs of the flexibility achieved would then be the duplication of the normal costs of changing the tax schedule. The analysis of this system was based on the assumption that the individual's income is spread evenly through the year. Once this assumption is dropped it is necessary to acknowledge the possibility that some individuals' incomes after the change in the tax schedule may be less than the additional liability it implies. Nor can it be assumed that the rebates he would be owed would necessarily be greater than the additional liability incurred. This argument is set out in Note 2 at the end of this chapter, and it can be shown that such a situation is more likely to occur the larger the fall in the individual's income, the larger the change in the tax schedule and the later in the year that change is introduced. It is likely that the number of individuals who would find themselves in such a position would be rather small, and there is no reason to believe they would be more numerous than the 'exceptional cases' arising under the present system. Nevertheless, the costs of dealing with these cases must be taken into account in judging the desirability of such a system.

4.   Regulatory Changes on a Non-Cumulative Principle

An alternative possibility would be to forgo any attempts to integrate regulatory changes in income tax with the PAYE system. Instead a simple income tax surcharge could be levied at x per cent of tax liability in those periods for which the surcharge is in operation. This would involve relatively simple calculations, which could be incorporated in a single set of tables covering the potential rates at which the surcharge may be levied. However, minor problems would still remain: what for instance would be the status of PAYE rebates arising when allowances exceed income in the period – would the tax on tax imply a similar rebate on rebate? More crucial is the question of variations in income over the course of the tax year: with a surcharge in operation for only part of the period, two individuals in circumstances identical in every respect except the timing of their income receipts could end up with differing tax bills for the year. This would conflict with the fundamental requirement of horizontal equity in the tax system, unless a system of year-end adjustments were introduced to ensure equality of treatment. This latter option, however, amounts to tacking a non-cumulative element subject to adjustments onto a cumulative system. This seems far from desirable, and the option of an income tax surcharge would appear to have practical feasibility only if the cumulative PAYE system were abandoned in favour of a non-cumulative system.

The cumulative nature of our PAYE system would therefore seem to present, if not entirely insuperable, at least very substantial impediments to introducing flexibility into the system. Some of these problems are already apparent in the consequences of introducing the tax schedule after the start of the tax year, and it would be useful to have more information on how great the costs are in these cases, and how satisfactorily the methods for dealing with them operate, for instance, in relation to companies' payment of Advance Corporation Tax and the withholding of interest, or in the cases of those individuals whose allowances are reduced. It is almost certainly the case that any scheme for introducing flexibility into the PAYE system would duplicate these costs, and it may be that this would be considered decisive against such a scheme. Such a decision would reinforce those arguments in favour of announcing the tax schedule in advance of the start of the fiscal year, and not interfering with it thereafter. On the other hand, if the flexibility of the income tax system is considered necessary, this would strengthen the arguments in favour of replacing cumulative PAYE with a non-cumulative system.

Note 1 to Chapter X

Let

$$y_i = \text{income in week } i, \quad i = 1, \ldots, n, \ldots 52$$
$$Y_{52} = \text{annual income } \Sigma_{i=1}^{52} y_i$$
$$EY_{52}^i = \text{estimated annual income at week } i$$
$$t_i = \text{tax due in week } i$$
$$T_{52} = \text{annual tax liability}$$
$$ET_{52}^i = \text{estimated annual tax liability at week } i$$

A = personal allowances
m = marginal tax rate.

Annual income may be estimated on the basis of income earned to date as

$$EY_{52}^{n+1} = \sum_{i=1}^{n} y_i + y_{n+1}(52 - n).$$

Estimated tax liability can then be found by applying the new marginal tax rate to this estimate of annual income *less* personal allowances:

$$ET_{52}^{n+1} = m'\left[\sum_{i=1}^{n} y_i + y_{n+1}(52 - n) - A'\right].$$

Total tax due in the $(n + 1)$th week can then be found by dividing the outstanding tax liability by the number of weeks remaining in the tax year:

$$t_{n+1} = \frac{ET_{52}^{n+1} - \sum_{i=1}^{n} t_i}{(52 - n)}.$$

The necessary tax tables would operate as follows:

Table 1: Given week number and income for that week, estimate income for the rest of the year, i.e. $y_{n+1}(52 - n)$. This figure is then added to previous income to obtain estimated annual income. The individual's allowances, as indicated by his code number, are then deducted from this total to give estimated annual taxable income,

i.e.

$$\sum_{i=1}^{n} y_i + y_{n+1}(52 - n) - A'.$$

Table 2: This applies the marginal tax rate (m') to estimated annual taxable income to produce estimated annual tax liability, ET_{52}^{n+1}. Total tax paid to date is then deducted from this to give outstanding estimated liability, i.e.

i.e.

$$ET_{52}^{n+1} - \sum_{i=1}^{n} t_i.$$

Table 3: Given week number and outstanding estimated liability, this indicates the amount of tax due this period t_{n+1}.

Note 2 to Chapter X

Suppose an individual earns income at a constant weekly rate of y_i for the first n weeks of the year. The introduction of the new tax schedule in week $(n + 1)$ coincides with his becoming unemployed.

Estimated annual income up to week n $\quad = 52y_i = Y.$

Actual annual income at year end $\left.\vphantom{\begin{matrix}a\\b\end{matrix}}\right\}$ $= \sum\limits_{i=1}^{n} y_i = \dfrac{n}{52} Y.$

Estimated annual income at week $(n + 1)$

Tax paid up to week n $\quad = \dfrac{n}{52} m(Y - A).$

Tax due at year end $\quad = m'\left(\dfrac{n}{52} Y - A'\right).$

Outstanding tax liability $\quad = m'\left(\dfrac{n}{52} Y - A'\right) - \dfrac{n}{52} m(Y - A),$

$$= \dfrac{n(m' - m)}{52} Y - \left(m'A' - \dfrac{n}{52} mA\right);$$

if $\quad m' > m \quad$ then $\quad \dfrac{n(m' - m)}{52} > 0;$

if $\quad A' > A \quad$ then $\quad m'A' > mA \quad$ and $\quad m'A' > \dfrac{n}{52} mA.$

We require that outstanding liability be non-positive:

$$\dfrac{n(m' - m)}{52} Y \leqslant \left(m'A' - \dfrac{n}{52} mA\right)$$

$$Y \leqslant \left(m'A' - \dfrac{n}{52} mA\right) \dfrac{52}{n(m' - m)}$$

or
$$Y \leqslant \frac{52m'A' - nmA}{n(m' - m)}$$

The critical level of Y that satisfies this inequality falls as n increases, $(m' - m)$ increases and $(A' - A)$ falls.

CHAPTER XI

The Use of a Wages Tax
as a Regulator

The present chapter examines means of achieving regulator powers in taxation of wages. It first examines whether variations in the surcharge on employers' national insurance contributions could be used for regulator purposes. The conclusion is that this would not be possible with the present arrangements for its collection. It then considers what alterations to the machinery for the collection of the surcharge would make this feasible, and raises the possibility of a surcharge on employees' contributions. It finally looks briefly at the problems of establishing a new tax on the wages bill that could be used for regulator purposes.

1. Background

It could be argued that there are good reasons for having taxes on wages levied in as flexible a manner as possible on *both* employers and employees. It is to be expected that the impact of changes in these two types of taxes might be rather different from other tax changes, thus expanding the potential scope for economic policy. It is also to be expected that variations in the two types of taxes would have rather different effects from each other. Variation of the employers' tax would in the first instance bear on employers' costs, and so would act through causing employers' behaviour to change; variation of the employees' tax would bear on employees' income and act through changes in their expenditure. It could be maintained that, whatever approach to economic policy-making is favoured, there are advantages in being able to change either or both types of tax in a flexible manner, since there are advantages in extending the range of instruments of control available to the government. The aim of this chapter is to discuss what practical difficulties might be encountered if regulatory changes in such taxes were introduced.

Proposals to use alterations in a wages or payroll tax to regulate total money expenditures on goods and services have been made in the past. In the White Paper on Employment Policy of 1944 the government advocated varying the weekly national insurance contributions to be paid by employers and employed for this purpose. The intention was to achieve a speedy corrective influence 'which would come into play automatically ... and in accordance with rules determined in advance and well understood by the public' (Minister of Reconstruction, 1944, p. 23). But the plan was never implemented. Attention returned to this issue in 1961 with proposals for a wages or payroll tax collected through PAYE machinery. After much discussion these were altered to proposals for variation in the employers' share of the national insurance stamp. The main reason for the change was the comparative ease of collection through the stamp. In the budget of 1961, the government was given the power to collect a surcharge by attaching it to the employers' share of the national insurance stamp and the power to vary this surcharge by order as a regulator. However this power was never used. More recently, surcharges on employers' national insurance contributions have been used for the purpose of influencing total money expenditures, but variations in the rate of surcharge have been rare and the surcharge has certainly not so far been used as a tax with regulator power.

2. Present Arrangements for the National Insurance Surcharge

The arrangements for the imposition and collection of the present national insurance surcharge (NIS) are determined by the arrangements for national insurance contributions (NIC).* The rates and levels of the NIC are set from the start of each year. The NIS, which is paid by the employer, is equal to 3.5 per cent of the earnings on which NIC are payable; for all practical purposes the NIS is treated as if it were part of the employer's contribution and is not separately identified on the annual deduction documents on which the employer records income tax and contributions deductions, or in the monthly remittances that employers send to the Collector of Taxes. The Department of Health and Social Security (DHSS) in due course receive the money remitted in respect of the NIC and NIS from the Inland Revenue and is responsible, in accordance with directions given by the Treasury, for determining the amount of the surcharge and paying it into the Consolidated Fund.

This close link with the NIC system means on the one hand that the NIS is in general collected with no additional administrative inconvenience to employers and (because in normal circumstances it does not disturb the arrangements for NIC) with virtually no additional collection cost to the government; on the other hand, it also means that any attempt to vary the rate or coverage of the NIS independently of the NIC can undermine these advantages and have serious repercussions for the NIC system.

The liability for NIC, and hence for NIS, is non-cumulative; it is assessed on all the employee's earnings in a week (or month) up to the upper earnings limit (£200 a week), provided that they reach the lower earnings limit (£27 a week). Because liability is non-cumulative, changes in

---

*Throughout this chapter we use NI for national insurance, NIC for national insurance contributions and NIS for national insurance surcharge.

rates cannot be applied retrospectively as they can with PAYE; the employer must have up-to-date information on rates. There are thirty-three combinations of employee and employer rates, depending on whether the employee is contracted out, opted out (if a married woman) or over retirement age, and whether the employer is exempt from contributions and surcharge or surcharge only, with further variations for HM forces, mariners, and registered dock workers. The different rates are contained in eight volumes of tables, the main one being sent to about 1 million employers on the Inland Revenue mailing list, and the others being distributed to various special groups (employers with contracted-out employees, embassies, charities, etc.). It takes two months from the point at which a decision on rates is made to pass the necessary legislation and to compile, print and mail the tables, and employers argue that they must get the tables two months before implementation to enable them to make the necessary arrangements, including reprogramming where the payroll is computerised. The contributions that employers deduct for each individual have to be checked by the DHSS and recorded in that individual's account. This is because the contributions paid to the NI scheme partly determine the value of the benefits payable to the contributor, for example if he is unemployed or sick or in retirement.* It is therefore essential that, in the interest of contributors, the DHSS should be able to verify as far as possible that the correct amounts of contributions are credited to the records of the individual contributors. The need to check that individual contributions are right, to record them and to sort out significant mistakes makes the NIC system in some respects expensive to administer.

3.   Flexibility within the Present System

The DHSS now have practical experience of the considerable difficulties involved in effecting a mid-year change of rate. The method in 1978 was to issue a new full set of tables, to replace existing tables from a specified date. Employers were not asked to make any retrospective changes, or to provide sub-totals on the annual deduction cards for deductions made before and after the change; indeed either of these two courses would almost certainly have been impossible for them.

There are three severe sets of problems with such a mid-year change in the rate of surcharge. The first is the difficulty of quickly getting a whole new set of NI tables into use. It would be possible to speed this up somewhat if legislation were passed that enabled the surcharge to be altered by order, rather than it being necessary on each occasion to wait until legislation had been passed by Parliament. This would shorten the required

*See Note to this chapter.

timetable by perhaps one and a half weeks, but it would still be necessary to print and distribute new tables for the changed rates, and, unless alternative tables had already been prepared in advance in case a change should prove desirable, this would take some six-and-a-half weeks. Any further reduction in the four-month timetable would be dependent on employers being able to implement changes in a shorter time than two months.

The second problem is to get a whole new set of NI tables correctly used. Many wages clerks understandably find the system difficult to understand and the issue of new tables causes further confusion. Computerised payrolls present a problem because the data on which they operate has to be changed.

The third problem arises in checking deduction documents provided to the DHSS to determine whether correct NI payments have been made. Wherever there is a mid-year change in surcharge rate, the liability for a full year to national insurance payments inevitably depends upon the distribution of earnings between the periods during which different rates rule. Such dependence makes for difficulty in checking total surcharge payments, and therefore total employer contributions (since the surcharge is not identified separately but added into the total employer contributions). One of the methods of checking NI contributions used by the DHSS is to compare the ratio of employee contributions to total employee plus employer contributions (including surcharge). But where there is a mid-year change in surcharge rate this ratio will depend upon the distribution of earnings. The DHSS are then faced with the prospect of investigating for possible error all NI payments for which this ratio is abnormal, even in cases where this non-normality is due not to error but to changes in the earnings distribution. If DHSS contribution records are to be kept as free of error as possible, such investigations must actually be carried out.*

These three considerations suggest that, although it might be possible to contemplate variations in the NIS once during a year, the use of the NIS in its present form as a regulator is unthinkable.

4. A Regulator Power Using the Existing National Insurance System

One approach to the problem of providing for flexible regulator changes in NI charges would be to move away from the present system where the surcharge is amalgamated with the employer contributions and to introduce a separately recorded surcharge on employer contributions. If this were done it might prove possible to introduce at the same time a second

---

*Given the present dependence of some benefits upon contributions, in the manner explained in the Note to this chapter, this seems necessary.

separately recorded flexible surcharge on employee contributions, a development that may be considered desirable for the reasons stated in Section 1.

Under such a system there would be no need to print and distribute a whole new set of NI tables whenever a change was made in the rates of the surcharge(s), and no problem for employers in getting such new tables into use. All that would be needed would be a very simple single sheet showing the new ruling rate(s) of the surcharge(s). Furthermore, the checks applied by the DHSS on NI contributions would be no more difficult than they are at present. Thus the separation of the surcharge would solve the three difficulties with the present system identified above.

However, there would remain other problems. In contrast to the present arrangements (under which the surcharge really collects itself with very little extra work for officials and no extra work for employers), a scheme on these lines would involve more work both for officials and for employers. Officials would need a new means of checking the amounts of surcharge(s) paid that could cope with the fact that the rates of surcharge could change during the course of the year. This would require recording of sub-totals for each of the periods during which different rates ruled. For employers, the introduction of separate sub-totals would increase costs by requiring them to extend the number of their calculations. There would also be problems for them in reporting liability for the surcharge(s) to the authorities, since the design of existing deduction cards is cramped, and redesign to make sufficient space for such sub-totals could well be difficult. But these difficulties, whilst pointing to the costliness of introducing flexibility and suggesting that any such introduction would need time, do not seem insurmountable.

The treatment of the self-employed would raise difficult questions. If they were not subject to the surcharge, then this could encourage traders to become self-employed rather than incorporated businesses. On the other hand, any surcharge on the self-employed would probably have to be based on profits rather than wages and this could introduce distortions in the other direction. It could also raise questions of inequality as between self-employed and other income tax payers. The experience of selective employment tax would provide a guide here.

To ease the implementation of this system it might be possible to impose a set of constraints on the flexibility with which the changes in the surcharge(s) were undertaken.

(1) The surcharge(s) would be levied on that earnings figure for which NI contributions liability arises (i.e. all the earnings up to the upper earnings limit providing that the lower limit had been reached). It might be thought even simpler, and therefore preferable, to compute liabilities for surcharge(s) as simple proportions of the level of employer (and employee) *contributions*, but this would produce

inequalities between employees who are contracted in and out of the national pensions scheme and between employers who are at present exempt and not exempt from employer contributions. This degree of simplicity could be achieved only if the NIC system were itself radically simplified.

(2)   The number of rates that could be levied might be limited to half percentage point rates, e.g. surcharge rates might be levied at 3.0 per cent or 3.5 per cent of earnings but not 3.25 per cent. This restriction would have the advantage not only of ensuring relative ease of calculation in most cases, but also, by limiting the set of possible rates, of enabling a limited set of ready reckoners covering all likely rates of the surcharge(s) to be produced for the use of employers.

(3)   The magnitude of rate changes could be limited in such a way that the rate could never be changed by more than some fixed amount, e.g. 1 percentage point on any one occasion.

(4)   There could be some limitation on the frequency with which rate changes occur. For example, the restriction might be specified in such a way that rate changes could occur only on specific dates at three-month intervals. This would reduce to four the number of sub-totals that needed to be recorded for each surcharge by employers.

Constraints 3 and 4 taken together would imply a maximum range in which surcharge rate(s) might change in any twelve-month period. If rate changes were restricted to 1 per cent on any one of the quarterly periods, the maximum rate change in any year would be 4 per cent. But if this restriction were relaxed for the date of change following the budget, normally the beginning of the tax year, then larger changes could be achieved, with up to 3 per cent variation on either side of the budget rate during the course of the year up until the next budget.

Any attempt to set up taxes with regulator powers through variations in NI charges (on either employers or employees) raises the question of how far NI charges are viewed as payments into an insurance fund in which outgoings balance inpayments. If this belief is a widespread one, then the public may view changes in charges as signifying changed entitlement to unemployment and pension benefits. The economic response to such changes might then be rather different from what it would be if the changes were viewed as changes in wages taxation, and it would not enable effective regulator powers to be easily established. But this problem is unlikely to arise under the schemes proposed above where changes in charges would be brought about by changes in separately identified surcharges, rather than by changes in NI basic contribution rates.

5.   A Separate Tax on the Wage Bill

A more radical alternative would be to replace the NIS with some other form of tax on wages, either on employers or on employees or on both.

Just as with the previous alternative, there would be additional administrative costs, which in this case would be the administrative costs of operating what would in effect be a separate system on top of the existing PAYE and NI machinery. The only reason for this way of achieving regulator flexibility seeming desirable is if there was some way of achieving greater simplicity by the use of such a separate tax system. This would be possible if the tax were levied on employers only, and took as its base not wage payments to individual employees but the total of all wage payments made by employers within a specified period of time. Each employer would then simply have to calculate and report his total wage payments and total tax liability for the specified period of time.

This tax could straightforwardly be levied in a flexible manner. To ease its implementation, it might be possible to impose a set of constraints on its operation like those discussed in Section 4, particularly constraints on the magnitude of rate changes and on the limitations in frequency of rate changes.

The following questions would need resolution in any consideration of such a new tax:

(1)   There would be problems in defining the tax base; would, for example, employers' payments to superannuation funds be taxable? The length of the tax period (perhaps three months) would need to be settled.

(2)   Should the new arrangements take the form of a tax normally levied at a given positive rate, the height of which could be varied, or should it take the form of a variable tax/subsidy normally levied/ paid at a zero rate? The former would be administratively easier, but it would give rise to the danger of the tax being used as a convenient and attractive source of revenue and being raised over time to the point where upward regulator movements became politically unfeasible.

(3)   The new tax could mean the end of any NIS on employers if the new tax were sufficiently buoyant to raise (on average and abstracting from regulator variations) sufficient revenue to replace that raised by the NIS.

(4)   From an administrative point of view, it would be essential to have a lower earnings limit; otherwise the earnings of every casual employee who works for one or two hours a week would be brought into the tax net. At present, an employer does not have to record earnings of such casual employees who are below certain limits for tax purposes. One possible way to administer a lower limit would be simply to bring into the tax net the earnings of all those employees whose earnings are recorded for NI or for tax purposes. There would not be for this tax an upper limit on the level of wages per employee that were taxed.

(5)   The treatment of the self-employed would raise the same questions as those discussed in the previous section.

(6)   It might be thought desirable for regulator purposes to have a tax that applies to employees as well as employers, for reasons discussed in Section 1; but the system under discussion here would obviously not provide the means of doing this, since its nature is that taxes are levied on employers' total wage payments and not separately on the wages of each employee. If this system were introduced, any regulator tax on employees would still have to be instituted through either the PAYE or NI systems.

6.   Conclusions

It appears that regulator changes in the NIS, as presently administered, are not feasible. It seems possible to introduce flexible surcharges on both employers' and employees' contributions with some alterations to the present system. Another alternative is a new separate flexible tax on the total wage bill levied on employers only. Both of these possibilities have costs, which this chapter has attempted to identify.

Note to Chapter XI on National Insurance Benefit Entitlement

The extent to which benefits are related to contributions varies. Payment of basic unemployment benefit and of basic sick pay is conditional upon a particular threshold level of contributions having been made. Payment of earnings-related unemployment benefit (which is being phased out) and of earnings-related sick pay likewise depends upon a threshold level of contributions having been made. The levels of payment also depend upon actual levels of contribution (see DHSS leaflets NI. 12 and NI. 16). Payment of basic pension depends upon having made sufficiently many contributions. Payment of additional (earnings-related) pension no longer depends upon actual contributions paid but simply upon the level of earnings upon which NI contributions were paid (whether these were paid at a correct or incorrect rate) (see leaflet NP. 32). Payment of supplementary benefit does not depend upon a contribution record (see leaflet SB. 8).

This is a complex set of criteria, and the whole system could be enormously simplified if all dependence of payments upon contribution records were abolished, and any earnings-related benefits were related simply to recorded earnings. This would separate the recording of the basis for entitlement (earnings) from the recording of payments of contribution and would mean that checks on the latter would need to be only as thorough as checks on other tax payments (e.g. income tax).

Part Four

The Derivation of Control Rules
for Economic Policy

CHAPTER XII

Feedback Systems and Economic Policies

1. Some Special Models and Policies

Consider a dynamic economy, whose behaviour is characterised by some economic variables. We distinguish the following five kinds of variable:

(1)   policy instruments, which we shall denote by the vector u,
(2)   endogenous variables, the control of which constitutes the objective of economic policy, denoted by the vector y,
(3)   endogenous variables that can be observed, but that are not themselves objectives of economic control, denoted by η,
(4)   exogenous variables that can be observed, denoted by δ, and
(5)   exogenous disturbances that cannot be observed, denoted by d.

We shall call the variables in category 1 'inputs' and those in category 2 'outputs', and will treat those in categories 3 and 4 as constituting what may be called 'potential indicators'.

The problem of policy formulation that we consider is how to manipulate the 'inputs' to control the 'outputs', such that they behave in a desirable manner, in spite of the fact that these 'outputs' are constantly being buffeted by the effects of the exogenous disturbances. Indications for the more effective manipulation of the 'inputs' may be provided by the information available from movements in all or some of the 'potential indicators'.

We assume that the behaviour of the economy can be described mathematically by the difference equation

$$\begin{pmatrix} y_k \\ \eta_k \end{pmatrix} = f_k(u_k, u_{k-1}, \ldots, y_{k-1}, y_{k-2}, \ldots, \eta_{k-1}, \eta_{k-2}, \ldots,$$

$$\delta_k, \delta_{k-1}, \ldots, d_k, d_{k-1}, \ldots) \tag{1}$$

where the subscript k denotes the kth period. We remark that this equation is in 'reduced form'. Although such an equation always exists for an economic model, it is in general difficult to obtain the reduced form from the 'structural form' in which economic models are usually formulated.

DEMAND MANAGEMENT

To save printer's ink we shall adopt a shorthand notation: u_k^- will denote the set of all values of u in periods up to and including the kth period. Thus equation (1) can be written more concisely as:

$$\begin{pmatrix} y_k \\ \eta_k \end{pmatrix} = f_k(u_k^-, y_{k-1}^-, \eta_{k-1}^-, \delta_k^-, d_k^-). \tag{2}$$

f_k is some function that is determined by the details of one's economic model. It may depend on the period k, and is usually non-linear.

We are interested in devising a policy that can be expressed as a *policy rule*, in particular as a difference equation

$$u_k = \pi_k(y_k^-, \eta_k^-, \delta_k^-, u_{k-1}^-). \tag{3}$$

Notice that u_k cannot depend on d_k^- since these exogenous disturbances cannot be observed. The appearance of the outputs on the right-hand side of this equation leads to the terms 'feedback policy' or 'closed-loop policy'. If the relationship between the economy and the policy is represented by a block diagram, as in Figure XII.1, the reason for these terms becomes apparent. (For an excellent introduction to the use of block diagrams, see Allen, 1967.) Of course, in this general sense every economic policy is a feedback policy, since every practical policy takes

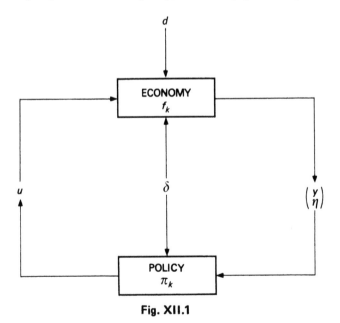

Fig. XII.1

some account of what the economy is actually doing. However, we shall shortly restrict ourselves to a much narrower meaning of 'feedback policy'.

Firstly, we assume that there is a vector of variables r, whose time path defines the trajectory that it is desired that the output variables y should follow. Thus the time path of these 'reference variables' defines the targets of economic policy. Note that there is an ambiguity in the term 'targets', as used by economists. It can mean either the desired levels of certain variables or those variables themselves. In this and succeeding chapters we shall use it only with the first of these meanings. The variables y and r will be called the 'output' and 'reference' variables, respectively.

Suppose that the sequence of inputs u_k^* would result in the outputs exactly following the reference trajectory, if *nothing unexpected occurred*. In mathematical terms,

$$\binom{r_k}{\eta_k^*} = f_k(u_k^{*-}, r_{k-1}^-, \eta_{k-1}^{*-}, \delta_k^{*-}, d_k^{*-}). \tag{4}$$

In this equation δ_k^* and d_k^* stand for the known or expected values of the exogenous variables, so that η_k^* and u_k^* represent the values of η_k and u_k that keep $y_k = r_k$ if nothing unexpected happens.

It is important to emphasise that, throughout this book, we assume that there is only one economic model. That is, we assume that there is a single set of functions $\{f_0, f_1, f_2, \ldots\}$, which is fixed at the outset, and which describes the behaviour of the economy over the whole fourteen-year interval which we consider. In practice, in addition to continuous revisions of forecasts of exogenous variables, the policy-maker would be constantly revising his model – possibly adding or removing equations, and certainly re-estimating parameters – so that policy would in fact be made on the basis of a *sequence* of models.

The input sequence $(u_0^*, u_1^*, \ldots)$ constitutes an 'open-loop' policy, since it is not affected by what actually happens to the economy. If this policy were followed, the economy would be blown rapidly 'off course' by the unexpected behaviour of the exogenous variables. (It would also be blown 'off course' because the model used for policy formulation is bound to be imperfect. However, we can account for any modelling errors, if they are not too gross, in the vector of unobservable disturbances d.) Finding the open-loop policy u_k^* is not a serious problem. Once the reference trajectory r_k has been decided upon, u_k^* may be determined from the economic model and the expected values of δ_k and d_k. (u_k^* may not be unique, for example if there are more instruments than controlled outputs, and it may not even exist if an unrealistic choice of reference trajectory is made. But these possibilities do not pose major problems.)

The policy formulation problem with which we are concerned is that of deciding how u_k^* should be modified to keep the economy 'on target', and it is this problem that is difficult.

If we write

$$u_k = u_k^* + u_k'$$ (5)

and

$$y_k = r_k + y_k'$$ (6)

then u_k' and y_k' represent the deviations of the actual time paths of u_k and y_k from the paths they would follow if nothing unexpected occurred. Also, η_k' will represent the deviations from η_k^*, the anticipated time path of the uncontrolled endogenous variables, while δ_k' and d_k' will denote the deviations of the exogenous variables from their expected values, δ_k^* and d_k^*.

Now if we assume that the feedback policy, when in place, will be sufficiently effective to keep the magnitudes of the deviations y_k' and η_k' small, and that the magnitudes of δ_k' and d_k' will be small, then we can design this policy on the basis of the approximation

$$\binom{y_k'}{\eta_k'} \doteq \sum_i \frac{\partial f_k}{\partial u_{k-i}} u_{k-i}' + \sum_i \frac{\partial f_k}{\partial y_{k-i}} y_{k-i}' + \sum_i \frac{\partial f_k}{\partial \eta_{k-i}} \eta_{k-i}'$$

$$+ \sum_i \frac{\partial f_k}{\partial \delta_{k-i}} \delta_{k-i}' + \sum_i \frac{\partial f_k}{\partial d_{k-i}} d_{k-i}'.$$ (7)

The partial derivatives in this equation (which are matrices, in general, since y, u, η, δ and d are vectors) are evaluated on the anticipated trajectory $(u_k = u_k^*, y_k = r_k, \eta_k = \eta_k^*, \delta_k = \delta_k^*, d_k = d_k^*)$, and consequently depend on the period k, even if the function f_k is itself independent of k (i.e. even if $f_0 = f_1 = f_2 = \ldots$). However, for the purposes of policy design we shall make the further approximation that these partial derivatives do not depend on k, so that (7) becomes a *constant-coefficient, linear difference equation*

$$\binom{y_k'}{\eta_k'} = \sum_i a_i u_{k-i}' + \sum_i b_i y_{k-i}' + \sum_i \theta_i \eta_{k-i}'$$

$$+ \sum_i \psi_i \delta_{k-i}' + \sum_i \phi_i d_{k-i}'.$$ (8)

These approximations may seem reckless, but it should be remembered that any policy that is designed on the basis of these approximations can and should be tested on the original model. We re-emphasise that the results presented in Chapter VIII were obtained with the full non-linear model described in Appendix A.

Equation (8) can be re-written as

$$\begin{pmatrix} y'_k \\ \eta'_k \end{pmatrix} = L_1(u_k'^-) + L_2(\delta_k'^-) + L_3(d_k'^-) \tag{9}$$

where L_1, L_2 and L_3 represent *linear* dynamic operators. The details of how this representation can be obtained are the subject of the next section. Corresponding to equation (9) we can draw Figure XII.2, which shows each of the variables u'_k, δ'_k and d'_k being operated on by L_1, L_2 and L_3, respectively, and the outputs added together to yield the endogenous variables.

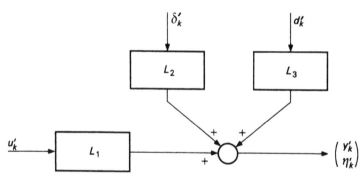

Fig. XII.2

Now consider u'_k to be composed of two parts, u_k^f and u_k^b:

$$u'_k = u_k^f + u_k^b \tag{10}$$

and suppose that we could make

$$u_k^f = -L_1^{-1}[L_2(\delta_k'^-)], \tag{11}$$

where L_1^{-1} denotes an operator whose effect is the inverse of that of L_1. Then the input u_k^f would have the effect of 'cancelling out' the observed disturbance δ'_k, and equation (9) would become

$$\begin{pmatrix} y'_k \\ \eta'_k \end{pmatrix} = L_1(u_k^{b-}) + L_3(d_k'^-). \tag{12}$$

The determination of u_k^f according to equation (11) is known to control engineers as 'feedforward control', and can be represented diagrammatically as in Figure XII.3. This shows the way in which the observable exogenous variables δ might be used as helpful 'indicators' for the formulation of policy rules.

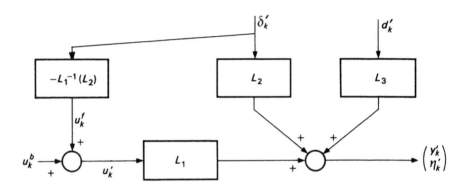

Fig. XII.3

If the feedforward control could be implemented exactly, so that equation (12) held, then the only problem remaining would be the determination of a suitable input u_k^b for dealing with the unobserved disturbance d_k'. In fact it is not possible to 'cancel out' the observed disturbances exactly, partly because the operators L_1 and L_2 are not known with great precision, and usually because L_1 cannot be inverted. However, it is possible to reduce the effect of δ_k' by feedforward control, and any residual effect can be conveniently assumed to be included in the catch-all vector of unobserved disturbances d_k'. In this book we do not investigate the possibility of using feedforward control at all, so the results reported in Chapter VIII are probably somewhat pessimistic.

Since the disturbance d_k is unobserved, and since it is the function of feedforward control to deal with the effects of δ_k', the control input u_k^b must depend on $y_k'^-$ and $\eta_k'^-$. That is, u_k^b must be a *feedback* control. In fact we have not made any investigation of the use of any of the endogenous 'potential indicators', η_k, in policy formulation, so for our purposes u_k^b will depend only on the deviations y_k' of the output y_k from the reference time path r_k.

It would be more accurate to say that we would like u_k^b to depend only on $y_k'^-$. But in practice it can depend only on measurements of $y_k'^-$, and these measurements are bound to be corrupted by errors of various kinds. We shall model this corruption in a particularly simple way, and assume

that a variable e, which is available to the agency implementing the policy
and may be called 'perceived error', is defined by

$$e_k = y'_k + m_k$$

$$= r_k - y_k + m_k. \tag{13}$$

The variable m_k here represents the error involved in measuring the output
y_k, and is of course unknown to the policy-maker at the time of policy
implementation. In this case the feedback policy rule that we need to
design is of the form

$$u^b_k = p_k(e^-_k, u^-_{k-1}). \tag{14}$$

But we shall simplify this further, and consider only policy rules that
are finite-order, constant-coefficient, linear difference equations of the
form

$$u^b_k = \sum_{i=0}^{\nu} \beta_i e_{k-i} + \sum_{i=1}^{\nu} \alpha_i u^b_{k-i} \tag{15}$$

where the α_is and β_is are constant matrices, and ν, the *order* of the
equation, is some positive integer. The main reason for this restriction is
necessity: it is only for this class of policies that anything like a systematic
design procedure exists. There is a second reason, which offers some
comfort. There are strong theoretical indications that this class of policies
is as large as one needs, at least when treating linear, constant models such
as equation (8). (See Kwakernaak and Sivan, 1972, for details.)

Before leaving this section, let us use some of the simplifying assumptions adopted for our policy design to simplify our representation
(equation (8)) of the economy still further. Since we shall not be
concerned with designing feedforward policies, but only feedback policies,
we do not need to consider the vector of observed disturbances δ_k
explicitly. It can either be considered to be eliminated by a feedforward
policy (which can be designed independently of the feedback policy,
because of the linearity of equation (8)), or it can be included with the
unobserved disturbances d_k. Furthermore, since we shall not be making
use of the indicators η_k, we need not exhibit them in our equations. Thus
our policy design will assume that the economic model is of the form

$$y'_k = \sum_{i=0}^{n} b_i u^b_{k-i} + \sum_{i=1}^{n} a_i y'_{k-i} + \sum_{i=0}^{n} c_i d'_{k-i}. \tag{16}$$

In subsequent sections and chapters, we shall write simply u_k instead of

u_k^b, y_k instead of y_k', and d_k instead of d_k'. For consistency of notation, the variable r will then denote the reference trajectory that the *deviations* of y from y^* are supposed to follow. Since we would like no deviations from y^*, the reference trajectory will be $r_k = 0$, for every k.

2. Transfer Functions

The essential features of feedback systems are greatly illuminated by regarding equations (15) and (16) as defining dynamic operators that transform the variable e into the variable u (in the case of equation (15)), or the variables u and d into y (in the case of equation (16)). To do this, we replace difference equations by 'transfer functions', in the following manner.

We first 'encode' whole sequences of variables into single functions: let $k = 0$ denote a starting period before which all variables take zero values. Then a time trajectory such as $u_0, u_1, u_2, \ldots$ can be 'encoded' into its 'z-transform' $u(z)$ by

$$u(z) = \sum_{k=0}^{\infty} z^{-k} u_k. \tag{17}$$

(Strictly speaking, this definition is only meaningful at those values of z for which the series converges, but the reader need not worry about this point while reading this book.) The trajectories of the variables y, d, r and others can be similarly encoded into their z-transforms $y(z), d(z), r(z)$, and so on. Furthermore, any such transform can be 'decoded' to yield the original time trajectory.

Suppose, for example, that u is scalar and that its time trajectory is

$$u_k = 0.5^k. \tag{18}$$

Then this can be 'encoded' into the z-transform

$$u(z) = 1 + \frac{0.5}{z} + \frac{0.5^2}{z^2} + \frac{0.5^3}{z^3} + \ldots \tag{19}$$

$$= \frac{z}{z - 0.5} \tag{20}$$

(using the usual formula for the sum of a geometric series). This can be evaluated for any value of z. For instance,

$$u(2) = \frac{2}{2 - 0.5} = \frac{4}{3}$$

$$u(3) = \frac{3}{3 - 0.5} = \frac{6}{5}$$

and so on. For reasons that will become clear in the following chapter, we allow z to take complex values, so that we can also write, for example,

$$u(3.5 + 4i) = \frac{3.5 + 4i}{(3.5 + 4i) - 0.5} = 1.06 + 0.08i.$$

If we were given the z-transform $u(z)$ in the form of equation (20), which is the most usual case, we could recover as many terms of (19) as required by 'long division', and could then recover the term u_k by reading off the coefficient of $(1/z)^k$. (Actually, the use of complex variable theory would allow us to recover equation (18) via 'contour integration', but we shall not need to do this.)

We refer the reader to Franklin and Powell (1980) for more details of z-transform theory.

The 'transfer function' $H(z)$ of a dynamic operator that acts on an input u to produce an output y is defined as the ratio of the two z-transforms $y(z)$ and $u(z)$:

$$y(z) = H(z)u(z). \tag{21}$$

Since $u(z)$ and $y(z)$ are vectors, in general, $H(z)$ must be a matrix (whose elements are functions of z). In general, this transfer function depends on the nature of the input u and, if the properties of the dynamic operator vary with time, it depends also on the time at which u is applied. However, if the operator can be described by a linear, constant-coefficient difference equation then its transfer function depends only on the coefficients of the equation, and is therefore a completely equivalent description of the dynamic operator.

Suppose, then, that the operator can be described by such an equation:

$$y_k = b_0 u_k + b_1 u_{k-1} + \ldots + b_n u_{k-n} + a_1 y_{k-1} + \ldots + a_n y_{k-n}. \tag{22}$$

Then we can multiply each side by z^{-k} to obtain

$$y_k z^{-k} = b_0 u_k z^{-k} + b_1 z^{-1} u_{k-1} z^{1-k} + \ldots + b_n z^{-n} u_{k-n} z^{n-k}$$
$$+ a_1 z^{-1} y_{k-1} z^{1-k} + \ldots + a_n z^{-n} y_{k-n} z^{n-k} \tag{23}$$

and hence

$$\sum_{k=0}^{\infty} y_k z^{-k} = b_0 \sum_{k=0}^{\infty} u_k z^{-k} + b_1 z^{-1} \sum_{k=0}^{\infty} u_{k-1} z^{1-k} + \ldots + b_n z^{-n}$$

$$\sum_{k=0}^{\infty} u_{k-n} z^{n-k} + a_1 z^{-1} \sum_{k=0}^{\infty} y_{k-1} z^{1-k} + \ldots + a_n z^{-n} \sum_{k=0}^{\infty} y_{k-n} z^{n-k}. \tag{24}$$

Since we assume that all variables are zero when k is negative, each of the summations in this equation equals either $u(z)$ or $y(z)$. Hence we have that

$$y(z) = (b_0 + b_1 z^{-1} + \ldots + b_n z^{-n})u(z)$$
$$+ (a_1 z^{-1} + \ldots + a_n z^{-n})y(z) \qquad (25)$$

or

$$A(z)y(z) = B(z)u(z) \qquad (26)$$

where

$$A(z) = Iz^n - a_1 z^{n-1} - \ldots - a_n$$
$$B(z) = b_0 z^n + b_1 z^{n-1} + \ldots + b_n$$

and I is a unit matrix of the appropriate dimensions. Since $A(z)$ is a square matrix, we can write

$$y(z) = A^{-1}(z)B(z)u(z). \qquad (27)$$

Hence the transfer function $H(z)$ is given by

$$H(z) = A^{-1}(z)B(z). \qquad (28)$$

We thus have a way of obtaining the transfer function corresponding to a linear, constant-coefficient difference equation in terms of that equation's coefficients.

Notice that there is a very simple rule that describes how one may perform this translation: regard the variable z as a 'forward-shift' operator, which has the effect of advancing the time index of any variable on which it operates. For example, consider 'zu_k' to be the same as 'u_{k+1}'. Similarly, regard z^{-1} as a 'backward shift' operator.* Then simply rewrite an equation such as (16) as

$$A(z)y(z) = B(z)u(z) + C(z)d(z) \qquad (29)$$

---

*The reader familiar with Laplace transform analysis of differential equations will recognise this procedure as completely analogous to the procedure of replacing the operator d/dt by the Laplace variable s.

where $\qquad\qquad A(z) = I - a_1 z^{-1} - \ldots - a_n z^{-n},$

$$B(z) = b_0 + b_1 z^{-1} + \ldots + b_n z^{-n},$$

and $\qquad\qquad C(z) = c_0 + c_1 z^{-1} + \ldots + c_n z^{-n}.$

One can multiply throughout by z^n to remove negative powers of z, but this is a matter of taste. Finally, one can pre-multiply by A^{-1} to obtain

$$y(z) = A^{-1}(z)B(z)u(z) + A^{-1}(z)C(z)d(z) \qquad (30)$$

$$= G_{yu}(z)u(z) + G_{yd}(z)d(z). \qquad (31)$$

The transfer function $G_{yu}(z)$ characterises the effect of u on y, while $G_{yd}(z)$ characterises the effect of d on y.

The following simple example will be useful in Chapter XIII. Suppose a single variable y is measured, but that it takes one whole period to perform the measurement. What is the transfer function corresponding to this delay? Let η represent the measurements of y that are obtained. Then, assuming the measurement is exact, the appropriate difference equation is

$$\eta_k = y_{k-1}. \qquad (32)$$

Using z as the shift operator this becomes

$$z\eta(z) = y(z) \qquad (33)$$

and the transfer function of the one-period delay is therefore

$$\frac{\eta(z)}{y(z)} = \frac{1}{z}. \qquad (34)$$

It can easily be seen that the transfer function of an m-period delay is $1/z^m$. If y were a vector of two variables, the first of which was measured with an m-period delay, and the second with an l-period delay, then the transfer function of the measurement process would be the 2×2 matrix

$$\begin{bmatrix} 1/z^m & 0 \\ 0 & 1/z^l \end{bmatrix}.$$

As a second example (which will also be useful later on) suppose that we wish to design an economic control policy in the form of equation (15), but which has the feature that the policy instrument u_k will only be set to zero if not only the error e_k is zero, but also the cumulative error

$\Sigma_{i=0}^{k} e_i$ is zero. A control policy with this feature is said by control engineers to incorporate 'integral action'. Such 'integral action' is often used, because it ensures that the error e_k is eventually returned to zero, even in the presence of sustained exogenous disturbances — such as a once-and-for-all rise in the price of oil, for example.

The following development shows that the transfer function of a policy that incorporates 'integral action' must contain $(z-1)$ as a factor of its common denominator. We will assume that both u and e are scalar variables. It can easily be verified that the required property is achieved if

$$u_k = v_k + w_k \tag{35}$$

where v_k depends on e_k in some manner such that $v_k = 0$ whenever $e_k = 0$, and where

$$w_k = \gamma e_k + w_{k-1}, \tag{36}$$

for some (real) constant γ. From equation (36) we obtain

$$w(z) = \frac{\gamma z}{z-1} e(z) \tag{37}$$

and substituting this in the transformed version of equation (35) gives

$$u(z) = v(z) + \frac{\gamma z}{z-1} e(z). \tag{38}$$

So if the policy is expressed as

$$u(z) = P(z)e(z) \tag{39}$$

then its transfer function $P(z)$ has the form

$$P(z) = \pi(z) + \frac{\gamma z}{z-1} \tag{40}$$

where $\pi(z)$ is some function of z. So $(z-1)$ must be a factor of the common denominator of $P(z)$, as claimed above.

For technical reasons one often works with a linear model in the form of a *pair* of vector equations

$$x_{k+1} = Ax_k + Bu_k, \qquad y_k = Cx_k + Du_k. \tag{41}$$

Here u and y have the same meanings as before, x is a so-called *state vector*, and A, B, C, D are constant matrices. It is important to be able to obtain the transfer function from such a representation of the model. Applying the rules described above, and eliminating x, gives

$$y(z) = [C(zI - A)^{-1}B + D]u(z), \tag{42}$$

so the expression in square brackets is the transfer function corresponding to equation (41).

In Chapter XIII we shall describe the design of economic policies in the form of transfer functions. It is of course a simple matter to reverse the procedure given above, in order to obtain difference equations such as (15) that correspond to these transfer functions.

The most important single reason for using transfer functions is that, with their aid, the effects of dynamic operators, and especially of connecting together such operators, are easily analysed. For example, the effect of u on y is given by an equation of the form

$$y_k = \sum_{i=0}^{k} h_{k-i}u_i, \tag{43}$$

an expression with which it is very much more difficult to work than with

$$y(z) = H(z)u(z). \tag{44}$$

Furthermore, if the transfer function relating variables e and u is $P(z)$, so that

$$u(z) = P(z)e(z), \tag{45}$$

then one can combine equations (44) and (45) to obtain

$$y(z) = H(z)P(z)e(z), \tag{46}$$

which is considerably simpler than

$$y_k = \sum_{i=0}^{k} h_{k-i}\left(\sum_{j=0}^{i} p_{i-j}e_j \right). \tag{47}$$

3.   The Benefits and Costs of Feedback

To recapitulate, we shall be concerned with designing an economic policy in the form

$$u(z) = P(z)e(z) \tag{48}$$

(which is the z-transformed version of equation (15)), for an economy modelled as

$$y(z) = G_{yu}(z)u(z) + G_{yd}(z)d(z) \tag{49}$$

(the transformed version of equation (16)), where

$$e(z) = r(z) - y(z) + m(z) \tag{50}$$

(the transformed version of equation (13)). For our present purposes we can define a new variable ξ by

$$\xi(z) = G_{yd}(z)d(z), \tag{51}$$

which is the effective exogenous disturbance as 'seen' at the output of the economy. We can now represent equations (48)–(51) by the block diagram of Figure XII.4.

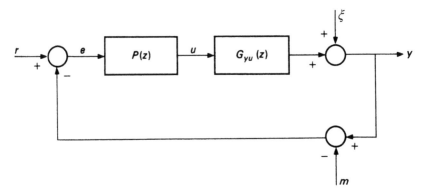

Fig. XII.4

Before proceeding to examine this feedback system in detail, notice one feature that is revealed very clearly by Figure XII.4. A colloquial phrase such as 'a change of economic policy' can mean one or other of two very different things. Either it can mean a change in the reference variable r, leaving the 'control law', namely the *system of policy rules* represented by $P(z)$, unchanged, or it can mean a change of $P(z)$ itself. In the exercises on rerunning history, presented in Chapter VIII, it was necessary to make occasional adjustments such as allowing the target trajectory of Money GDP to 'slip'. This kind of adjustment corresponds to the first meaning: the targets of economic policy, represented by the reference variable r, are changed, without altering the regulating mechanism that ensures that the economy is driven towards those targets. Adjustments of this kind are far more sanitary than *ad hoc* tampering with the policy rules $P(z)$, since it is known that the dynamic characteristics of the regulated economy remain unchanged. By contrast, there are no satisfactory techniques for investigating the effects of frequent adjustments to $P(z)$. ('Frequent' here means 'at intervals of less than five years', say.)

We now return to the analysis of the 'closed loop' depicted in Figure XII.4. For convenience we shall omit the suffix from $G_{yu}(z)$, and write it as $G(z)$. From Figure XII.4 we have

$$y(z) = \xi(z) + G(z)P(z)[r(z) - y(z) + m(z)] \tag{52}$$

or $$[I + G(z)P(z)]\, y(z) = \xi(z) + G(z)P(z)[r(z) + m(z)] \tag{53}$$

where I denotes a unit matrix of appropriate dimension, and hence

$$y(z) = [I + G(z)P(z)]^{-1}\{\xi(z) + G(z)P(z)[r(z) + m(z)]\}. \tag{54}$$

Let

$$T(z) = [I + G(z)P(z)]^{-1} G(z)P(z). \tag{55}$$

Then

$$I - T(z) = [I + G(z)P(z)]^{-1} \tag{56}$$

so equation (54) becomes

$$y(z) = [I - T(z)]\,\xi(z) + T(z)[r(z) + m(z)]. \tag{57}$$

$T(z)$ is called the 'closed-loop transfer function', since it relates the output variable y to the reference variable r, while $[I - T(z)]$ is called the 'sensitivity function', since it determines the sensitivity of the regulated output to the exogenous disturbance ξ.

Two vitally important features are revealed by equation (57). The first is that the regulated output y reacts in exactly the same way to measurement errors m as it does to changes in the reference variable r. The second is that the response of y to the exogenous disturbance ξ is completely determined by its response to r or m. It is not possible to modify the way in which y responds to any one of r, ξ, or m, without simultaneously modifying the way in which it responds to the other two. This lack of independence leads to a certain cost being *inevitably* associated with any benefit that is obtained by using feedback.

The first benefit that may be obtained by using feedback is that the effects of the disturbances ξ may be greatly reduced, by choosing the policy $P(z)$ such that $I - T(z) \simeq 0$. Simultaneously, the benefit of good tracking of the reference variable is obtained, since $\partial y(z)/\partial r(z) \simeq I$ in this case. The inevitable cost that accompanies these benefits is that $\partial y(z)/\partial m(z) \simeq I$ also, so that the regulated output in fact 'tracks' completely misleading measurement errors. On the other hand, if no feedback control is applied (i.e. $P(z) = 0$), then one incurs the cost that $\partial y(z)/\partial \xi(z) \simeq I$, but one obtains the benefit of $\partial y(z)/\partial m(z) = 0$. A suitable 'trade-off' of these two extremes against each other evidently depends on the relative strengths of the exogenous disturbances and the measurement errors.[*] (However, this is not the only 'trade-off' that is required: even if it is known that there are no measurement errors, the achievable benefits of feedback are limited by the need to maintain stability, as will be discussed in the next chapter.)

Now let us suppose that all the variables r, u, y and m are scalars, in order to keep the mathematics simple. Suppose that we have made an error in modelling the economy, so that the true relation of u to y is

$$y(z) = [G(z) + \Delta G(z)] u(z) \tag{58}$$

and $\Delta G(z)$ is unknown to us. Nevertheless we design $P(z)$ on the assumption that $\Delta G(z) = 0$. What will be the effect of this error on the behaviour of the economy with the feedback policy in place? We can answer this, for *small errors* $\Delta G(z)$, as follows. From equation (55), we obtain

$$\frac{\partial T(z)}{\partial G(z)} = \frac{P(z)}{[1 + G(z)P(z)]^2} \tag{59}$$

and hence

$$\frac{\partial T(z)/T(z)}{\partial G(z)/G(z)} = \frac{1}{1 + G(z)P(z)}$$
$$= 1 - T(z) \tag{60}$$

In other words, the proportional error in the *closed-loop* behaviour is the proportional error in the open-loop behaviour, reduced by the same sensitivity function as defined in equation (56). We see here another benefit of feedback, but again obtained at the same cost as the benefits derived earlier. A similar, but more complicated, relationship can be derived if the variables are vectors.

---

[*]It is usually appropriate to make the details of this 'trade-off' different for different values of z. Some details of how this may be done will be given in the next chapter.

There is another cost to be incurred if benefits are to be obtained from feedback. That is the necessity to move the policy instruments u vigorously. To see why this is so, we shall retain the simplifying assumption that all the variables are scalars. In this case $P(z)$, $G(z)$, $T(z)$, etc. are just complex numbers whose values depend on the value of z, and we can therefore write (from equation (55))

$$|1 - T(z)| = \frac{1}{|1 + G(z)P(z)|} \geq \frac{1}{1 + |G(z)P(z)|} . \tag{61}$$

To keep the sensitivity small, we clearly have to make $|G(z)P(z)|$ large. $|G(z)|$ may not be large enough, so the remedy is to make $|P(z)|$ large. However, from equation (48) we have

$$|u(z)| = |P(z)||e(z)|, \tag{62}$$

which tells us that any perceived error e will result in a large corrective action u.

The quantity $|G(z)P(z)|$ is known to control engineers as 'loop gain', because it is the amount by which any variable would be magnified if it were propagated once round the 'open' loop. Imagine that the lines joining the blocks in Figure XII.4 represent wires, and that the variables represent electrical signals. Suppose the wire entering the block $P(z)$ were cut, and that the signal $e(z)$ were applied to this block. Then, if $\cdot r(z) = \xi(z) = m(z) = 0$, the signal appearing at the cut end would be $-G_{yu}(z)P(z)e(z)$, so that the magnitude of its z-transform representation would be changed by the factor $|G_{yu}(z)P(z)|$.

When engineers build control systems they can usually increase the loop gain to any value they require simply by buying large enough amplifiers, motors, gearboxes, and so on (which of course incurs a financial cost, but is possible to do). If one is implementing an economic control policy, however, the limits on the achievable loop gain are imposed by administrative considerations, such as those discussed in Part Three, and by the disruptive effects of very large changes of policy instruments. It is very difficult, if not impossible, to increase these limits, and they must therefore be considered quite explicitly when designing an economic feedback policy.

4. The Structure of a New Keynesian Policy

The economic structure of a New Keynesian policy, such as we are advocating in this book, has already been explained in Part One. It is useful to derive the corresponding mathematical structure. For this purpose we shall simplify matters slightly by assuming that there is only one tax instrument to manipulate, although elsewhere in the book we have separated the direct and indirect tax instruments. Suppose that there are three variables in the input vector u, and that they are arranged in the following order: tax rate, foreign-exchange rate, wage rate. Further suppose that the output vector y also contains three variables: the money value of the gross domestic product at factor cost (Money GDP), the balance of payments on current account and the level of unemployment. The component variables of the 'perceived error' vector e then represent the perceived deviations of each of these output variables from their reference time paths.

If equation (48) is written out as three scalar equations, one for each component of u, it becomes

$$u_i(z) = p_{i1}(z)e_1(z) + p_{i2}(z)e_2(z) + p_{i3}(z)e_3(z) \qquad (63)$$

(for $i = 1, 2, 3$ in turn) where $p_{ij}(z)$ is the (i, j)th element of $P(z)$, $u_i(z)$ is the ith component of $u(z)$ and $e_j(z)$ is the jth component of $e(z)$. Now the hallmark of a New Keynesian policy is that the ith component of $u(z)$ should react only to the ith component of $e(z)$ (with the particular ordering of variables that we have chosen), and this is achieved by insisting that

$$p_{ij}(z) = 0 \quad \text{whenever} \quad i \neq j. \qquad (64)$$

Thus a New Keynesian policy is 'diagonal'* in the sense that the matrix $P(z)$ has the structure

$$P(z) = \begin{bmatrix} p_{11}(z) & 0 & 0 \\ 0 & p_{22}(z) & 0 \\ 0 & 0 & p_{33}(z) \end{bmatrix} \qquad (65)$$

An Orthodox Keynesian policy, by contrast, is one in which financial management is used to regulate the level of real activity and hence of employment, while wage rates are manipulated in order to restrain any resulting inflation: that is, $u_1(z)$ reacts only to $e_3(z)$, while $u_3(z)$ reacts only to $e_1(z)$. The matrix $P(z)$ corresponding to an Orthodox Keynesian policy is thus 'anti-diagonal':

$$P(z) = \begin{bmatrix} 0 & 0 & p_{13}(z) \\ 0 & p_{22}(z) & 0 \\ p_{31}(z) & 0 & 0 \end{bmatrix} \qquad (66)$$

*No mystic significance should be attached to the fact that the policy is diagonal. By reordering the input and output variables, the non-zero elements of $P(z)$ can be made to appear in different positions.

Both New and Orthodox Keynesian policies are severely constrained in their form, when compared with the policy that a control engineer would devise if he were free to ignore considerations of political acceptability and administrative feasibility. This would be a policy of the kind discussed in Chapter II, namely one in which a deviation of any one of the outputs from its desired time path would result in adjustments of all of the policy instruments. In this case the matrix $P(z)$ would have no entries that were required to be zero, as a result of which such a policy could certainly perform at least as well as either a New or Orthodox Keynesian policy. The question of how much better it could perform is one that is difficult to answer precisely, because it depends crucially on the extent of the errors that are likely to be made when formulating the model of the economy that is used for designing the policy. At present, very little is known about the nature and extent of such modelling errors.

However, our advocacy of New Keynesian policies is not likely to be greatly affected by increased understanding of these errors, since the problems of political and administrative acceptability and feasibility not only cannot be ignored, but in fact dominate the design of a realistic policy. But one could have a policy that was recognisably New Keynesian, yet that made some concession to the control engineer — namely, one in which the regulation of the domestic demand and of the foreign balance was co-ordinated, but in which the level of employment was determined by the actions of the reformed wage-fixing institutions, which were outlined in Volume 1. For such a policy the transfer function $P(z)$ has the 'block-diagonal' structure:

$$P(z) = \begin{bmatrix} p_{11}(z) & p_{12}(z) & 0 \\ p_{21}(z) & p_{22}(z) & 0 \\ 0 & 0 & p_{33}(z) \end{bmatrix} \qquad (67)$$

Again, a precise answer to the question of how much is really gained by this concession depends on the details of the likely modelling errors, which are as yet unknown.* But we can at least indicate what the answer depends on. For this purpose we shall suppose that the wage policy, $p_{33}(z)$, is fixed and is in operation, and that we therefore remove the wage rate from the vector of policy instruments, and the level of unemployment

---

*We have two students currently studying the questions raised in this section. N. Christodoulakis is engaged on characterising the discrepancies between three well-known macroeconomic models in such a way that the 'uncertainty' revealed by these discrepancies can be taken into account when designing a feedback policy. P. Westaway is examining, among other things, the benefits to be obtained from the use of a 'partly cross-coupled' policy.

from the vector of outputs. Both $P(z)$ and $G(z)$ become 2×2 matrices in this case. We define

$$Q(z) = G(z)P(z) \tag{68}$$

so that the sensitivity function is

$$I - T(z) = (I + Q(z))^{-1}$$

$$= \frac{1}{\det (z)} \begin{bmatrix} 1 + q_{22}(z) & -q_{12}(z) \\ -q_{21}(z) & 1 + q_{11}(z) \end{bmatrix} \tag{69}$$

where 'det (z)' denotes the determinant of $(I + Q(z))$.

The greatest shortcoming of the policy presented in Chapter XIV is that when exogenous disturbances on domestic demand are corrected by the manipulation of tax rates, there is considerable subsequent disturbance of the balance of payments on current account. Also, an exogenous disturbance on the balance of payments results in an appreciable disturbance of the Money GDP. From equation (57) we see that the mathematical remedy for these 'interactions' is the reduction in magnitude of elements $(1, 2)$ and $(2, 1)$ of the sensitivity function. From equation (69) we deduce that $|q_{12}(z)/\det (z)|$ and $|q_{21}(z)/\det (z)|$ should be reduced.

Now

$$q_{12}(z) = g_{11}(z)p_{12}(z) + g_{12}(z)p_{22}(z)$$

$$\tag{70}$$

and

$$q_{21}(z) = g_{21}(z)p_{11}(z) + g_{22}(z)p_{21}(z)$$

so the elements of policy $p_{12}(z)$ and $p_{21}(z)$ can certainly be used to try to reduce $q_{12}(z)$ and $q_{21}(z)$ to zero (if other considerations, such as the need to retain stability, allow). For example, the exchange rate can be appreciated whenever tax rates are raised, in order to offset the anticipated reduction in the volume of imports. As can be seen from equation (70), the amount of the required adjustment, and its temporal pattern, depend on the relationship between $g_{21}(z)$ and $g_{22}(z)$. However, the information required is not simply two numbers, but the two functions $g_{21}(z)$ and $g_{22}(z)$, which must be known (albeit approximately) for all values of the variable z.

There is another way of reducing the 'interactions' between the domestic and foreign sectors, and that is to increase the magnitude of 'det'. This can be done even if $p_{12}(z)$ and $p_{21}(z)$ are zero, since in this case

$$\det (z) = 1 + g_{11}(z)p_{11}(z) + g_{22}(z)p_{22}(z)$$

$$+ p_{11}(z)p_{22}(z)[g_{11}(z)g_{22}(z) - g_{12}(z)g_{21}(z)] \tag{71}$$

but $|\det(z)|$ can only be increased by increasing the loop gain. As we have already mentioned, the achievable loop gain is severely limited, so this route to reduced 'interaction' is probably not available. We content ourselves here with pointing out that the benefit to be obtained from allowing $p_{12}(z)$ and $p_{21}(z)$ to be non-zero increases as the accuracy of the economic model increases, and decreases as the achievable loop gain increases.

CHAPTER XIII

Frequency-Response Methods
for Policy Design

1. The Problem of Stability

A major problem to be faced when designing a feedback policy is that the resulting feedback configuration may be unstable, even though both the economy and the policy rules may themselves be stable. What we mean by 'unstable' is that even a short, isolated exogenous disturbance, or change in the level of the desired reference variable, will provoke a catastrophic, ever-increasing deviation of the economy from the desired time path. In mathematical terms, this will happen if the characteristic polynomial of the set of difference equations, which describe the behaviour of the economy under feedback control, has any roots that have magnitude greater than unity. (We maintain the assumption, made in the previous chapter, that the economy is described by a linear model.)

The designer has to work with 'open-loop' entities, namely the model of the economy without feedback, and the policy he is designing. The problem of deducing whether the 'closed-loop' system will be stable, from the open-loop information available to him, is solved by the Nyquist stability theorem, which will be presented in the next section. This theorem leads to a design technique that allows one to specify the transfer function of the economic policy in such a way as to obtain satisfactory closed-loop regulation properties, with the assurance that closed-loop stability is not lost.

2. The Nyquist Theorem

In this and the next three sections we shall limit ourselves to the consideration of the case in which only one output variable is to be regulated. Therefore all the variables and transfer functions that we shall use will be scalars (rather than vectors and matrices).

Suppose that an economic policy has been designed, which could be used in the feedback scheme shown in Figure XII.4. Imagine that the variable e shown in that figure can be manipulated at will, rather than being defined by equation (13) of Chapter XII. In particular, suppose that one could set the single variable e according to

$$e_k = \sin(2\pi f k). \tag{1}$$

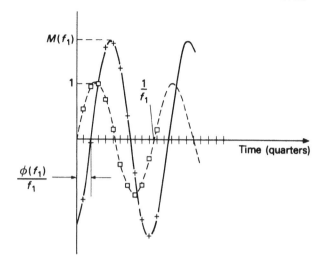

Fig. XIII.1(a)

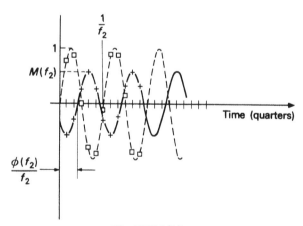

Fig. XIII.1(b)

If both the policy and the model of the economy behave as linear, constant-coefficient difference equations, and if they are both stable, then both the (single) policy instrument u and the output variable y would follow paths that approximate to sine waves of frequency f, and the approximation will improve as time proceeds. In particular, the output y would eventually be indistinguishable from

$$y_k = M(f) \sin [2\pi f k + \phi(f)], \tag{2}$$

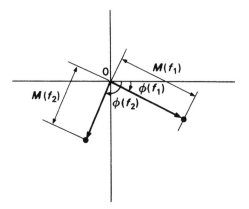

Fig. XIII.2(a)

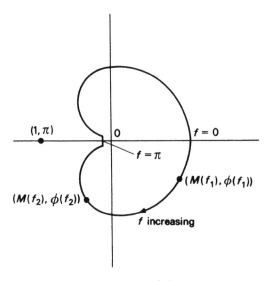

Fig. XIII.2(b)

in which expression the *magnification* (or *gain*) $M(f)$ and the *phase shift* $\phi(f)$ both depend on the frequency f.

The relationship between e_k and y_k is illustrated in Figure XIII.1 for two frequencies, f_1 and f_2. When the frequency f is very low, so that the variables are changing very slowly, the output y may be able to 'keep up' with the stimulating variable e, so that the phase shift $\phi(f)$ may be almost zero. But all dynamic economic models contain 'inertia', which manifests itself by the output being unable to 'keep up' with the input as the frequency

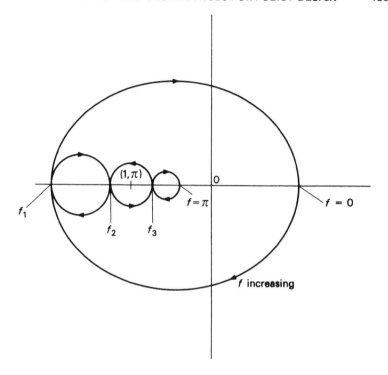

Fig. XIII.3

is increased. The output *lags* behind the input, or, in terms of equation (2), $\phi(f)$ takes on negative values. It may not decrease monotonically with f, and it may even be positive for some values of f. But the typical behaviour of $\phi(f)$ is that it becomes more negative as the frequency f increases.

The response of the combined policy and economic model, at each frequency, is conveniently represented by a vector whose magnitude is $M(f)$, and whose argument is $\phi(f)$, as shown in Figure XIII.2(a). If such a vector were drawn for each possible frequency, and all the 'tips' of the vectors were joined together, a continuous closed curve would result, like the one shown in Figure XIII.2(b). Such a curve is known as a 'frequency-response locus' or a 'Nyquist locus', and it is from this curve that closed-loop stability can be predicted.

The Nyquist stability theorem states that, if this closed curve makes no net encirclements of the point whose polar co-ordinates are $(1, \pi)$, then the system will remain stable when the negative feedback loop is closed as in Figure XII.4. The phrase 'makes no net encirclements' means that encirclements in opposite senses 'cancel' each other. If each anticlockwise encirclement is treated as $+1$, the algebraic sum of all the encirclements should be zero. For example, the system whose Nyquist locus is shown in Figure XIII.3 will remain stable when the negative feedback loop is closed. We assume throughout this discussion that the economic model itself, without feedback, is stable. Otherwise the statement of the theorem has to be slightly modified.

In simple cases, the Nyquist theorem confirms what one might intuitively expect: if at some frequency f^*, we have $\phi(f^*) = \pi$, so that the feedback loop becomes a *positive* feedback loop for oscillations of frequency f^*, then the loop will remain stable if $M(f^*) < 1$, that is, if an oscillation at that frequency is reduced in magnitude every time it is propagated around the loop. However, in cases like that shown in Figure XIII.3, the theorem gives stability conditions that are not at all clear from intuition. Three frequencies $f_1 < f_2 < f_3$ are marked on Figure XIII.3, at each of which the phase lag is π. As shown in the figure, $M(f_1) > M(f_2) > 1$, $M(f_3) < 1$; this combination of magnifications gives closed-loop stability. However, if $M(f_2)$ is *reduced*, so that it falls below unity, then the closed locus will encircle the point $(1, \pi)$ twice clockwise, and hence the system would be unstable if the feedback loop were closed.

In both Figures XIII.2(b) and XIII.3 we have shown the Nyquist loci to be symmetric about the line $(r, 0)$. We shall now show that these loci always exhibit this characteristic. Suppose that the frequency f of the stimulating variable e is such that $\frac{1}{2} < f < 1$. Let $f' = 1 - f$, so that $0 < f' < \frac{1}{2}$. Then, from equation (1) we have

$$e_k = \sin(2\pi f k) = \sin(2\pi k - 2\pi f' k)$$

$$= \sin(-2\pi f' k). \qquad (3)$$

Thus the oscillation of frequency f applied to the input of the combined policy and economic model has precisely the same effect as an oscillation with the lower frequency f', whose phase is reversed. From equation (2) we therefore obtain

$$y_k = M(f') \sin[-2\pi f' k - \phi(f')] \qquad (4)$$

but also, by definition,

$$y_k = M(f) \sin[2\pi f k + \phi(f)]. \qquad (5)$$

Comparing equations (4) and (5), and remembering that $f' = 1 - f$, we obtain

$$M(f) = M(f'), \qquad \phi(f) = -\phi(f'). \qquad (6)$$

This shows that the point on the Nyquist locus corresponding to frequency f' is the mirror image (about the line $(r, 0)$) of the point corresponding to frequency f.

If we now consider a still higher frequency f, such that $1 < f < 3/2$, and let $f'' = f - 1$, so that $0 < f'' < \frac{1}{2}$, then we have

$$
\begin{aligned}
e_k &= \sin(2\pi f k) \\
&= \sin(2\pi k + 2\pi f'' k) \\
&= \sin(2\pi f'' k)
\end{aligned}
\tag{7}
$$

so that, in this case,

$$
M(f) = M(f''), \qquad \phi(f) = \phi(f'').
\tag{8}
$$

This process can be repeated for any frequency higher than $\frac{1}{2}$. It is clear from this development that the Nyquist locus is entirely determined by the response of the system to oscillations with frequencies lying between 0 and $\frac{1}{2}$.* For frequencies between $\frac{1}{2}$ and 1 the locus is just the 'mirror image' of the locus for the lower frequencies. At frequencies above 1 the locus simply repeats itself.

Linear difference equations are continuous operators. This means that if the input oscillation $(e_0, e_1, e_2, \ldots)$ changes by an arbitrarily small amount, then the output response $(y_0, y_1, y_2, \ldots)$ should also change to an arbitrarily small extent. In particular, if f changes from $\frac{1}{2} - \epsilon$ to $\frac{1}{2} + \epsilon$, then the difference between $\phi(\frac{1}{2} - \epsilon)$ and $\phi(\frac{1}{2} + \epsilon)$ can be made arbitrarily small by making ϵ small enough. This, together with the fact (from equation (6)) that

$$
\phi(\tfrac{1}{2} + \epsilon) = -\phi(\tfrac{1}{2} - \epsilon),
\tag{9}
$$

implies that

$$
\phi(\tfrac{1}{2}) = -\phi(\tfrac{1}{2}).
\tag{10}
$$

Consequently, $\phi(\frac{1}{2})$ must be either 0 or π. This shows that the Nyquist locus is not only symmetric but also forms a closed curve, as shown in Figures XIII.2(b) and XIII.3. This argument using continuity breaks down if $M(f)$ is infinite. In the next section we shall see that $M(0)$ is often infinite, and we shall discuss how to apply the Nyquist theorem in such cases.

---

*The units of frequency are 'cycles per time unit'. If time is measured in quarters, they are 'cycles per quarter', etc. If the time interval of the model is T time units (e.g. if time is measured in months, but the model is quarterly, then $T = 3$) then the range $0 < f < \frac{1}{2}$ must be replaced by $0 < f < \frac{1}{2}T$.

In view of the fact that the entire Nyquist locus can be constructed from its initial section, it is conventional to draw it for frequencies between 0 and $\frac{1}{2}$ only. It is also very useful to use the frequency variable $\omega = 2\pi f$ instead of f. The range $0 < f < \frac{1}{2}$ corresponds to $0 < \omega < \pi$, and the units in which ω is expressed are 'radians per time unit'.

Before leaving this section, we must state an essential caveat about the use of the Nyquist stability theorem. The theorem uses only information about the combined frequency response of the policy $P(z)$ and the economic model $G(z)$ (cf. Figure XII.4). It therefore cannot detect any instabilities that are 'hidden' inside this combination. For example, suppose that the economic policy is

$$u_k = e_k + 2u_{k-1}, \tag{11}$$

which is unstable since it has a characteristic root at 2, and that the model is

$$y_k = u_k - 2u_{k-1}. \tag{12}$$

Writing these in transfer function form, we have

$$u(z) = \frac{z}{z-2}\, e(z) \quad \text{and} \quad y(z) = \frac{z-2}{z}\, u(z) \tag{13}$$

so that the two combine to give

$$y(z) = e(z) \tag{14}$$

and hence

$$y_k = e_k. \tag{15}$$

The entire Nyquist locus is therefore the single point $(1, 0)$, and the Nyquist theorem predicts stability if the feedback loop is closed by setting $e_k = r_k - y_k$. In fact, the instability introduced in equation (11) is still present, and would cause the policy instrument u to 'explode' even though the output y may behave satisfactorily. (In practice the explosive behaviour of u would take the original (non-linear) model out of the region in which it was linearised, and certainly give unsatisfactory behaviour of y.)

Fortunately, such hidden instabilities are usually easily avoided or removed, with the aid of results from the theory of linear systems. They arise from so-called 'uncontrollable' or 'unobservable' unstable modes, which can be detected by standard techniques (Kailath, 1980).

3. Frequency Responses and Transfer Functions

It would be prohibitively expensive to obtain Nyquist loci for economic models by performing actual frequency-response measurements on them. Indeed, most macro-economic models cannot be run for more than fifty or sixty time units, at most, so that it is usually impossible to carry out such measurements. However, Nyquist loci can be easily obtained by other means.

In particular, they can be obtained from transfer functions. It turns out that, if a transfer function $G(z)$ is evaluated at complex values of z such that $|z| = 1$ (i.e. if z takes values on the unit circle whose centre is the origin of the complex plane), then its values (which are complex numbers) lie on the Nyquist locus of the system defined by the transfer function. We can obtain the entire Nyquist locus by evaluating $G(z)$ at all values of z for which $|z| = 1$. To be more precise, the response of the system to a sinusoidal oscillation of frequency f can be obtained by evaluating $G(z)$ at $z = \exp(2\pi f i)$ (where $i = \sqrt{-1}$). In fact, the magnification $M(f)$ and phase shift $\phi(f)$ are given by

$$M(f) = |G(e^{2\pi f i})| \quad \text{and} \quad \phi(f) = \arg G(e^{2\pi f i}). \qquad (16)$$

For example, suppose that

$$y_k - 0.5 y_{k-1} = u_k. \qquad (17)$$

The transfer function corresponding to this difference equation is

$$G(z) = \frac{z}{z - 0.5}. \qquad (18)$$

Evaluating this on the unit circle gives (using $\omega = 2\pi f$, and omitting some of the steps):

$$G(e^{i\omega}) = \frac{e^{i\omega}}{e^{i\omega} - 0.5}$$

$$= \frac{\cos \omega + i \sin \omega}{\cos \omega + i \sin \omega - 0.5}$$

$$= \dots$$

$$= \frac{(1 - 0.5 \cos \omega) - 0.5 i \sin \omega}{1.25 - \cos \omega} \qquad (19)$$

From this it follows that

Table XIII.1

f	ω	$\|G(e^{i\omega})\|$	$\arg\,(G(e^{i\omega}))$ (radians)
0	0	2.00	0
$\dfrac{1}{2\pi}$	1	1.19	-0.523
$\dfrac{1}{\pi}$	2	0.775	-0.360
$\tfrac{1}{2}$	π	0.667	0

$$|G(e^{i\omega})| = \frac{1}{\sqrt{1.25 - \cos \omega}} \tag{20}$$

and

$$\arg G(e^{i\omega}) = -\tan^{-1}\left(\frac{0.5 \sin \omega}{1 - 0.5 \cos \omega}\right). \tag{21}$$

Table XIII.1 shows the values of expressions (20) and (21) at four points on the unit circle. Figure XIII.4(a) shows these points on the unit circle, while Figure XIII.4(b) shows the values of the transfer function at these points, drawn on the complex plane. Figure XIII.4(b) also shows the Nyquist locus for equation (17), for the frequency range $0 < \omega < \pi$ (i.e. $0 < f < \tfrac{1}{2}$). The remainder of the locus is obtained by drawing the mirror image about the real axis. In this simple case the Nyquist locus is seen to be a circle, but in general it can have a very complicated shape.

From Figure XIII.4(b) we can deduce that, if $u_k = \sin (\omega k)$ and y_k is generated by equation (17), then as ω is increased from zero, y begins to lag behind u, the greatest phase lag occurring near $\omega = 1$. As ω is increased further the lag decreases, until, at $\omega = \pi$, y is again able to 'keep up' with u. However, the magnitude of the oscillations of y will decrease monotonically as ω is increased from 0 to π.

It may be instructive to verify that the frequency-response information in Table XIII.1 does indeed correspond to the behaviour of equation (17). Table XIII.1 predicts that if $u_k = \sin (k)$ (i.e. $\omega = 1$), then

$$y_k = 1.19 \sin (k - 0.523). \tag{22}$$

We can check whether this is correct by substituting this expression in equation (17):

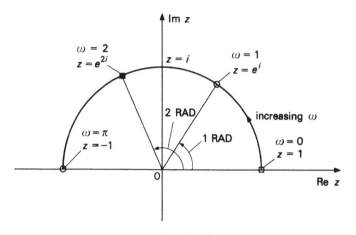

Fig. XIII.4(a)

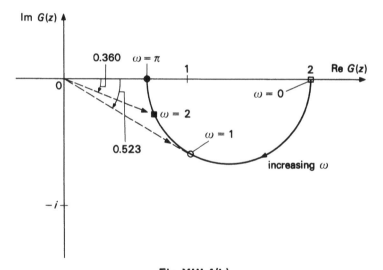

Fig. XIII.4(b)

$$y_k - 0.5 y_{k-1} = 1.19 \sin(k - 0.523) - 0.595 \sin(k - 1.523)$$

$$= 1.002 \sin k + 0.0006 \cos k \qquad (23)$$

$$= u_k \quad \text{(allowing for numerical truncation errors).}$$

If ω takes values very close to zero, then the Nyquist locus of Figure XIII.4(b) tells us how equation (17) behaves when the input u changes very slowly. In the limit, at $\omega = 0$, it tells us what happens if the input is

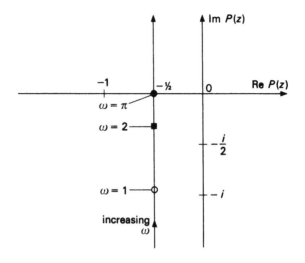

Fig. XIII.5(a)

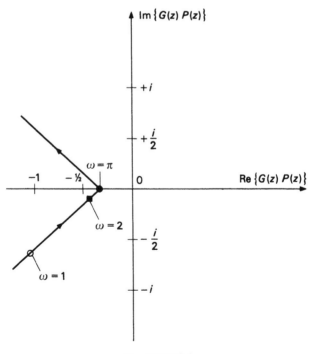

Fig. XIII.5(b)

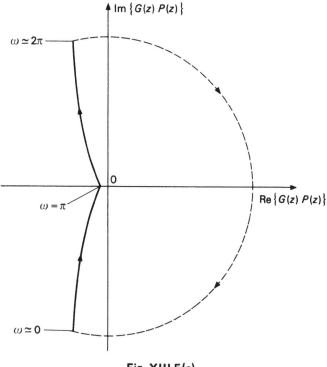

Fig. XIII.5(c)

a constant: the output is also a constant, whose value is twice that of the input. The correctness of this can be verified immediately from equation (17).

To predict closed-loop stability we require the Nyquist locus of the combination of the economic model with a proposed policy. If the transfer functions of the model and the policy are $G(z)$ and $P(z)$, respectively, then the combined locus is obtained by evaluating $G(e^{i\omega})P(e^{i\omega})$. For each value of ω this is just the product of the complex numbers $G(e^{i\omega})$ and $P(e^{i\omega})$.

Suppose that $u_k = u_{k-1} + e_{k-1}$, namely that the transfer function of the policy is $P(z) = 1/(z-1)$. As we saw in the previous chapter, this is a policy of 'integral control', namely one for which $u_k = 0$ only if both $e_k = 0$ *and* $\Sigma_{i=0}^{k} e_i = 0$. It exhibits the characteristic feature of integral control, which is that it gives infinite magnification at zero frequency (since $|P(1)|$ is infinite). Figure XIII.5(a) shows part of the Nyquist locus of this policy, while Figure XIII.5(b) shows part of the Nyquist locus of the policy combined with the model of the previous example.

In this case there is a problem with applying the Nyquist stability theorem, because the Nyquist locus is not a closed curve. However, it can be shown that if the 'loose ends' of the Nyquist locus are connected by an arc of a circle of large enough magnitude, *in a clockwise sense* as shown in Figure XIII.5(c), then the resulting closed curve can be used to predict closed-loop stability as if it were a Nyquist locus.

Using this rule, we see from Figure XIII.5(b) that we would obtain a stable closed loop if we set $e_k = r_k - y_k$, since our manufactured closed curve does not encircle the point $-1 + 0i$. Suppose that we modify the control policy, so that it is represented by

$$P_1(z) = \frac{\gamma}{z-1}$$

$$= \gamma P(z), \tag{24}$$

where γ is a real, positive number. Then, since $|P_1(z)| = \gamma|P(z)|$, the Nyquist locus corresponding to this policy is the same as in Figure XIII.5(b), but magnified by the factor γ. In Figure XIII.5(b), the Nyquist locus intersects the negative real axis at $-\frac{1}{3} + 0i$. If $P(z)$ is replaced by $P_1(z)$, the intersection will be at $-(\gamma/3) + 0i$. Consequently closed-loop stability will be obtained for any value of γ between 0 and 3, but higher values of γ will result in instability.

If the negative feedback loop is closed, the difference equation relating the output y to the reference variable r is

$$y_k + (\gamma - 1.5)y_{k-1} + 0.5y_{k-2} = \gamma r_{k-1}, \tag{25}$$

so the characteristic equation is

$$z^2 + (\gamma - 1.5)z + 0.5 = 0. \tag{26}$$

Even in this simple example, determining the limit of stability by finding the value of γ at which one root of (26) becomes larger than 1 is quite complicated.

We saw in the previous chapter that the sensitivity of the controlled system both to exogenous disturbances and to modelling errors can be made small by making the 'loop gain' $|G(z)P_1(z)|$ large. In the present example, one may therefore wish to make γ as large as possible. (But this will depend on the extent of any measurement errors, and on the vigorousness of control action that one can tolerate.) However, the application of the Nyquist stability theorem shows that the range of allowable values of γ is quite limited.

The process of designing a feedback control policy can be viewed as one of manipulating the Nyquist locus until it satisfies the designer's requirements. One starts with the Nyquist locus of the economic model, and proceeds to 'bend' it by devising policies in the form of appropriate

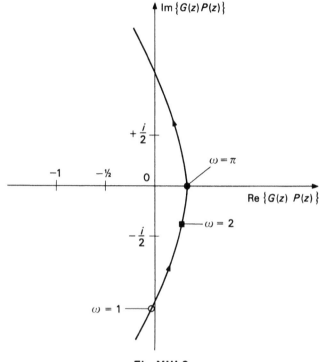

Fig. XIII.6

transfer functions. It is frequently convenient to do this in stages, at each stage concentrating on one aspect of the locus. For instance, in the example just considered, the policy $P_1(z)$ may be the first step of a design intended to introduce 'integral control'. But the limitation $\gamma \leqslant 3$ may not be acceptable. (We shall see in the next section how its acceptability may be judged.) In this case the Nyquist locus of $G(z)P_1(z)$ may be modified by a suitable transfer function $P_2(z)$, and a complete policy $P(z)$ obtained as $P(z) = P_1(z)P_2(z)$. In principle, one can assemble a policy from as many such factors as one likes, but in practice one is prevented from using more than three or four by the requirement of having a reasonably simple policy.

If we take $P_2(z) = z$, for example, then, since $|P_2(e^{i\omega})| = 1$ and $\arg P_2(e^{i\omega}) = \omega$, the Nyquist locus shown in Figure XIII.5(b) is modified to that shown in Figure XIII.6. With this modification the closed-loop will be stable with *any* positive value of γ, since the locus now intersects the real axis at a positive value instead of a negative one. (With a more realistic economic model it would be impossible to retain stability for an infinite range of γ.)

When modifying policies in this way, one must ensure that the transfer function of the complete policy has a denominator polynomial whose degree is at least as large as the degree of the numerator. Otherwise the corresponding difference equation will be *unrealisable* in the sense that its output will depend on future inputs. In the above example, we have

$$P_1(z)P_2(z) = \frac{z}{z-1}, \qquad (27)$$

which corresponds to the realisable difference equation

$$u_k = u_{k-1} + e_k. \qquad (28)$$

But if we had chosen $P_2(z) = z^2$, then we would have had

$$P_1(z)P_2(z) = \frac{z^2}{z-1} \qquad (29)$$

or

$$u_k = u_{k-1} + e_{k+1}. \qquad (30)$$

There is no way of implementing the policy represented by this equation.

4. Frequency Response and System Performance

In Section 3 of the previous chapter it was shown that the performance of a linear feedback system is determined by the sensitivity function $1 - T(z)$ $(= 1/[1 + G(z)P(z)])$ and by the closed-loop transfer function, $T(z)$ $(= G(z)P(z)/[1 + G(z)P(z)])$. In this chapter, we have seen that the behaviour of the function $G(z)P(z)$ on the unit circle $|z| = 1$, namely the open-loop frequency-response behaviour, can be used to predict closed-loop stability, and that this behaviour can be manipulated by the policy designer.

In order to bring these facts together into a coherent design technique, we must answer two questions. Firstly, what constitutes 'good', or at least 'acceptable', behaviour of $G(z)P(z)$ on the unit circle? Secondly, even if we answer the first question, and manage to obtain good frequency-response behaviour, what should we do about $G(z)P(z)$ at other values of z?

Consider the second question first, since it can be answered more concisely. The response of a system defined by linear, constant-coefficient difference equations to *any* input function is determined entirely by its response to (all possible) harmonic input functions of the form sin (ωk). Consequently, if one specifies the transfer function of such a system on the unit circle, then one also determines it at all other points on the complex plane. It is therefore enough to specify it on the unit circle, which simplifies the design problem enormously.

To answer the first question we make use of two mathematical results. The first is that there is a close correlation between the shape of a system's frequency-response locus and the 'shape' of its time response in the face of a constant disturbance. Consequently dynamic characteristics such as damping factor, speed of response, degree of overshoot and tracking error can be estimated from the Nyquist locus. The second result is that one way of representing random disturbances and measurement errors is as distributions of sinusoidal functions. If such a representation of a random function shows a concentration of content over some particular frequency range, and the function acts at the input of a linear dynamic system, then the variations of the output will be small if the system's magnification is small over that frequency range, and, conversely, they will be large if the magnification is large at those frequencies.

(i)   *Stability Margin and 'Underdamping'*

Let us examine more closely the question of correlating the frequency response with the time response. According to the Nyquist stability theorem, if the open-loop Nyquist locus is distorted until it passes through the point $-1 + 0i$, then the closed-loop system changes from being stable to being unstable (if it was originally stable). Naturally, this does not happen suddenly. As the Nyquist locus approaches the critical point $-1 + 0i$, so at least one of the *closed-loop* characteristic roots of the system approaches the unit circle, which is the stability boundary. If a pair of these roots is located at $r \exp (\pm i\theta)$ then the output of the closed-loop system will contain oscillatory terms of the form $Ar^k \sin (\theta k - \psi)$, for some numbers A and ψ. If $r \simeq 1$ then these terms will decay very slowly with time; system behaviour of this kind is said to be very 'underdamped'.

Figure XIII.7 illustrates the effect of increasing the positive constant γ in the policy $P(z) = \gamma/z - 1$, when it is applied to the model $G(z) = z/z - 0.5$. We saw earlier (from Figure XIII.5(b)) that γ could be increased to 3 before the closed-loop system became unstable. In Figure XIII.7 we show what happens to the output of the system when the negative feedback loop is closed, all variables are initially at zero, and a constant disturbance is suddenly added to the output (i.e. $\xi_k = 1$ for $k = 0, 1, 2, \ldots$, in Figure XII.4). The reference variable r is held at zero, so the action of the feedback loop should be to drive the output y back to zero. The three graphs show the behaviour of the output for three values of γ: 1, 2 and 2.8. As γ approaches its limiting value very closely, the control quality

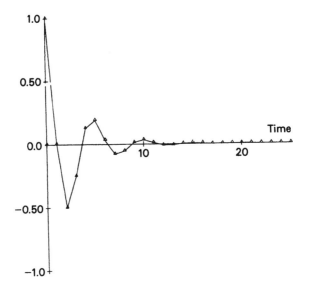

Fig. XIII.7(a)   gamma = 1

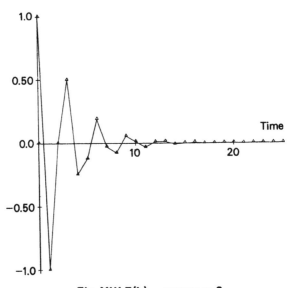

Fig. XIII.7(b)   gamma = 2

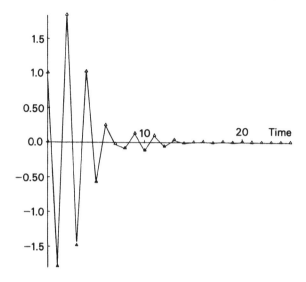

Fig. XIII.7(c)   gamma = 2.8

clearly becomes very poor. The output 'overshoots' its required value of zero, and this overshoot becomes very large. Simultaneously, the output becomes oscillatory and these oscillations become underdamped. Although the response becomes faster as γ increases, in the sense that the initial reduction of the output towards zero is faster, the time taken for the effect of the disturbance to be effectively corrected begins to increase if γ is increased too much. Consequently the most satisfactory value of γ is some way short of its maximum allowable value.

If the shape of the Nyquist locus is changed so that, with the same values of γ, it does not approach the point $-1 + 0i$ so closely, then much better closed-loop response characteristics may be obtained. Figure XIII.8 shows the recovery from a constant disturbance when $P(z) = \gamma z/z - 1$ and $\gamma = 1$, that is, of the system whose open-loop Nyquist locus is shown in Figure XIII.6.

Underdamped behaviour arises from complex conjugate roots of the closed-loop characteristic polynomial lying close to the unit circle. Consequently, the denominator polynomial of the *closed-loop* transfer function

$$T(z) = \frac{G(z)P(z)}{1 + G(z)P(z)} \tag{31}$$

will also have at least one pair of roots that are close to the unit circle, since the two polynomials are usually the same. We can therefore write the

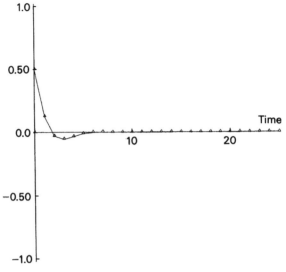

Fig. XIII.8   gamma = 1

closed-loop transfer function as

$$T(z) = \frac{T'(z)}{z - z^*} \qquad (32)$$

where z^* is one of the roots close to the unit circle, and we choose z^* to be the root in the upper half of the complex plane. Let $z^* = r^* \exp(i\omega^*)$. Then

$$e^{i\omega^*} - z^* = (1 - r^*)e^{i\omega^*} \qquad (33)$$

but $r^* \simeq 1$, so $|e^{i\omega^*} - z^*|$ is small, with the consequence that $|T(e^{i\omega^*})|$ is large in view of equation (32). In other words, the frequency-response of the output y in the face of oscillatory behaviour of the reference variable r (see Figure XII.4), with the negative feedback loop closed, exhibits large magnification over some (often small) range of frequencies. This phenomenon is known as *resonance*.

As discussed in the previous chapter, the greatest benefits are obtained from the use of feedback if $T(z) = 1$ approximately. Consequently, a typical graph of $|T(e^{i\omega})|$ against ω for a well-designed feedback system has the appearance of Figure XIII.9, in which the magnitude of the peak indicates the degree of underdamping exhibited by the time response. Much empirical evidence suggests that the time response is unsatisfactory if the peak value of $|T(e^{i\omega})|$ exceeds $\sqrt{2}$, approximately. This criterion

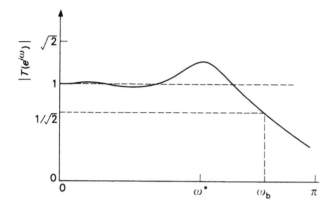

Fig. XIII.9

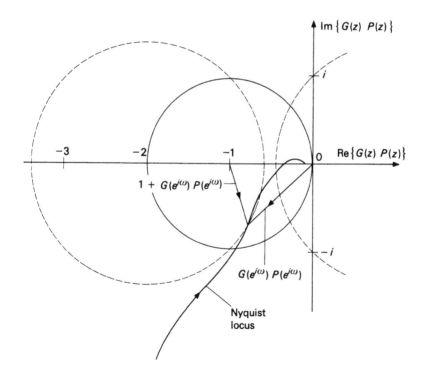

Fig. XIII.10

can be easily translated into a requirement on the *open-loop* Nyquist locus $G(e^{i\omega})P(e^{i\omega})$. Figure XIII.10 shows part of such a locus, and the two complex numbers $G(e^{i\omega})P(e^{i\omega})$ and $1 + G(e^{i\omega})P(e^{i\omega})$ are shown as vectors for a particular frequency ω. Now $|T(e^{i\omega})|$ is just the ratio of the lengths of these two vectors, in view of the definition (31). We have drawn the vectors in Figure XIII.10 so that the ratio of their lengths is exactly $\sqrt{2}$, and we have also shown, by a broken line, the circle that is the locus of all the points p such that $|p|/|1 + p| = \sqrt{2}$. If a point p lies inside this circle, then $|p|/|1 + p| > \sqrt{2}$. Consequently we have a criterion that specifies how close to $-1 + 0i$ the Nyquist locus is allowed to come: it should lie outside the left-most circle shown in Figure XIII.10.

This is not a rigid rule that must always be adhered to. There are other aspects of the performance of a feedback system that are important, apart from the degree of damping of its time response, and it may be impossible to make those aspects satisfactory without allowing the locus to stray inside the circle. But it does provide a very useful guide, and a Nyquist locus that penetrates deeply into the circle almost always indicates an unacceptable design.

(ii) *Stability Margin and Robustness*

One of the other important aspects of a feedback design is its robustness, in the face of uncertainty about the economic model on which it is based. It is inevitable that the performance of the policy in practice would be different from its designed performance, because the economic model used for the design is bound to be inaccurate. But if the extent of the inaccuracy can be estimated, then an attempt can be made to devise a policy that retains adequate performance when applied to the real economy. In particular, it is essential to ensure that the real economy is stable when the policy is used to regulate it.

The errors made in modelling the economy can be thought of as errors in the magnification and phase-lag characteristics of the model. If the Nyquist locus of the nominal design lies very near the point $-1 + 0i$, then there is a large chance that the locus of the policy combined with the real economy will encircle that point, and that the regulated economy will be unstable. Hence we have another reason for ensuring that the Nyquist locus is well clear of the point $-1 + 0i$. As far as robustness is concerned, no general-purpose guideline can be given for the location of the locus. A satisfactory location can be determined only when the extent of the modelling inaccuracies has been estimated.

(iii) *Bandwidth*

Of course it is not sufficient, for satisfactory performance of a policy, that the Nyquist locus should lie outside the left-most circle shown in Figure

XIII.10. This condition could be satisfied, for example, by putting $P(z) = 0$, namely having no policy at all, since the locus would then consist of the single point at the origin.

If an exogenous disturbance takes the form of an oscillation of very low frequency, a good feedback policy should be capable of leaving the regulated output almost undisturbed. Therefore the magnitude of the sensitivity function $|1 - T(e^{i\omega})|$ should be small for very low values of ω. This is achieved by making the loop gain $|G(e^{i\omega})P(e^{i\omega})|$ large at these values of ω. The desirable extreme of being able to remove completely the effect of a constant disturbance (as shown in Figures XIII.7 and XIII.8, for example) is achieved if $|1 - T(1)| = 0$. This occurs if the loop gain is infinite at $\omega = 0$, which, as we saw earlier, is precisely the effect of introducing integral control.

Since the phase lag of all except the simplest models eventually increases with frequency, the loop gain must almost always be kept low at high frequencies (near $\omega = \pi$). Otherwise the Nyquist locus would encircle the point $-1 + 0i$, and instability of the closed loop would result.

How should the transition from high gain at low frequencies, to low gain at high frequencies, be accomplished? We have already said that Figure XIII.9 shows how the *closed-loop* magnification $|T(e^{i\omega})|$ varies with frequency for a well-designed feedback policy. The slight peak may or may not be there, but there is always a frequency at which the magnification begins to fall significantly below 1. Let us define this frequency, somewhat arbitrarily, as the frequency at which $|T(e^{i\omega})| = 1/\sqrt{2}$; we denote this frequency by ω_b, and we call the range of frequencies between 0 and ω_b the closed-loop *bandwidth*. The bandwidth is the feature of Figure XIII.9 that determines, more than any other, the performance of the closed-loop system.*

Before describing how the bandwidth affects system performance, let us see how it is related to the open-loop Nyquist locus. Whenever the Nyquist locus intersects the left-most circle shown in Figure XIII.10 we know that $|T(e^{i\omega})| = \sqrt{2}$. The frequencies at which $|T(e^{i\omega})| = 1/\sqrt{2}$ are those at which the locus intersects another circle, with the same radius as the first, but whose centre is at $+1 + 0i$ instead of $-2 + 0i$. Part of this circle is also shown by a broken line in Figure XIII.10. The closed-loop bandwidth is therefore given by the lowest frequency at which the locus intersects this second circle. In practice, this frequency is usually quite close to the lowest frequency at which $|G(e^{i\omega})P(e^{i\omega})| = 1$, so the main feature of the transition from high to low loop gain is established by the stipulation that the distance of the Nyquist locus from the origin should

---

*Whenever we discuss $T(z)$ we assume that it results from a reasonably good design. In particular, we assume that the peak in Figure XIII.9 is not too high, in other words that the closed-loop system is not very underdamped.

Table XIII.2

ω_b	α	k^*
0.01	0.99	120
0.1	0.91	13
0.2	0.82	6
0.4	0.67	3
1	0.40	2
2	0.22	1

be approximately one at the frequency that is to be the closed-loop bandwidth.

But how is this bandwidth to be determined? If the graph of the closed-loop gain $|T(e^{i\omega})|$ (Figure XIII.9) has no peak in it, the closed-loop transfer function can often be approximated by

$$T(z) = \frac{(1-\alpha)z}{z-\alpha}, \qquad (0 < \alpha < 1). \tag{34}$$

It is easy to find the value of α that corresponds to a given closed-loop bandwidth by evaluating $T(e^{i\omega})$. Some pairs of values of ω_b and α are shown in Table XIII.2. The response of the output y, when the reference variable r takes the values

$$r_k = 1, \qquad (k = 0, 1, 2, \ldots) \tag{35}$$

and the feedback loop is closed, is approximately

$$y_k = 1 - \alpha^k. \tag{36}$$

From equation (57) of the previous chapter, we see that if, instead of increasing the reference variable, we apply an exogenous disturbance

$$\xi_k = 1, \qquad (k = 0, 1, 2, \ldots) \tag{37}$$

to the system, then its output will be

$$y_k = \alpha^k. \tag{38}$$

Thus the parameter α determines the 'speed of response' of the system, which is therefore related to the closed-loop bandwidth. The third column of Table XIII.2 shows the value of k^*, which is the number of time steps that must elapse before 70 per cent of a constant disturbance is removed by the feedback action:

$$k^* = \min(k: \alpha^k \leqslant 0.3). \tag{39}$$

The time taken to remove 90 per cent of a constant disturbance is approximately $2k^*$. From Table XIII.2 one can see that the closed-loop bandwidth is approximately the inverse of the 'time constant', k^*, of the regulated system at least in this simple case. One also expects, from Table XIII.2, that an economic regulation policy should give a closed-loop bandwidth of about 0.1 radians/quarter at least, if it is to be worth having. That is, it should certainly take no longer than thirteen quarters to remove 70 per cent of a constant disturbance.

In many cases this simple relationship between the bandwidth and the 'time constant' (as measured by the time taken to remove 70 per cent of a constant disturbance) remains approximately true. This is often so even if the system behaviour shows some oscillation and the graph of $|T(e^{i\omega})|$ exhibits resonance – in other words, even if a first-order transfer function such as (34) gives a very poor approximation to the real transfer function. On the other hand, there are also systems in which the reciprocal of the bandwidth is very different from the 'time constant'. But in these cases the 'time constant' is always longer than the value predicted from the bandwidth – a comparison of Figures XIV.2 and XIV.6 in the next chapter provides an example of this.

The conclusion to be drawn from all this is that to achieve a required speed of response, the closed-loop transfer function of the controlled system must exhibit *at least* a certain bandwidth. The faster the speed of response, the greater must the bandwidth be.

Of course, a large bandwidth can only be obtained by the vigorous use of control action. This is evident both from the rapid response of the system, and from the fact that the loop gain $|G(e^{i\omega})P(e^{i\omega})|$ must be large (certainly larger than 1) from $\omega = 0$ up to a high value of frequency. The actual extent of policy-instrument movement required to achieve a given bandwidth depends entirely on the details of the economic model, since it depends on how much of the required loop gain is supplied by the magnification of the model, namely by $|G(e^{i\omega})|$.

(iv) *Rejection of Disturbances*

Suppose that an exogenous disturbance

$$\xi_k = X \sin(\omega k) \qquad (40)$$

impinges on the economy. Is its effect always reduced by the feedback action? If the resulting output is (eventually) given by

$$y_k = Y \sin(\omega k - \psi), \qquad (41)$$

then we see from equation (54) of the previous chapter that

$$\left|\frac{Y}{X}\right| = \left|\frac{1}{1 + G(e^{i\omega})P(e^{i\omega})}\right| \tag{42}$$

so that the effect of the disturbance is actually exacerbated if

$$|1 + G(e^{i\omega})P(e^{i\omega})| < 1. \tag{43}$$

This occurs if the point of the Nyquist locus corresponding to the frequency ω lies inside the circle which has centre at $-1 + 0i$ and radius 1. This circle is shown by the solid line in Figure XIII.10. In practice it is impossible to prevent the Nyquist locus entering the circle for some range of frequencies – because of the Nyquist stability theorem – so there are always some potential disturbances whose effect is *worse* than it would be if no regulation were attempted.

The explanation of this is that the 'inertia' in both the economy and the policy causes sufficient phase lag, at some frequencies, for the feedback loop to become 'positive' instead of 'negative' at those frequencies. Consequently the effect of policy is to reinforce an exogenous disturbance that acts at one of those frequencies, rather than reduce it. The possibility of this perverse effect was first pointed out in the economics literature in the classic paper by Friedman (1953), who used statistical arguments. The frequency-response analysis shows that it is not only possible, but virtually inevitable, that disturbances should be magnified at some frequencies. But this should not be taken to mean that negative feedback does more harm than good. The policy should be so designed that the damage done at these frequencies is more than outweighed by the benefits obtained at others.

At which frequencies will the inequality (43) hold? That is, at which frequencies will feedback regulation be harmful rather than beneficial? If $|T(e^{i\omega})| < \sqrt{2}$, as prescribed in Section 4(i), then inequality (43) will hold only if $|G(e^{i\omega})P(e^{i\omega})| < \sqrt{2}$. So it will only hold if the loop gain is rather low, which should be the case only at frequencies above a certain value. If the Nyquist locus is similar to that shown in Figure XIII.10, then it can be shown that this value does not differ from the closed-loop bandwidth by a factor of more than 2 (approximately). This suggests that one should always try to achieve as large a bandwidth as policy-instrument movements will allow, in order that exogenous disturbances might be magnified over as small a range of frequencies as possible.

(v)   *The Effects of Measurement Errors*

It will be recalled from the previous chapter that the closed-loop transfer function $T(z)$ relates the regulated output not only to the reference variable r, but also to the variable m, which represents errors made in measuring the output. If this variable is imagined to have the form of a sinusoidal oscillation, then its effect on the true output will be significantly attenuated only if its frequency is higher than the closed-loop bandwidth. Thus, if considerable measurement error is known to be present, there may be grounds for keeping the bandwidth lower than the achievable limit.*

The reader may feel that little is to be gained by considering disturbances and measurement errors in the form of highly idealised oscillations. But, as we have already mentioned, it is possible to represent random functions by distributions of sinusoidal functions, using the techniques of *spectral analysis* (see Jenkins and Watts, 1968). Disturbances that affect the true output variable of a model are themselves the results of social and economic processes, which occur either at home or abroad. They therefore tend to contain more gradual, or 'low frequency', changes than rapid ones. Measurement errors, on the other hand, are generated more randomly, and therefore tend to contain a more even distribution of frequency components. Indeed, since long-term measurement errors are probably detected and corrected, it is likely that measurement errors are more concentrated at high frequencies than at low ones.

Thus, to regulate the economy effectively in the face of both exogenous disturbances and measurement errors, one would like the magnitude of the sensitivity function, $|1 - T(e^{i\omega})|$, to be small at low frequencies, even though this must be accompanied by $|T(e^{i\omega})| \doteq 1$, and one would like the magnitude of the closed-loop transfer function, $|T(e^{i\omega})|$, to be small at high frequencies, even though this would probably be accompanied by $|1 - T(e^{i\omega})| > 1$ (cf. Section 4(iv)). At low frequencies the resulting reduction of the effects of exogenous disturbances would probably outweigh the effects of measurement errors appearing unattenuated at the outputs, while at high frequencies the attenuation of measurement errors would probably outweigh the magnification of exogenous disturbances.

These desirable characteristics of $|T(e^{i\omega})|$ and $|1 - T(e^{i\omega})|$ are achieved if the loop gain $|G(e^{i\omega})P(e^{i\omega})|$ is high at low frequencies, and low at high frequencies. We have already seen that this is how the loop gain must vary if closed-loop stability is to be maintained. But in order to devise some 'optimal' transition from high gain at low frequencies to low gain at high frequencies, one would need a detailed and reliable assessment of the spectral characteristics of both disturbances and measurement errors. No such assessment is available, and, even if it were, the resulting optimal transition might well conflict with the requirements of having a reasonable stability margin and sufficient speed of response to deal with occasional, sustained disturbances. For these reasons we designed our

---

*We are making a general point here. In fact, the bandwidths that result from the policies advocated in this book *are* limited by the amount of policy instrument variation that is feasible.

proposed policy by focusing on speed of response and on stability margins, rather than on considerations of random disturbances and measurement errors. But in the next chapter we shall see that such considerations are nevertheless helpful when comparing alternative policies.

5. Factors Limiting Performance

In the previous section we have shown how the details of a proposed Nyquist locus are related to various aspects of the closed-loop system performance. What prevents the policy designer from achieving any locus he wants, and thus obtaining any performance characteristics that he specified? Factors of two kinds impede him. There are factors that are inherent to the mathematics and to the particular economy with which he is working — we assume that he can do nothing to make the economy itself easier to control — and there are factors that arise from practical considerations — how vigorously he can move the policy instruments, for instance, and how complex the policy can be. In this section we shall focus on the inherent limitations to policy performance.

The most important of these is the fact that $|G(e^{i\omega})|$ and arg $G(e^{i\omega})$ cannot be varied independently of each other. A simple Nyquist locus is shown in Figure XIII.4(b), in which a *reduction* of the magnification (with increasing frequency) is accompanied by a phase *lag* (i.e. negative phase angle). This combination is always obtained together, if the system is stable. A system that exhibits phase lead will always show increased magnification at high frequency, compared with that at low frequency.

Furthermore, at any frequency a given rate of decrease of magnification with frequency must be accompanied by at least a certain phase lag and this minimal lag increases with the rate of decrease of magnification. Consequently, one may not be able to achieve a transfer function $G(z)P(z)$ that corresponds to an arbitrary Nyquist locus, because no such transfer function need exist. (It should be remembered that the frequency calibration along a Nyquist locus is as important as its shape.)

Thus the transition from the 'low frequency, high loop-gain' regime to the 'high frequency, low loop-gain' regime is constrained by the interdependence of the magnification and phase shift of the Nyquist locus. If one attempts to squeeze this transition into too small a frequency interval, then the Nyquist locus will inevitably exhibit large negative phase shifts that will bring the locus near to the point $-1 + 0i$. This will result in a low margin of stability, underdamped dynamic characteristics, and, possibly, amplification of exogenous disturbances over a large range of frequencies, as we have discussed in the previous section.

Another inherent limitation on the achievable performance of policy arises if the economic model, represented by its transfer function $G(z)$, is such that $G(z_0) = 0$ for some complex number z_0 such that $|z_0| > 1$.

Models with this property can often be identified from a peculiar characteristic of their time responses. If a constant input

$$u_k = 1, \qquad k = 0, 1, 2, \ldots$$

is applied to such a model, its output will, in many cases, initially move in the 'wrong' direction. It will either become negative at first, and eventually positive, or the other way round. An economic example of such behaviour is provided by the 'J-curve' effect, which is observed when one attempts to improve the balance of payments by depreciating the exchange rate. One expects intuitively that systems that exhibit such behaviour should be difficult to control, and this indeed turns out to be the case: we can also show that the attainable closed-loop bandwidth – and hence the speed of recovery from an exogenous disturbance – of such systems is limited to a value that depends on z_0.

Let

$$Q(z) = G(z)P(z), \tag{44}$$

then $Q(z_0) = 0$ if $G(z_0) = 0$. We can factorise $Q(z)$ as

$$Q(z) = M(z)A(z) \tag{45}$$

where

$$A(z) = \frac{1}{|z_0|} \frac{z - z_0}{z - 1/z_0}, \tag{46}$$

so that $A(z_0) = 0$ and $M(1/z_0) = 0$. Now $A(z)$ has the property that $|A(e^{i\omega})| = 1$ for every ω, and $\arg A(e^{i\omega})$ decreases with ω (from π at $\omega = 0$ to 0 at $\omega = \pi$, if z_0 is real and positive). Thus the magnification of $Q(e^{i\omega})$ is the same as that of $M(e^{i\omega})$, while its phase *lag* is that of $M(e^{i\omega})$, increased by the phase lag of $A(e^{i\omega})$.*

To satisfy the Nyquist stability theorem, the frequency ω_c at which

$$|Q(e^{i\omega_c})| = 1 \qquad (= |M(e^{i\omega_c})|) \tag{47}$$

must be sufficiently low for the condition

$$\arg Q(e^{i\omega_c}) = \arg M(e^{i\omega_c}) + \arg A(e^{i\omega_c}) > -\pi \tag{48}$$

---

*Systems whose transfer functions become zero at points outside the unit circle are known as 'non-minimum phase' systems because of this factorisation. The factor $A(z)$ is called 'all-pass' since it neither attenuates nor magnifies its input at any frequency.

Table XIII.3

z_0	ω^*
1.0	0
1.1	0.095
1.2	0.181
1.3	0.259
1.5	0.395
2	0.644
3	0.927
∞	$\pi/2$

Negative real values of z_0 give $\pi/2 < \omega^* \leqslant \pi$

to be satisfied. In fact, to retain not just stability but also reasonable performance, we must have some margin of stability, so that we need

$$\arg M(e^{i\omega_c}) + \arg A(e^{i\omega_c}) > \mu - \pi \qquad (49)$$

where the 'phase margin' μ is at least $\pi/5$ if severe underdamping is to be avoided. Since $M(z)$ will inevitably show some phase lag itself at this frequency, ω_c is limited approximately by the value of ω^* such that

$$\arg A(1) - \arg A(e^{i\omega^*}) = \pi/2. \qquad (50)$$

Table XIII.3 shows what this limiting value is for several *real* values of z_0. The achievable closed-loop bandwidth is approximately twice this value.

In the balance of payments loop of our linearised model we found — with the *gdp* loop closed — that $G(z_0) = 0$ for $z_0 = 1.44$. This limits the achievable bandwidth to about 0.7 radians/quarter. But we found that the bandwidth of the balance of payments loop was in fact limited to about 0.1 radians/quarter by limitations on the permissible amount of exchange-rate movement.

6. Multivariable Systems

So far in this chapter we have discussed the control of a single economic variable, and the use of a single policy instrument to do so. But in this book we are concerned with using several instruments to control several output variables, which has become known as the *multivariable* control problem. Fortunately, all the concepts that we have introduced in the previous sections can be applied to the multivariable problem, with appropriate modifications.

The transfer function $Q(z) = G(z)P(z)$ is now a square matrix of functions, rather than a single function, but $Q(e^{i\omega})$ still conveys frequency-response information. The (i,j) element $Q_{ij}(e^{i\omega})$ gives the eventual magnification and phase shift of the ith output variable y^i, relative to the jth input variable e^j, when this variable oscillates with frequency ω. That is, if

$$e^j_k = \sin(\omega k) \tag{51}$$

then y^i will eventually be indistinguishable from

$$y^i_k = \sum_j |Q_{ij}(e^{i\omega})| \sin[\omega k + \arg Q_{ij}(e^{i\omega})] \tag{52}$$

(if the open-loop system is stable). A diagram that simultaneously displays the Nyquist locus of each element of $Q(z)$ can be drawn, and is called a 'Nyquist array', but closed-loop stability cannot be deduced directly from this. Instead, another set of loci, the so-called 'characteristic loci' or 'generalised Nyquist loci' must be drawn. These are loci of the *eigenvalue* functions $\lambda_j(e^{i\omega})$ of $Q(e^{i\omega})$, namely functions that solve the equation

$$\det[\lambda_j(e^{i\omega})I - Q(e^{i\omega})] = 0. \tag{53}$$

(I denotes the unit matrix). There are as many of these cnaracteristic loci as there are outputs to be controlled, and taken together (but not necessarily separately) they form a set of closed curves. If the open-loop (i.e. uncontrolled) system is stable, then the *generalised Nyquist stability theorem* states that the closed-loop system is stable if and only if these closed curves do not encircle the point $-1 + 0i$ (Postlethwaite and MacFarlane, 1979).

If any of the characteristic loci approach the point $-1 + 0i$ too closely — if one or more enter the left-most circle shown in Figure XIII.10, for example — then at least one of the outputs will exhibit underdamped behaviour when the feedback loop is closed.

The characteristic loci can often be used to assess the performance of a proposed policy, much as the ordinary Nyquist locus is used with single-variable control problems. But unfortunately they are not always reliable in this role. The source of the problem is that there is now no single loop gain. A variable appearing at any point of the loop shown in Figure XII.4 is a vector in the multivariable case, and the extent to which it is magnified (or attenuated) as it is propagated around the loop depends on its 'direction'. For example, if there are two variables to be controlled, then the error vectors

$$e_k = \begin{bmatrix} \sin(\omega k) \\ 0 \end{bmatrix} \quad \text{and} \quad e_k = \begin{bmatrix} 0 \\ \sin(\omega k) \end{bmatrix} \tag{54}$$

result in the output vectors

$$y_k = \begin{bmatrix} |Q_{11}(e^{i\omega})| \sin [\omega k + \arg Q_{11}(e^{i\omega})] \\ |Q_{21}(e^{i\omega})| \sin [\omega k + \arg Q_{21}(e^{i\omega})] \end{bmatrix} \qquad (55)$$

and

$$y_k = \begin{bmatrix} |Q_{12}(e^{i\omega})| \sin [\omega k + \arg Q_{12}(e^{i\omega})] \\ |Q_{22}(e^{i\omega})| \sin [\omega k + \arg Q_{22}(e^{i\omega})] \end{bmatrix} \qquad (56)$$

respectively, if the loop is open. If we measure the lengths of vectors using the Euclidean norm, then the 'loop gain' is $\sqrt{(|Q_{11}(e^{i\omega})|^2 + |Q_{21}(e^{i\omega})|^2)}$ in the first case, but $\sqrt{(|Q_{12}(e^{i\omega})|^2 + |Q_{22}(e^{i\omega})|^2)}$ in the second. Note that only the direction of e_k is different between the two cases, not the frequency.

Clearly, one has to replace the concept of a single 'loop gain' by a band of possible 'loop gains'. It can be shown that a suitable band can be defined, and that the magnitudes of the characteristic loci all lie within this band. Now the individual characteristic loci are subject to constraining relationships between their moduli and phases, in the same way as ordinary Nyquist loci are. Consequently the performance of a multi-variable control system is limited in essentially the same ways as is the performance of a feedback system which controls only one variable.

To assess and compare the performance of policies we shall use Nyquist arrays, not of the open-loop transfer function $Q(z)$, but of the closed-loop transfer function $T(z)$ and of the sensitivity function $I - T(z)$. These are particularly useful when drawn so that each element displays the variation with frequency of the magnitude of the corresponding element of the matrix. In this form, each diagonal element of the Nyquist array of $T(z)$ looks like the graph shown in Figure XIII.9. The bandwidth of each loop can therefore be obtained from the array. The attenuation of measurement errors can also be deduced, as in the case of single-variable systems. This information cannot be obtained directly from a Nyquist array of $Q(z)$, because, unlike the case of single-variable systems, the elements of $Q(z)$ are now related to the elements of $T(z) = Q(z)[I + Q(z)]^{-1}$ in a very complicated manner.

The elements of $T(z)$ and of $I - T(z)$, on the other hand, are related to each other in a very simple way. One could therefore assess the effectiveness of a policy in dealing with exogenous disturbances directly from the Nyquist array of $T(z)$. However, to do this, one would require both the magnitudes and phases of the elements to be drawn. Since only the magnitude information is required for performance assessment, and since

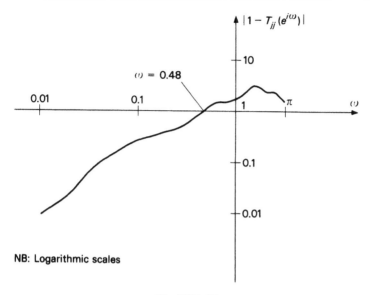

Fig. XIII.11

the only practical way of generating displays of the Nyquist arrays is by means of a computer, it turns out to be more convenient to display the Nyquist array of $I - T(z)$ separately, again in such a form that the variation of magnitudes with frequency is shown. A diagonal element (i.e. one in position (j,j) for some j) of a typical array is shown in Figure XIII.11. This shows the effect of the jth exogenous disturbance ξ^j on the jth output y^j when the feedback policy is in place. From the diagram one can deduce that for frequencies up to $\omega = 0.48$ such a disturbance is attenuated (relative to the effect it would have if no control action was taken), but that above this frequency it is magnified. Just as in the single-variable case, it is usually impossible to avoid magnifying disturbances at some frequencies. Obviously, one can also see from the diagram the extent to which disturbances of various frequencies are attenuated or magnified.

We model exogenous disturbances as being additive at the output of the model of the economy. Consequently, if the model were uncontrolled, the action of a disturbance on only one of the outputs would leave the other output variables undisturbed. But when all the outputs are being controlled, a disturbance on one output causes corrective action to be taken by at least one policy instrument, and this has the effect of disturbing all the outputs to some extent. Errors made in measuring one of the output variables also eventually affect all the outputs, through the feedback mechanism. The extent to which either a disturbance or a measurement error on output y^j disturbs output y^i is measured by the magnitude of element (i,j) of the sensitivity function $I - T(z)$, or of the closed-loop transfer function $T(z)$, so this information can again be obtained from an appropriate Nyquist array.

However, such information must be interpreted with care, since exogenous disturbances do not usually act on individual outputs in isolation (although measurement errors on different variables *are* independent of each other). For example, exogenous changes in real output appear as combinations of disturbances on the (Money) GDP, on the balance of payments on current account and on unemployment, and these combinations can be corrected more easily than a change on only one of these output variables. The reason for this is that a decrease in real output, for example, appears as a fall in Money GDP, a rise in the balance of payments and a rise in unemployment. The measures required to correct each of these are consistent with each other. If, however, a fall in Money GDP occurs alone, the stimulation of demand required to correct for this conflicts with the requirement of keeping the other two output variables undisturbed. Consequently, the Nyquist array of $I - T(z)$ could lead to too pessimistic an assessment of policy performance.

But suppose that a realistic disturbance ζ (such as a fall in real output) generates a disturbance vector ξ at the output according to

$$\xi(z) = H(z)\zeta(z).$$

Then the extent to which the regulated economy is disturbed by ζ can be assessed from the modified sensitivity function $[I - T(z)]H(z)$. We make use of such modified sensitivity functions in the next chapter, in order to assess the performance of alternative policies in the face of exogenous disturbances in import prices and in consumer spending. Of course the transfer function $H(z)$ is different for each of these disturbances.

7.   Design Techniques

Most traditional methods of designing single-variable control systems are based on directly modifying the shape of the Nyquist locus of $G(z)P(z)$, and they use various mixtures of trial-and-error, mathematical results and computer assistance to do so. The attempt to extend these techniques to multivariable problems leads naturally to methods that try to modify the shapes of the characteristic loci. Methods of this kind have been developed, and their further development is the subject of much current research, but it is impossible to preserve any required structure of policy – such as 'New Keynesian' – when using them. The control policies that result always require the use of all available policy instruments for the control of each output variable.

When one requires – as we do – a 'diagonal' policy, namely one that uses only one instrument for the control of each output variable, there are two possible ways of proceeding, and we have used both of them. One is to regard the design problem as a succession of single-variable control problems. One starts by having one instrument, a composite tax rate, which one will use to regulate one output variable – Money GDP. This is a single-variable problem, and one designs a feedback policy to solve it. Next, one keeps this policy in place, and one is faced with another single-variable problem: the use of the exchange rate to control the balance of payments. One proceeds to design a policy to solve this problem, and one hopes that this policy does not upset the behaviour of the regulated Money GDP too much. One goes on like this until a control policy has been designed for each output variable, whereupon one may go back to the first variable and repeat the process. With luck, one eventually obtains satisfactory performance of all variables. This procedure may appear crude, but it is straightforward and often successful.

The other way of proceeding is to define a structure for the multi-variable control policy, somehow to define an ideal performance specification, and then to allow a computer to optimise the policy so as to approach the ideal performance as closely as possible. This approach has the merit that the design of each part of the control policy takes into account all the other parts. On the other hand it is not guaranteed to succeed, and is difficult to use. The difficulty arises from the fact that when one is beginning a design, one usually has only a hazy idea of what would constitute acceptable performance, and of what is possible with the particular model one is using. The initial performance specification may well have mutually contradictory aspects, whose existence and lack of suitability has to be gradually discovered as the design proceeds. For example, one may initially specify a closed-loop bandwidth for each controlled variable, but one may simultaneously impose a constraint on instrument variations that makes it impossible to achieve that bandwidth. Such conflicts have to be resolved by an iterative evolution of the performance specifications, and the direction of that evolution is more of an art than a science.

The manner in which we specify performance specifications is by defining a desired closed-loop transfer function $T_d(z)$, and then using an optimisation algorithm, due to Edmunds (1979), which attempts to minimise the error between $T_d(e^{i\omega})$ and the actual closed-loop frequency response $T(e^{i\omega})$ at a number (typically 40) of frequencies. The designer must supply the optimisation algorithm with denominator polynomials for those elements of the policy $P(z)$ that are to be non-zero, and with the relative weights that are to be attached to errors in the various elements of the closed-loop transfer function matrix. The algorithm then 'tunes' the appropriate numerator polynomials of $P(z)$, so that the resulting control policy is presented to the designer in the form of a transfer function matrix.

Constraints on instrument variations can be specified by means of a trick. The economic model is replaced by an augmented model, which has the feature that every policy instrument also appears as an output (but one that is not to be controlled). This allows the designer to specify the transfer function that is to hold between the reference variables *r* and the policy instruments *u* (see Figure XII.4) when the feedback loop is closed. This is equivalent to specifying the trajectory that each instrument is to follow when a reference variable suddenly changes, or when an exogenous disturbance appears on one of the outputs.

Of course, the performance of the policy designed by the optimisation algorithm is analysed by the use of appropriate Nyquist loci and their generalisations, and by simulation.

8.   Why Not 'Optimal Control'?

Most of the control-theoretic literature of the past twenty-five years has been concerned with 'optimal control'. It deals with questions such as: find a control policy that will minimise the cost

$$J = \sum_{k=0}^{T} (y_k' Q y_k + u_k' R u_k) \tag{57}$$

where *y* and *u* represent vectors of outputs and instruments as usual, *Q* and *R* are weighting matrices and *T* is some 'time horizon'. Many variations on the form of this cost function are possible, although its quadratic nature is usually retained. This body of literature makes little use of the frequency-response concepts that we have introduced — it is quite possible to design a policy using 'optimal control' methods without knowing anything about Nyquist diagrams, bandwidths or resonances. Most economic applications of control theory have used these methods (notable exceptions are the pioneering papers by Phillips, 1954; 1957). Why, then, have we not also used them?

First, let us dispose of a common misapprehension, which is that the methods we use are somehow inferior, because they are not 'optimal'. An 'optimal' policy is merely one that solves a mathematical optimisation problem. There is no guarantee that it is a good, or even a satisfactory, solution to the economic problem that faces the policy-maker. That depends largely on how well the mathematical formulation of the problem represents the real economic problem. Clearly, a considerable gap exists between the formulation of a cost function such as the one defined by equation (57) and a complete statement of the design problem. This is not to say that the gap cannot be narrowed. There is much need for skill and ingenuity when deciding the details of the cost function. By including appropriate terms with appropriate weights one may well obtain a satisfactory policy, but normally only after a process of trial and error.

One can solve an optimal control problem for either a non-linear or a linearised model. If one works with the non-linear model then very little theoretical support is available for the analysis of the resulting policy. Whereas linear optimal control theory yields a control policy in the form of a feedback *rule*, in the non-linear case one obtains only a required time profile of policy instruments conditional upon assumed values for the exogenous variables. (It is also possible to assume a particular functional form for a control rule, and then to optimise the details of this rule. But this approach does not give a truly 'optimal' solution.) Because of this, extensive numerical studies are necessary to ensure that the solution is satisfactory. Two categories of investigation are particularly important.

(1)   The sensitivity of the proposed solution to unexpected exogenous disturbances must be studied. This corresponds to examining the dynamic characteristics of a policy rule, such as overshooting, persistent oscillations, speed of response, and so on. Also sensitivity to the choice of time horizon should be examined.

(2)   The sensitivity of the solution to modelling errors must also be studied. In particular, errors in modelling future consequences of observed exogenous variables assume great importance, since at any time the policy is 'driven' as much by modelled future consequences for the output variables of the already observed exogenous variables, as by the already observed values of the output variables.

If one works with a linearised model, on the other hand, there is a considerable amount of theory to aid the design process, but only if one stays within the confines of a standard formulation of the problem. For example, the solution to the multivariable linear optimal control problem yields a cross-coupled policy with each instrument being used to control each output. An insistence that the policy should have a New Keynesian structure removes the problem from the realm of standard theory, and one has to proceed in some more or less *ad hoc* manner. Furthermore, recent developments in linear optimal control theory (for example, Doyle and Stein, 1981) emphasise the use of frequency-response concepts for both the analysis *and specification* of policy performance, with parameters of the mathematical problem, such as weighting matrices, being increasingly relegated to a merely technical intermediate role.

In other words, the optimisation of a cost function such as (57) is no longer regarded as an underlying economic problem, but only as a device for imposing some structure on the task of searching for an acceptable policy. Viewed in this light, the status of 'optimal control' methods is quite comparable to that of the frequency-response methods that we have used. They are simply alternative ways of tackling the problem of designing control policies, and neither has any inherent advantages over the other, although there is considerable evidence that the assessment of policy performance is more conveniently performed by using frequency-response concepts. We trust that this chapter has provided some of this evidence. The question of which alternative to choose when embarking on policy design is best answered by taking account of the expertise of the persons involved in developing the design, and on the availability of suitable computer software. In our case both considerations led us to the use of frequency-response methods.

CHAPTER XIV

The Design and Performance of New Keynesian Policies

1. Introduction

In this chapter several alternative sets of policy rules will be presented. One of these sets — the one discussed in Section 5 — is the policy that was used for 'rerunning history', which has already been extensively discussed in Chapter VII. The other rules are included here to give some indication of how the recommended design evolved. The chapter contains an extensive discussion of the dynamic properties — both time-response and frequency-response characteristics — obtained with our model, and is therefore somewhat tedious. But this discussion will allow the reader to gain an insight into the conflicts that exist between the various desirable properties that an ideal policy might possess.

2. Obtaining a Linear Model

The design of the policy made extensive use of the theory outlined in the previous two chapters. In order to make use of this theory, a linear time-invariant model of the UK economy is required. In Chapter XII it was shown how such a model could in principle be obtained from the non-linear model described in Appendix A, by calculating appropriate partial derivatives and approximating them by constant values (see equations (7) and (8) of Chapter XII). However, this procedure is too time consuming and error prone to be attempted by hand, and an automated version of it must be used.

There are several ways of linearising models automatically, each with its own strong and weak points. The method we used is the following. The non-linear model is first run with Base Run values of inputs and exogenous variables. The run is then repeated with the same values of exogenous variables, but with one of the input variables differing from the Base Run values in just one period. By comparing the values of the output variables in the two runs, an 'impulse response' of the model to that input variable is obtained. This is repeated for each of the input variables, so that a complete matrix of 'impulse responses' is established.

A linear model in the form of equations (41) of Chapter XII is then found, whose impulse response closely approximates the impulse response of the non-linear model. The algorithm for finding such a model is based on deep results of linear systems theory, and a detailed description of it would be out of place here. The reader is referred to Maciejowski and Vines (1982) and to Kung (1979) for details and an explanation of the algorithm. The linear model itself is available in Maciejowski and Vines (1983), and from the authors.

The model obtained in this way depends on the Base Run trajectory about which the non-linear model is being linearised. The Base Run trajectory should be the trajectory that the controlled economy is supposed to follow, in accordance with the development of equation (8) of Chapter XII. However, the implementation of the non-linear model was such that it was difficult to make the Base Run different from the trajectory defined by the actual histories of the exogenous and endogenous variables over the period 1970–9. This was therefore the trajectory about which the linearisation was performed. Although this was not the most appropriate trajectory, the resulting model was good enough for our purposes, since the performance of the policy rules obtained from it was very similar when applied to either the linear or the non-linear model.

A linear model obtained by our procedure also depends on the period in which the impulsive input perturbations are applied. But with our model this dependence is very slight. When our policies are implemented on the non-linear model, and an exogenous disturbance is suddenly applied, the ensuing trajectories of both input and output variables depend very little on the period in which the disturbance is first applied. This suggests that the behaviour of the model changes little with time, at least so far as input–output characteristics are concerned.

The model obtained by the use of the automatic linearisation procedure was slightly modified before being used for designing policies. Firstly, a feedback path was closed between the price level (an output) and the rate of interest (an input). As explained in Section 6 of Chapter V, the change in the rate of interest in each period was set equal to the change in the rate of price inflation since the previous period. Secondly, as also explained in Section 6 of Chapter V, the real exchange rate was treated as an input. This real exchange rate was manufactured from the nominal exchange rate and the wage rate after allowing for a one-period lag; it is thus related to the nominal exchange rate and the wage rate by

$$v_k = e_k + w_{k-1} \tag{1}$$

where v_k, e_k and w_k represent the differences between the values of the real exchange rate, nominal exchange rate and wage rate, respectively, and their Base Run values. The subscript 'k' identifies the time period. In the remainder of this chapter, 'exchange rate' should be understood as 'real exchange rate'. Finally, the outputs Money GDP and balance of payments on current account were delayed by one quarter, to simulate the effect of a delay in implementing the feedback policy, as discussed in Chapter VII.

With these modifications, the resulting linear model has four input and four output variables. The inputs are: the rate of indirect tax, the real exchange rate, the wage rate and the rate of employees' national insurance contributions. The outputs are: Money GDP (delayed), the balance of payments on current account (delayed), the level of unemployment and the price level. Note that the rate of interest has become an internal variable, and no longer appears as an input.

3. The Initial Design

(i) The Specification of Requirements

Although the modified linear model has four output variables, only the first three of these are to be regulated. The feedback policy, when expressed as a transfer function, will therefore have the form

$$
P(z) = \begin{bmatrix} p_{11}(z) & 0 & 0 \\ 0 & p_{22}(z) & 0 \\ 0 & 0 & p_{33}(z) \\ p_{41}(z) & 0 & 0 \end{bmatrix}
\tag{2}
$$

rather than the form shown in equation (65) of Chapter XII. The reason is that there are now two instruments that can be used to regulate Money GDP, namely, the rate of indirect tax and the rate of employees' national insurance contributions. $p_{11}(z)$ and $p_{41}(z)$ represent the transfer functions between the deviation of Money GDP from its target value and these two instruments.

The initial design was aimed at achieving satisfactory recovery from sudden 'step' disturbances of the output variables, without requiring unacceptably large movements of the inputs. 'Satisfactory' was defined as follows. Suppose that any one of the three controlled output variables were subjected to an exogenous disturbance that would have the effect, *in the absence of corrective feedback action*, of producing a sustained deviation of constant magnitude from that output's target trajectory. Then the feedback policy should reduce the effect of that disturbance by half within four quarters of its first appearance, and should remove it almost entirely within ten quarters. Furthermore, while the corrective action is taking place the deviation of each of the other two controlled outputs, from their target trajectories, should not exceed half of the magnitude of the original disturbance.

It is possible to make direct comparisons of the deviations of the various outputs in this way, if they are measured in appropriately normalised units. In this chapter we measure the input and output variables as follows. The exchange rate, the wage rate, Money GDP and unemployment are all measured in percentage deviations from their target trajectories. The rates of indirect tax and employees' national insurance contributions are measured in differences in percentage rates from their target trajectories. The balance of payments is measured in differences from its target trajectory, but expressed as a percentage of the Base Run value of Money GDP.

Constraints on the movements of policy instruments were specified as follows. Maximum movements away from targets that the policy rule is designed to deal with were chosen by inspection of the data for the 1970s (deliberately on the low side so that the policy rules would represent the maximum that could conceivably be achieved) as 1.5 per cent per quarter for Money GDP and 1 per cent per quarter for the current balance. Constraints on the instrument movements were then set: indirect tax rate, 2 percentage points per quarter; rate of employees' national insurance contributions, 1 percentage point per quarter; real exchange rate, 5 percentage points per quarter (the figures for indirect taxes and national insurance contributions are those suggested in Part Three, the figure for the exchange rate seemed to be the extreme upper limit attainable by the methods of policy proposed in Chapter V). These figures define the permissible instrument variations to accompany the correction of a step disturbance. In response to a 1 per cent disturbance of Money GDP, the rate of indirect tax should change by no more than 1.3 per cent per quarter, and the rate of employees' national insurance contributions should change by 0.7 per cent per quarter at most. If the balance of payments on current account is disturbed by 1 per cent, the exchange rate should change by no more than 5 per cent per quarter. Finally, the wage rate was required to change by no more than 1 per cent per quarter in response to a change in the level of unemployment of 1 per cent, this seeming to be the extreme upper limit to the amount of wage flexibility attainable.

These specifications of both the output and instrument movements were converted into a specification of a desirable closed-loop transfer function, by postulating possible trajectories of these variables and obtaining their z-transforms (see Section 2 of Chapter XII). After a considerable amount of trial and error, a specification of a closed-loop transfer function was found that gave a reasonable initial design, using the methods outlined in Section 7 of Chapter XIII.

(ii) *Recovery from Exogenous Output Disturbances*

It became apparent that the restrictions imposed on instrument movements were incompatible with the initial requirements for recovery from an output disturbance. Several alternative policies were obtained by the methods outlined in the previous chapter, and one was chosen that came closest to satisfying all the specifications defined above. (For details of the design procedure see Maciejowski and Vines, 1983.) The policy rules corresponding to this design are given in the form of difference equations in Appendix B. Each of these equations has a characteristic root at $1 + 0i$. Thus, as shown in Section 2 of Chapter XII, each incorporates 'integral action'.

The performance achieved with these rules can be inferred from Figures XIV.1–XIV.3. Each of Figures XIV.1(a), XIV.2(a) and XIV.3(a) shows the response of the output variables when the reference (or target) value of one controlled output variable is suddenly increased by 1 per cent. As shown by equation (57) of Chapter XII, this is the same as the recovery from a sustained exogenous *decrease* of 1 per cent in the output variable, except for an obvious shift of the horizontal axis. Figures XIV.1(b), XIV.2(b) and XIV.3(b) show the corresponding movements of the four policy instruments.

All these figures show the *deviations* of the variables from their target values. The continuous lines show the behaviour of the linear model, while the dots show the behaviour of the original non-linear model, when the same manoeuvres are attempted with the same policy rules in place. The agreement between the behaviour of the two models is very close, and we have found a similar degree of agreement in all the policy simulations that we have performed. Consequently, the remaining figures in this chapter show the performance of the linear model only. (We reiterate that the rerun of history of Chapter VIII was performed on the original non-linear model.)

Figure XIV.1 shows that half of a sustained disturbance of 1 per cent on Money GDP would be eliminated in only one quarter. There is also the one-quarter delay in implementation (see Section 2 above), which is not shown on any of the figures in this chapter. After two quarters little is left of the disturbance, but there is some overshooting, followed by a sustained oscillation of Money GDP, with a period of four quarters. But this behaviour is obtained at the cost of very large instrument movements. The indirect tax rate changes by 1.4 per cent in the second quarter, which slightly exceeds the limit we have specified, but the rate of national insurance contributions changes initially by 1.6 per cent, which is nearly double our limit. These changes induce deviations of the balance of payments (which first worsens as a result of the increased spending that follows tax cuts) and of unemployment (which initially falls for the same reason). The feedback rules manage to contain the peak deviation of unemployment to 0.25 per cent, but the balance of payments moves by about 0.7 per cent from its target, before deviating by 0.5 per cent in the other direction. It takes about fifteen quarters for the system to 'settle down' after the onset of the disturbance. (The four-quarter oscillation of

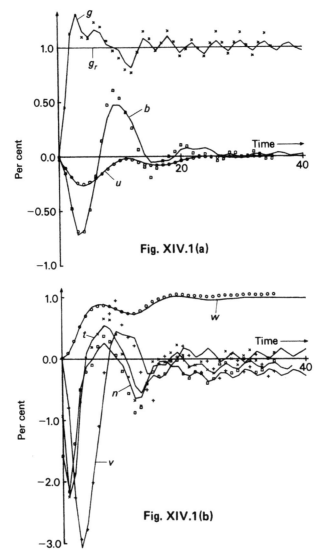

Fig. XIV.1(a)

Fig. XIV.1(b)

Key to Figs. XIV.1–XIV.9 and XIV.12–XIV.20

g = Money GDP
b = balance of payments on current
    account
u = unemployment
r (subscript) denotes reference (i.e.
    desired) level of g, b or u
t = rate of indirect taxation

n = rate of employee's national
    insurance contributions
v = real exchange rate
w = wage rate
p = price level

All the above are measured in % units, as defined in section XIV.3. Time is measured
in quarters. Frequency is measured in radians per quarter.
Note: Figs. XIV.6–XIV.9 and XIV.17–XIV.20 have logarithmic scales.

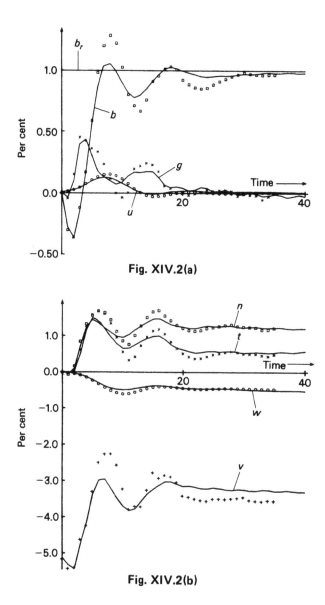

Fig. XIV.2(a)

Fig. XIV.2(b)

Money GDP which remains is an artefact due to the peculiar properties of the non-durable consumption function – see equation (67) in Appendix A – which, being in fourth differences, contains a 'hidden integrator'.) The system settles down on target because we have inserted integral control in all of the policy rules (see Section 4 of Chapter XIII). The long-term effect of the policy rules is, as we would expect, higher prices, a higher wage rate and all real variables almost unaltered.

Figure XIV.2 shows that, with the initial design of policy rules, half of a sustained 1 per cent disturbance on the balance of payments is eliminated in about five quarters. It takes another two quarters to recover from it completely, but there is then a further deviation, which lasts about ten quarters. The induced deviations of Money GDP and unemployment are within our initial specifications. The system 'settles' (on target because of 'integral action') in about twenty quarters. The movement of the exchange rate is at the limit of acceptability, being just over 5 per cent in the first quarter. In the long term, an exogenous fall of 1 per cent in the balance of payments is corrected by reducing the exchange rate by 3.4 per cent and the wage rate by 0.6 per cent, and by increasing the rates of tax and national insurance contributions by about 0.6 per cent and 1.2 per cent, respectively. These long-run instrument movements are consistent with the parameter values of the non-linear model.

The 'J-curve' effect is clearly exhibited in Figure XIV.2(a), in which the devaluation has the effect of worsening the balance of payments for three quarters before its beneficial effect becomes visible.

The process of elimination of an exogenous 1 per cent fall in unemployment can be inferred from Figure XIV.3, and the more interesting case of recovery from a 1 per cent rise in unemployment can be described simply by a reversal of the signs in the following discussion. In the first case the resulting rise in the wage rate means that the policy rules operate so as to reduce real domestic activity, and the level of unemployment is increased until it is back at its initial level. The required movements of the wage rate are excessive; in the second quarter it must change by 2 per cent which is twice the maximum change which we have stipulated. Even so, the speed of recovery from the disturbance is slower than our requirement: half of the disturbance is eliminated in about five quarters, but it takes a further fifteen quarters to recover completely (which it does because of the presence of integral control action). The induced deviations of Money GDP and the balance of payments are also both uncomfortably large. The behaviour of the balance of payments is particularly alarming, since it deviates by over 1.5 per cent from its target trajectory, and it takes about twenty-five quarters to bring it back to within 0.2 per cent of its target. In the long term the wage rate is raised by 3.4 per cent and the exchange rate by 5.8 per cent. The rate of indirect tax and employees' national insurance contributions are increased by 0.6 per cent and 1.4 per cent respectively. These long-run instrument movements make sense, given a knowledge of the underlying parameters of the non-linear model.

(iii) *Recovery from more Realistic Disturbances*

Although Figures XIV.1–XIV.3 are disappointing, it should be remembered that exogenous disturbances that act on one output only, and that

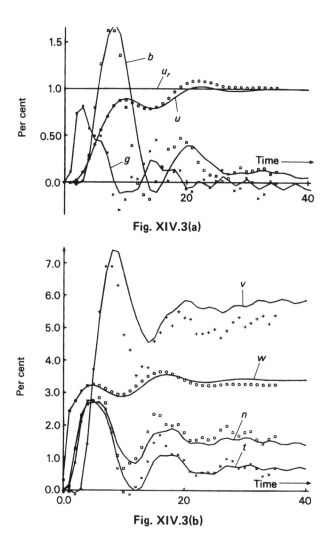

Fig. XIV.3(a)

Fig. XIV.3(b)

would leave the other outputs undisturbed in the absence of feedback, do not occur in practice. Consequently, we have also simulated the effects of two realistic exogenous disturbances, namely an exogenous fall in consumer spending and an exogenous increase in the price of imports.

When consumer spending falls so as to cause an immediate and sustained fall of exactly 1 per cent of real output in the uncontrolled economy, Money GDP falls immediately by 1 per cent, unemployment rises smoothly by 0.4 per cent within six quarters, and the balance of payments improves smoothly by 0.5 per cent (of Base Run GDP) within four quarters.

Figure XIV.4 shows the response of the controlled economy. Taxes are

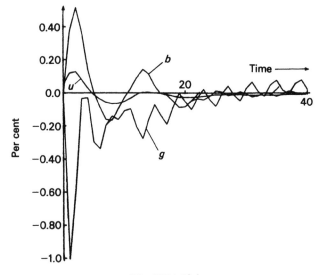

Fig. XIV.4(a)

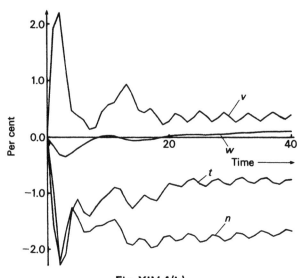

Fig. XIV.4(b)

cut and this quickly restores Money GDP and real output; unemployment quickly disappears. The short-term improvement in the balance of payments induces an unnecessary exchange-rate appreciation but this is also soon gone. Although significant deviations from targets persist until about twenty quarters have elapsed, the magnitudes of these are kept small.

When there is a sustained 1 per cent increase in import prices the effects on the uncontrolled economy are as follows. The current balance immediately worsens by about 0.2 per cent of GDP. The price level rises by about a third of the rise in import prices within about five quarters (wages are exhypothesis unchanging). Unemployment slowly rises, but only by 0.02 per cent, as spending falls, but improves as a result of substitution against imports and as higher domestic prices work through into higher export unit values (thus partially remedying the worsening of the terms of trade). Money GDP initially *falls* by 0.1 per cent. (Money GDP equals money exports plus money domestic expenditure minus money imports; the last of these initially rises, but lags in the marking up of domestic prices mean that the first two take time to rise commensurately.) Within two-and-a-half years the fall in Money GDP has disappeared; the rise in unemployment is gone in five years.

This pattern of disturbances is much more difficult to deal with. Figure XIV.5 shows what happens in the controlled economy. The real exchange rate depreciates to correct the worsened current balance. Initially taxes are cut to counter the fall in money incomes but because prices and output rise after the exchange-rate depreciation this movement must be more than reversed. There is a substantial cut in real wages implicit in the movements of the price level and the (real) exchange rate in Figure XIV.5; a small cut in money wages is also necessary to ensure that when full employment is restored the rise in profits coming from devaluation is counteracted, so as to enable Money GDP to be unchanged. The necessary temporary increase in unemployment is not large but takes about sixteen quarters to be removed. The disturbances in Money GDP and the balance of payments take an even longer time to be removed.

(iv)   *Frequency-Response Properties*

We shall now examine the frequency-response properties of the initial design. Figure XIV.6 shows the magnitudes of the diagonal elements of the closed-loop Nyquist array. (This is defined in Section 6 of Chapter XIII.) In the terminology of equation (55) of Chapter XII, Figure XIV.6 shows graphs of $|T_{ii}(e^{i\omega})|$ against ω for $i = 1, 2, 3$, both axes having logarithmic scales. These show that the bandwidths (see Section 4(iii) of Chapter XIII) of the three feedback loops (Money GDP, balance of payments and unemployment) are 1.74, 1.00, and 0.54 radians/quarter, respectively. These should be compared with Figure XIV.7, which shows the magnitudes of the diagonal elements of the sensitivity function – i.e. graphs of $|1 - T_{ii}(e^{i\omega})|$. They show that exogenous disturbances appearing independently on each of the three controlled outputs are attenuated at frequencies below 0.46, 0.17 and 0.21 radians/quarter, respectively, and are actually magnified at higher frequencies. From the point of view of regulating against frequent, random disturbances, the control of Money

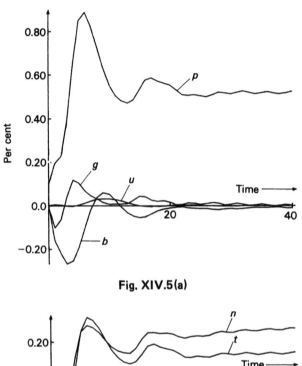

Fig. XIV.5(a)

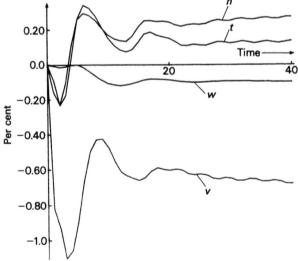

Fig. XIV.5(b)

GDP and of the balance of payments is 'inefficient' in the sense that policy instruments react strongly to measurement errors (because $|T|$ is close to 1) even at frequencies that are four to six times higher than those at which the instrument movements cease to have any beneficial effect

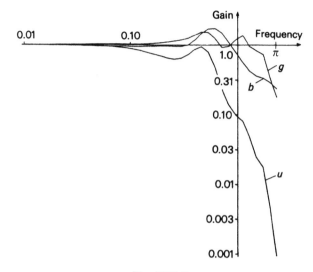

Fig. XIV.6

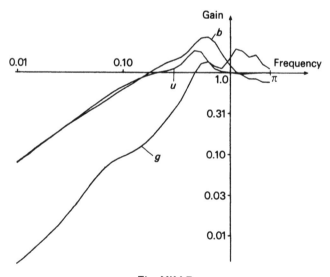

Fig. XIV.7

(namely those at which $|1 - T| = 1$). Control of unemployment is more 'efficient' in this respect, since the ratio of the two frequencies is only 2.6 in this case.

Since Figure XIV.7 gives information only about regulation in the face of independent, and hence unrealistic, exogenous disturbances, it is of

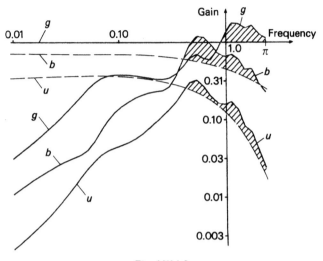

Fig. XIV.8

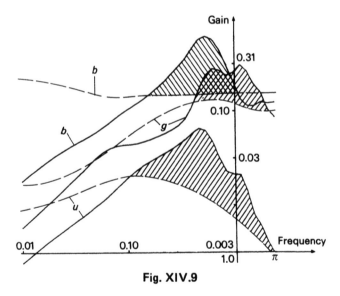

Fig. XIV.9

interest to assess the performance of the initial policy design when the
economy is subjected to exogenous changes in consumer spending and in
import prices, and which recur frequently with random magnitudes.
Figure XIV.8 shows the magnitude of the deviation of each of the
controlled outputs, both with and without feedback action, caused by
exogenous changes in consumer spending. The horizontal axis measures

the frequency of the change. Figure XIV.9 shows the corresponding graphs when the price of imports is exogenously changed. In each figure the broken lines indicate the effects of the exogenous changes when no feedback regulation takes place. However, in Figure XIV.8 only two broken lines are visible, since the third, which shows the one-for-one effect of changes in consumer behaviour on Money GDP, lies (at unity) along the horizontal axis. The hatched areas highlight those frequency ranges at which the feedback policy magnifies rather than attenuates the effects of the exogenous changes.

From Figure XIV.8 it can be seen that the high bandwidth of the initial design is not as wasteful as it appears from Figure XIV.7. The effects of changes in consumer spending on Money GDP are attenuated at frequencies up to 0.88 radians/quarter, which is only a factor of 2 below the GDP bandwidth. Effects on the balance of payments are attenuated up to 0.40 radians/quarter, and on unemployment up to 0.42 radians/quarter. The high bandwidths are therefore being used quite effectively, so long as the principal source of exogenous disturbances is consumers' spending behaviour.

Figure XIV.9, on the other hand, shows that the effects of changes in the price of imports on the three controlled outputs are amplified by the feedback policy at frequencies above 0.42, 0.16 and 0.11 radians/quarter, respectively. All of these are very low in comparison with the three bandwidths. Even the regulation of unemployment, which appeared 'efficient' on Figure XIV.7, is seen to be effective only up to one-fifth of the unemployment bandwidth.

4.   A More Robust Design

The policy presented and analysed in the previous section performs disastrously if the delay in implementing tax and exchange-rate policies is two quarters, rather than one quarter. Any single disturbance causes both the instruments and the controlled outputs to oscillate, with very little damping of the oscillations. The regulated system is on the verge of instability.

The explanation of this is clear in frequency-response terms. The transfer function of an additional delay is $1/z$. Its effect on a Nyquist locus is therefore to rotate it clockwise by the angle ω at frequency ω (since $1/z$ evaluated at $z = \exp(i\omega)$ is $\exp(-i\omega)$), thus bringing it nearer to the point $(-1 + i0)$ and destabilising the feedback loop. The effect of an additional delay in two out of three loops on the three characteristic loci (which give stability information in the multivariable case, as explained in Section 6 of Chapter XIII) is similar in nature. Figure XIV.10 shows the characteristic loci obtained with the initial policy design in this case. One

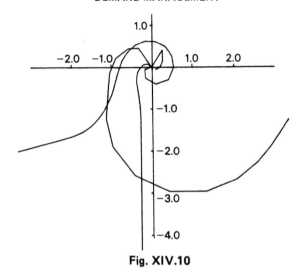

Fig. XIV.10

of the loci can be seen to be extremely close to $(-1 + 0i)$, implying that the system is indeed almost unstable.

A second policy was designed to give reasonable performance with either a one-quarter or a two-quarter delay in policy implementation. This was achieved by designing the policy while assuming the existence of two-quarter delays, and then checking that its performance was still acceptable if the delays were reduced. Details of the design process are available in Maciejowski and Vines (1982).

The revised, more robust policy rules are given in Appendix B. It will be noticed that the Money GDP and the unemployment rules are simpler than those of the initial design, in the sense that their dynamic orders are lower (2 rather than 3). This simplification is possible because the bandwidths of all three loops are lower with the robust design than with the initial design.

The characteristic loci obtained with these rules in place are shown in Figure XIV.11, for both one-quarter and two-quarter delays. The loci corresponding to two-quarter delays are shown by broken lines. Both sets of loci are well clear of the point $-1 + i0$.

An important feature of these rules is that the movement of the indirect tax rate and of employees' national insurance contributions in response to a sudden disturbance of Money GDP is only half of that required by the initial policy design. Thus these movements no longer violate our initial specification. Also, movements of the exchange rate are reduced by 30 per cent. Clearly the search for robustness in the face of variable delays has led to 'caution' in the use of policy instruments.

The principal price paid for achieving robustness in the face of delay variations is a considerable deterioration in the regulation of the balance of payments on current account, even when one-quarter delays are assumed.

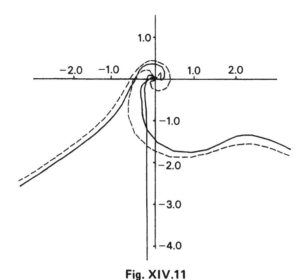

Fig. XIV.11

However, some benefits are obtained as well. The four-quarter oscillation of Money GDP, and consequently of the policy instruments, which is evident in Figures XIV.1 and XIV.4, no longer occurs when the robust policy is used. In addition, the bandwidth of each loop is considerably decreased, without too much loss of regulation against random disturbances.

We do not put forward this robust policy as a practical one, however, because rerunning history with it in place revealed that the required movements of the exchange rate would still be unacceptably large, and that these would cause unacceptably large interactions on Money GDP, and oscillations in taxes, in spite of the reduction that has already been achieved over the initial design.

5. The Proposed Policy

(i) *Derivation of the Policy*

The policy that we examine in this section is the one used for rerunning history, in Chapter VIII, with one-quarter implementation delays. It is obtained from the robust policy, discussed in the previous section, by first halving the movements of the exchange rate and leaving all other details of the rules unchanged. This adjustment results in movements of the exchange rate that we judge to be acceptable. The exchange-rate behaviour is then further improved, without significant loss of regulation, by an adjustment that will be explained in the next sub-section.

When this policy is used with two-quarter implementation delays it retains reasonable stability margins. However, the additional delay allows larger deviations of Money GDP to build up, with the consequence that movements of the indirect tax rate and of national insurance contributions become excessively large. We therefore reduce the movements of these two instruments by 33 per cent, but *only when two-quarter delays are present*.

The analysis of policy performance that follows applies when one-quarter delays exist, and without this 33 per cent reduction of tax instrument movements.

(ii)   A Simple Interpretation of the Policy Rules

When the robust policy has been modified by halving the exchange-rate movements, the transfer function of each of the policy rules can be written in the form

$$p(z) = \phi(z)\left(k_p + k_I \frac{z}{z-1} + k_D \frac{z-1}{z}\right). \tag{3}$$

The three terms in the second factor represent proportional, integral and derivative action, respectively, while $\phi(z)$ serves to smooth or shape the resulting instrument movement before applying it to the economy. The terms 'proportional', 'integral' and 'derivative' are used in the following sense.

Suppose that the output variable being controlled is 1 per cent above its target value. Then the appropriate component of the error (variable e in Figure XII.4) is -1 per cent. The proportional action is then $-k_P$ per cent, and this is the basic component of negative feedback action, driving the output towards its target value. If the error between the output and its target value were a *steady* 1 per cent, then the integral component of the control action would be a 'ramp', that is a steadily increasing instrument movement, with slope $-k_I$ per cent per quarter. The transfer function $k_I z/(z-1)$ thus behaves rather like an integrating element would behave in a continuous-time context. The purpose of the integral action is to ensure that, if the economy is subjected to a sustained exogenous disturbance (i.e. d_k = constant in Figure XII.4), then the only equilibrium condition of the controlled economy is one in which the output variable achieves its target value (i.e. $e_k \to 0$ in Figure XII.4).

So long as the error between the output and its target value is steady, the derivative component of the control action contributes nothing. But if the error is changing at a steady rate of 1 per cent per quarter, then the derivative component takes the value k_D per cent. Thus, if the error itself is small, but it is rapidly approaching zero, the derivative component should provide some braking in order to prevent excessive overshoot of the

Table XIV.1

Policy rule	$p_{ij}(z)$ (c.f. eqn XIV.2)	k_P	k_I	k_D	$\phi(z)$
GDP error-to-indirect tax rate	$p_{11}(z)$	-0.994	-0.040	$+0.571$	$\dfrac{z}{z-0.693}$
GDP error-to-national insurance rate	$p_{41}(z)$	-0.797	-0.115	$+0.121$	$\dfrac{z}{z-0.662}$
balance of payments error-to-exchange rate	$p_{22}(z)$	-0.364	-0.326	-1.108	$\dfrac{z(z-0.909)}{(z-0.5)(z-0.6)}$
unemployment error-to-wage rate	$p_{33}(z)$	$+0.650$	$+0.350$	-0.650	1

target value. In other words, the purpose of the derivative action is to prevent the controlled economy from being excessively underdamped.

The values of k_P, k_I and k_D, as well as of the 'shaping' operators $\phi(z)$, for each of the policy rules, are given in Table XIV.1. It will be seen that k_P and k_I are negative in the tax and exchange-rate rules, but positive in the wage-rate rule. This is because an increase in the wage rate leads to a *rise* in unemployment, whereas an increase in any of the other instruments eventually leads to a *fall* in the corresponding output variable. Thus the difference in sign is necessary to ensure that each control loop has *negative* feedback.

More surprisingly, the signs of k_D in the Money GDP and unemployment policy rules are opposite to the signs of k_P and k_I in those rules. This means that, far from anticipating an overshoot and acting to reduce it, the derivative action in these rules makes the overshoot worse and increases the degree of underdamping! The reasons for this can be seen if k_D is set to zero in these rules (but not in the balance of payments rule). In that case the time responses of the output variables to step disturbances are very similar to those obtained with values of k_D as in Table XIV.1. This shows that the magnitudes of the k_Ds are sufficiently small for them to have no appreciable effect on the damping, for either better or worse.

However, the very important effect that the retention of the k_D terms does have is a significant moderation of the initial magnitudes of instrument movements upon the appearance of a sudden exogenous disturbance. For example, if consumer spending suddenly falls exogenously by 1 per cent, the indirect tax rate initially falls by 0.46 per cent if $k_D = 0.571$ (as in Table XIV.1), but by 1.03 per cent if $k_D = 0$. Equally important is the effect that the k_D terms have on the loop gain at high frequencies (i.e. in the region of $\omega = \pi$). At these frequencies the loop gain should be as low as possible in order to minimise futile instrument movements, which have no chance of affecting the outputs beneficially. Removing the derivative action from the Money GDP and unemployment rules results in the gain of the tax rule being increased by nearly 700 per cent at high frequencies. The increases in the gains of the national insurance and wage-rate rules are more modest, being 40 per cent and 74 per cent respectively, but these are nevertheless very significant.

The coefficient k_D in the exchange-rate rule has the same sign as k_P and k_I, so it has the expected effect, namely that of increasing the damping of the balance of payments control loop. But of course it has this effect at the cost of an increased initial exchange-rate movement in response to the sudden appearance of an exogenous disturbance, and at the cost of a higher loop gain at high frequencies. Since the balance of payments loop appears overdamped rather than underdamped, one questions whether the derivative action is really necessary.

Setting k_D to zero in the exchange-rate rule reduces the initial exchange-rate depreciation, in the face of an exogenous fall of 1 per cent in the balance of payments on current account, from 1.8 per cent to 0.7 per cent. It also reduces the loop gain at the frequency $\omega = \pi$ by over 400 per cent. The cost to be paid for these improvements is minimal, at least as far as effectiveness of the feedback rules is concerned. The main penalty is that the 'J-curve' effect is a little more prolonged. It takes five quarters instead of four for an exchange-rate depreciation to produce an improvement in the current balance. But thereafter there is very little difference between the effects of the two policy rules (i.e. with $k_D = -1.108$ and $k_D = 0$). Indeed, the time taken to eliminate 50 per cent of an exogenous disturbance is slightly shorter (12 quarters) without the derivative action than with it (thirteen quarters). With either policy, 70 per cent of a disturbance is eliminated in twenty-four quarters. In other respects both the time- and frequency-response properties of the two policies are nearly identical.

Of course, the time trajectory of the exchange rate, in response to a single, sustained exogenous disturbance of the balance of payments, is very different in the two cases, and this provides an argument for the retention of the derivative action. It is desirable that the exchange-rate rule should be such that successful speculation about future exchange-rate movements should be as difficult as possible. In an environment of stochastic exogenous disturbances this is achieved if the high-frequency magnification of the exchange-rate rule is high rather than low, since the pattern of exchange-rate variations is then 'more random', not only in the sense that its variance is greater, but − and this is the more important point − that the accuracy of the best possible predictor of the exchange rate is smaller. Broadly speaking, the requirement of a large high-frequency magnification translates into the requirement that the initial reaction of the exchange rate to an exogenous disturbance should be violent rather than mild. Our initial design (see Figure XIV.2(b)) does well in this respect. The exchange rate initially falls by 5 per cent, and then rises rapidly by 2 per cent. In our proposed design, the corresponding movement of the exchange rate is (approximately) an initial fall of 1.8 per cent, followed by a small rise, and then a sustained fall to 3 per cent below its initial level, if we retain $k_D = -1.108$ in the exchange-rate rule. If, however, the derivative action is removed from the exchange-rate rule, the exchange rate initially falls by only 0.7 per cent, and then falls smoothly to 3 per cent below its initial level. Thus the removal of the derivative action may make life more profitable for currency speculators.

But we do not consider the above argument to be a strong one. We prefer to opt for less violent exchange-rate movements. Consequently the policy that we propose is as set out in Table XIV.1, but with $k_D = 0$ in policy rule $p_{22}(z)$. This rule is also given in difference-equation form in Appendix B.

The smoothing operators $\phi(z)$ in the tax and national insurance rules are simple lags of the kind discussed in Section 4 of Chapter XIII. They both have a 'time constant' of three quarters. The wage-rate rule has

$\phi(z) = 1$, that is, there is no smoothing. The exchange-rate rule has a relatively complex, second-order transfer function for its smoothing operator. Its response to a step change in its input is shown in Figure XIV.21, which reveals its shape to be a mirror image of the 'J-curve' exhibited by the balance of payments when the exchange rate is suddenly changed.

(iii)   *Recovery from Single Exogenous Disturbances*

Figures XIV.12, XIV.13 and XIV.14 show what happens when the reference value of each of the controlled outputs is suddenly increased by 1 per cent. They should be compared with Figures XIV.1, XIV.2 and XIV.3, which show the system's responses when the initial policy design is used.

The behaviour of Money GDP is, if anything, rather improved (Figure XIV.12). Although it takes two quarters instead of one to halve the deviation from target, the smoother trajectory is much more satisfactory, since the instruments are no longer required to oscillate for ten years. The peak induced deviation of the balance of payments is smaller than in Figure XIV.1(a), but a small deviation remains uncorrected for over forty quarters.

Figure XIV.13 shows the main penalty for restricting the magnitude of exchange-rate movements. The response of the balance of payments is much slower than in Figure XIV.2(a). Reduction of the initial deviation by 50 per cent takes twelve quarters instead of five, and by 70 per cent takes twenty-four quarters instead of six. The exchange rate has to be reduced by 0.7 per cent initially, and then gradually reduced by another 2.3 per cent. In Figure XIV.2(b) it is reduced by 5 per cent and then rapidly raised again by 2 per cent.

The response of unemployment, shown in Figure XIV.14(a), is a little changed from that of Figure XIV.3(a). The initial deviation is reduced by 50 per cent in eight quarters instead of five. However, it takes only nine quarters (instead of seven) to reduce it by 70 per cent. The induced deviation of the balance of payments is not as large as in Figure XIV.3(a), but it is reduced much more slowly. Even after forty quarters the balance of payments is off target by about 0.5 per cent. Figure XIV.14(b) shows that the greatest change required of the wage rate in any one quarter is less than 1 per cent, whereas in Figure XIV.3(b) it is 2 per cent.

Figure XIV.15 shows the recovery from a 1 per cent exogenous fall in consumer spending. The deviation of Money GDP is not corrected quite as quickly as in Figure XIV.4, but the balance of payments is brought back on target more quickly than in Figure XIV.4, because the exchange rate moves away less from its long-run value.

Figure XIV.16 shows recovery from a 1 per cent rise in import prices. Initially this looks very similar to Figure XIV.5, but after about ten

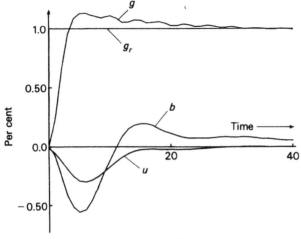

Fig. XIV.12(a)

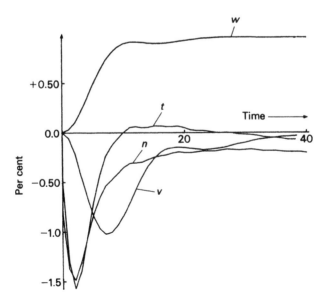

Fig. XIV.12(b)

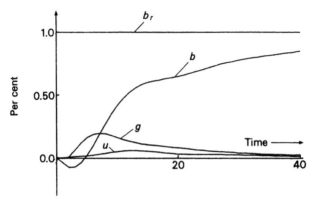

Fig. XIV.13(a)

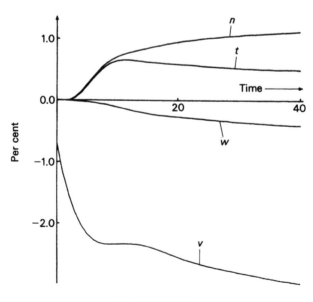

Fig. XIV.13(b)

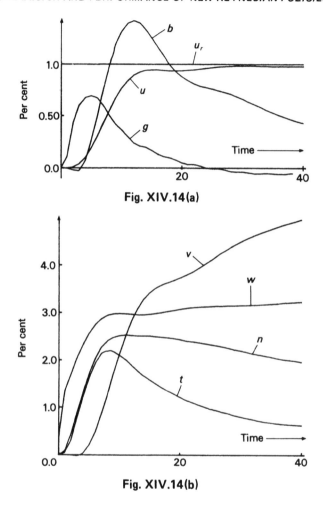

Fig. XIV.14(a)

Fig. XIV.14(b)

quarters the elimination of the deviations of both Money GDP and the balance of payments becomes much slower.

(iv) *Frequency-Response Characteristics*

The magnitudes of the diagonal elements of the closed-loop Nyquist array are shown in Figure XIV.17. This shows that the bandwidths of the Money GDP, balance of payments and unemployment loops are 1.00, 0.059 and 0.301, respectively, and are substantially lower than the values 1.74, 1.00, and 0.54, which were obtained with the initial design (cf. Figure XIV.6). The diagonal elements of the sensitivity function are displayed in

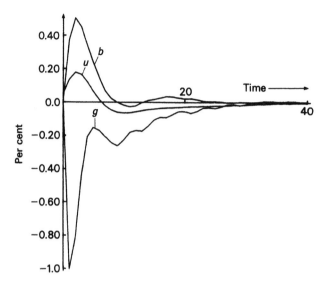

Fig. XIV.15

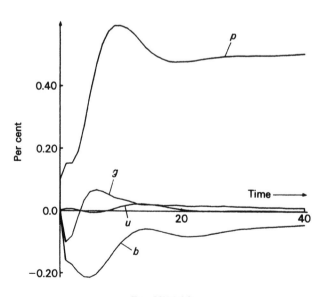

Fig. XIV.16

Figure XIV.18. It can be seen that exogenous disturbances acting independently on each of the three outputs are attenuated up to 0.43, 0.11 and 0.14 radians/quarter, respectively. These frequencies are not much lower than the corresponding frequencies for the initial design, which are 0.46, 0.17 and 0.21 (cf. Figure XIV.7). The proposed design is clearly more 'efficient' than the initial design, in the sense that much less of the frequency range is used in futile reactions to measurement errors, without much loss of frequencies at which useful regulation is performed. Indeed, disturbances on the balance of payments are attenuated even at frequencies above the bandwidth of that loop.

From Figure XIV.19 one can deduce how successful the proposed policy is in regulating against changes in consumers' spending behaviour. Improvement over the unregulated economy is obtained up to 0.56 radians/quarter on Money GDP, up to 0.36 radians/quarter on the balance of payments, and up to 0.34 radians/quarter on unemployment. These values compare with 0.88, 0.40 and 0.42 for the initial design (Figure XIV.8). There is therefore a considerable loss of regulation of Money GDP, compared with the initial design, but very little loss on the balance of payments and unemployment.

Regulation of all three outputs, in the face of random changes in the price of imports, is almost as good as – or perhaps we should say not much poorer than – it is with the initial design. Figure XIV.20 shows that the resulting variations of the outputs are decreased at frequencies below 0.33, 0.09 and 0.14 radians/quarter, respectively, which compare with 0.42, 0.16 and 0.11 for the initial design (Figure XIV.9).

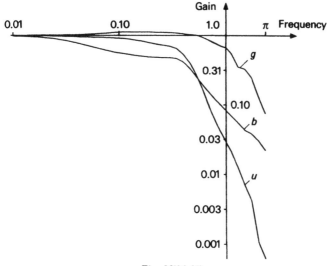

Fig. XIV.17

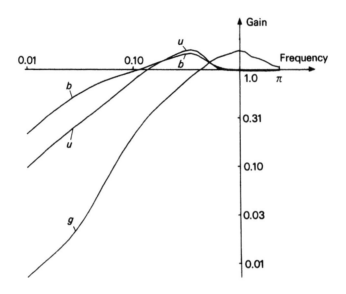

Fig. XIV.18

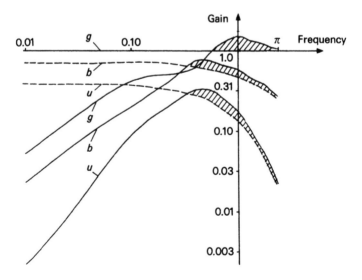

Fig. XIV.19

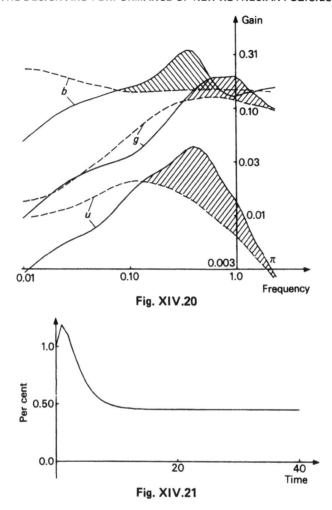

Fig. XIV.20

Fig. XIV.21

6. A Summary of Policy Performance

The reruns of history discussed in Chapter VIII show that the policy rules that we are proposing could be an effective means of combating stag-flation, even in difficult economic circumstances such as those experienced in the 1970s. But the analysis carried out in this chapter reveals surprising limitations on the performance of feedback policies for regulating the economy.

If corrective action is taken against a single sustained exogenous disturbance, the following outcomes are observed. Money GDP can be well controlled: we can obtain fast response, good rejection of disturbances and small interactions on other target variables. The cost of this is regulator movements in taxes that, although within the bounds that we set ourselves, are large. By contrast, control of the current balance of payments using the exchange rate is really rather difficult. (This one would expect from the long lags in the export function; equation (27) in Appendix A.)

Control of unemployment by means of wage flexibility *can* be achieved quite rapidly without the very large movements in wages required in our initial design. This makes the policy proposals seem more feasible than our earlier paper (Vines and Maciejowski, 1982) suggested. But, as the results in Chapter VIII emphasise, the really important requirement for our policies not to be defeated on the 'wages front' is that the influence of price inflation on wage inflation be minimised.

If exogenous disturbances are thought of as sustained oscillations rather than as single shocks, effective regulation against them can be provided only if the oscillations are very slow. For example, if the price of imports is oscillating steadily, regulation of the balance of payments is effective only if the period of oscillation is longer than ten years, even if the (faster) initial policy design is adopted. If our (slower) proposed policy is used, the period has to be longer than fourteen years. On the other hand, regulation of Money GDP is effective if the period of the import-price changes drops to five years (with the use of the slower policy).

It must therefore be expected that circumstances will sometimes arise in which the control of the balance of payments and of unemployment will be worse than it would have been with no feedback regulation, but that this is a necessary sacrifice if the control of Money GDP is to be improved. There will also be circumstances, but these will be less frequent, in which all three outputs would be better regulated by doing nothing rather than by taking corrective action. (Note that 'doing nothing' here means leaving the real exchange rate unadjusted, for example. It does *not* mean leaving the exchange rate to be adjusted by market forces, which would constitute the replacement of our policy by some other feedback action. The option of really 'doing nothing' hardly exists in a developed economy.)

All this is not to say that feedback policies are necessarily ineffective at regulating the economy, but merely that they are less effective than one may have hoped. They are very effective at combating the effects of slowly changing disturbances, and of disturbances that exhibit a bias or a trend. For example, the world slump (amongst other things) creates severe difficulties for the balance of payments in the 1970s, but our proposed policy has been shown to be capable of returning the economy to a prescribed target path by the end of the 1970s despite this trend. Similarly, the policy is capable of ensuring that employment keeps pace with the trend increase in the labour supply.

It may be asked to what extent the limitations of the policy that we have proposed are inherent limitations of any such policy. It is probably possible to 'tune' the details of the policy — without straying from the New Keynesian structure — to make it more satisfactory in one or more respects. But it is very unlikely that any major improvement can be obtained. The evidence for this is provided by a brief study in which a New Keynesian policy was designed by 'optimal control' rather than by 'frequency response' methods. In spite of the very different design philosophy, the performance which was obtained was very similar to that obtained with our initial design (Westaway and Maciejowski, 1983).

Major improvements of performance are only likely to be obtained by one or more of the following means:

(1) supplementing our feedback rules with feedforward control (see Section 3 of Chapter VI and Section 1 of Chapter XII);
(2) finding ways of allowing greater instrument movements — or devising additional instruments (see Chapters IX–XI);
(3) reducing the interval between adjustments of instruments — for example, adjusting the tax rate monthly rather than quarterly (see Chapter VII and its Note);
(4) reducing the lags of responses in the economy. Although we accept the 'Lucas critique' that a correct model of the economy itself depends on policy (see Chapter I), we find it hard to believe that the critical lags in our model would be significantly *shortened* by the introduction of the policy that we propose.

Improved performance might also be attainable if the policy were implemented in a period during which exogenous disturbances were milder than they were in the period we have considered. In that case the resulting instrument movements would be less violent, and it would be possible, in consequence, to move away from our proposed policy towards a more vigorous policy, such as our initial design. The actual experience of the early 1980s suggests that much improved international co-operation is necessary for this to be a possibility.

APPENDIX A

The Economic Model

1. The Purpose of the Model

The dynamic, macro-economic model of the United Kingdom economy presented here is essentially based on the Treasury Model and may be regarded as a shortened and compressed version of that model. The parameters and time lags in the model are not estimated econometrically, and so we do not report standard errors or other statistical measures. They are instead derived directly or indirectly (e.g. by aggregation) from those used in the Treasury Model, except in those few cases that are noted in the following description.[*]

The model has been used for the purpose of rerunning history in a manner described in Chapters VII and VIII. For this purpose more detail was required of the incomes and expenditures of the different economic sectors than could have been obtained with a truly small econometric model which we could have estimated ourselves. On the other hand, the plethora of detail made available by the full Treasury Model with its 700-plus equations would have also thwarted our exercise: to construct a Base Run back to 1972, revise it in the manner described in Chapter VII, and simulate a rerun of history for thirteen years would have proved an impossible task. That is why we have adopted the somewhat unusual procedure of creating by hand the small model described here from the large Treasury Model.[†] A bonus is that the small size of the present model aids an understanding of the basic dynamic relationships that underly its performance and that determine the outcomes described in Chapters VII and VIII.

---

[*]For the source of the equations below the reader is referred at the appropriate places to HM Treasury, *Macroeconomic Model Technical Manual 1979*, October 1979 (Treasury, 1979), HM Treasury, *The Unified Model: Specification of Equations and Listing of Variables*, January 1980 (Treasury, 1980), Alan Ritchie, 'The Small Model; A Shrunken Version of the Treasury Model', HM Treasury UMDG Paper, April 1980 (Ritchie 1980), and G.R. Horton, 'Small Model – Standard Simulations', HM Treasury Academic Panel Paper, July 1980 (Horton, 1980). The present model is somewhat different from the Ritchie–Horton model, for it was designed for a different purpose.

[†]It could be that one of the other small UK quarterly econometric models – e.g. the National Institute Model or the London Business School Model – could have well served our purpose. We are at present investigating whether the use of these other models greatly changes the outcome of our study.

The model describes the dynamic relationships between 99 variables. It is presented in this chapter in the form of a numbered list of these 99 variables, followed in each case with a definition of the variable. Where the variable is assumed to be exogenously determined, this is simply stated; where the variable is assumed to be dependent upon the value of another variable or set of variables, the equation describing the relationship is given together with a short commentary on its meaning.

The model has been used for the purpose of comparing what in Chapter VII has been called the Base Run with the Control Run. The logic of the relationships between the uses of the economic model for these two purposes has been described at some length in that chapter and will not be repeated here. It is sufficient to note that certain variables that in the Base Run are treated as exogenous (rates of interest, of foreign exchange, and of tax) are in the Control Run used as policy-control instruments and thus made to depend upon what is happening to other variables in the system; and in the case of the wage rate the factors that determine it in the Base Run are assumed in the Control Run to have been suitably modified in the interest of managing the economy. In all these cases in which a variable is determined differently in the Control Run than it was in the Base Run, both the Base Run determination and the Control Run determination of the variable are shown separately. Where no distinction is made in the list of variables between Base Run and Control Run determination it is implied that the principles of determination are the same in both cases.

2. The Basic Structure of the Model

The model is constructed on the basis of four sectors: (1) the personal sector, (2) the company sector, which includes the banks and other financial institutions, (3) the public sector, which in addition to central and local government includes public corporations, and (4) the overseas sector.

The model is essentially a Keynesian one in the sense that the level of economic activity is determined by the level of effective demand for final goods and services, the levels of employment being adjusted (with appropriate time lags) to those that are needed to meet the demand for their outputs. Similarly the level of the capital stock of plant, machinery, etc. that producers desire to possess is dependent upon the level of the effective demand for their output; and investment in new capital equipment is made in order to keep the existing capital stock in line with the desired level (once again with appropriate time lags).

These relationships are outlined in Table A.1. The first row enumerates the various elements making up the effective demand for final output: (1) in the personal sector the demands for non-durable (*CND*) and durable

Table A.1 Goods and Labour Markets: Real Demand and Supply

		Personal	*Company (including banks, etc.)*	*Government (including public corporations)*	*Overseas*
Goods and services (£m., 1975)	Demand	Consumption plus personal sector residential investment $CND + CDUR + IPRD$	Investment plus stockbuilding $ICP + SB$	Public expenditure on goods and services $CGPO + IPU + CGE$	Exports of goods and services X
	Supply	Gross domestic product at constant market prices $Y + FCA$			Imports of goods and services M
Labour ('000s)	Demand	Self-employment ES	Company employment ECP	Government employment EG	
	Supply	Labour supply $D - (D - ET)$			

($CDUR$) consumption goods and for investment in housing ($IPRD$); (2) in the company sector, the demands for investment in fixed equipment (ICP) and in stock building (SB); (3) in the public sector, the demands for procurement of goods for current purposes ($CGPO$), for public investment (IPU), and for the services of the public servants directly employed by the government (CGE); and (4) in the overseas sector, the demands for the country's exports (X).

Row 2 of the table shows part of these demands being met by imports (M) and the rest being met by home production ($Y + FCA$), where Y represents the factor-cost element in home production and FCA the element in home production that is creamed off in indirect taxation and never reaches the factors (labour, capital, etc.) employed in the production.

Row 3 of the table shows the labour required for these productions, whether employed by self (ES), by companies (ECP), or by the government (EG). The divisions between these categories have been so drawn as to emphasise the fact that a very large part of the effective demand of the personal and public sectors is in fact met by employment in the company sector, which produces the goods for use by the other sectors.

Finally Row 4 shows the labour supply that meets this demand for labour. The total available supply (D) is assumed to be exogenously given; but the total demand for labour ($ET = ES + ECP + EG$) will be somewhat less than D so that ($D - ET$) measures the amount of unemployed labour.*

For purposes of simplification in the model presented later in this appendix it is assumed that there is only one single home-produced good, which represents an aggregate of the very large range existing in the real world, and that there is only one grade of labour, which similarly represents an aggregate of the wide diversity in the real world. The price of the home-produced good on sale in the home market is assumed to be set by means of a profit mark-up on the variable costs of production (i.e. on the cost of the labour and imported materials needed for its production); and the amount produced is then that which is necessary to satisfy the demand at this selling price. The price of the inputs of labour and of imported materials and the price at which goods can be sold for export are all separately treated in the model.

The elements in Table A.1 are all expressed in terms of real quantities. They become comparable in value only when the money prices of the various elements have been determined; when this is done, it is possible to consider the complicated dynamic flows of money payments between the various sectors that lie behind the simple relations shown in Table A.1. The structure of the money payments between the four sectors that is

---

*($D - ET$) will be greater than the amount of registered unemployment by the number of persons who would take a job if it were available but do not register themselves as seeking work.

Table A.2 Income and Expenditure by Sector

Inflow (+), outflow (−) of £ payments	Private sector — Personal	Private sector — Company (and banks)	Public sector (incl. public corps & govt.)	Overseas sector
1 Supply of goods and services		GDP at market prices + $GDPM^*$		Imports of goods and services + M^*
2 Taxes on expenditure		Taxes on expenditure (incl. NI surcharge) − TXC − $TXPD$ − TXX − $TXNI$		
3 Rents		Rents − RN		
4 Stock appreciation		Stock app. + SAC		
5 Employment	Wages + self employment + $(ECP + EG)$ × $ERPR/1000$ + SE + OCR + $YPNIR$	Wages + self-employment + other contributions − $(ECP + EG)$ × $ERPR/1000$ − SE − OCR		
6 Employer NI contributions		Employer NI contributions − $YPNIR$		
7 Public sector trading surplus		Public sector trading surplus − FYG	Public sector trading surplus + FYG	
8 Income from trading and employment = 1 + 2 + 3 + 4 + 5 + 6 + 7	Income from employment and self-employment + $(ECP + EG)$ × $ERPR/1000$ + SE + OCR + $YPNIR$	Company profits + $FYCPR$	Public sector trading surplus + FYG	Imports of goods and services + M^*

	Personal sector	Company sector	Public	Overseas
9 Rent dividends and interest	Dividends, debt interest and rent $+ DDIRPE$ + part RN	Dividends, debt interest and rent $- DDIPCP$ + part RN	Dividends, debt interest and rent $- DDIPGG$ + part RN	IPD credits and debits $- CIPD + DIPD$
10 Taxes on income and transfers	Taxes on personal income $- TYPP$ Grants to persons $+ YPCG^*$	Taxes on company income $- TCP$	Grants to persons & transfers overseas $- YPCG^* - NTD$ Taxes on income $+ TYPP + TCP$	Transfers $+ NTD$
11 Taxes on expenditure, and NI contributions	Employee NI contributions $- NIPE - YPNIR$		Taxes on expenditure, and NI contributions $+ TXC + TXPD + TXX + YPNIR + NIPE + TXNI$	
12 Stock appreciation		Stock appreciation $- SAC$		
13 Sectoral incomes $= 8 + 9 + 10 + 11 + 12$	Personal sector disposable income $+ YPDY^*$	(not defined)	(not defined)	(not defined)
14 Goods and services	Consumption and private residential investment $- CND^* - CDUR^* - IPRD^*$	Company sector investment, stock-building $- ICP^{*g} - SB^*$	Public expenditure on goods & services $- CGPO^* - CGE^* - IPU^*$	Exports of goods and services $- X^*$
15 Sectoral net acquisition of financial assets $= 13 + 14$	$NAFPE$	$NAFCO$	$NAFPU$	$NAFOS$

embodied in the economic model presented later in this appendix is indicated in Table A.2.

The general structure of Table A.2 shows, as one reads down the elements in any one of the four columns, inflows of money payments into that sector from another sector (+) less outflows of money payments from that sector into another sector (−). Thus the personal sector receives wages (line 5) and dividends, interest and rent (line 9), receives social benefits but pays taxes (line 10), pays national insurance contributions (line 11), and spends money on non-durable and durable consumption goods and on house purchases (line 14). What is left over after such transactions (line 15) can be used by the personal sector for the purchase of financial assets from other sectors, i.e. shares of companies, government debt, or overseas assets.*

Similarly, columns 2, 3 and 4 enumerate the flows of £ funds into (+) or out of (−) the sector in question, ending up in each case in line 15 with the net surplus available for the purchase of financial assets from another sector or the net deficit needing to be financed by the sale of its financial liabilities to the other sectors.

The payments noted in Table A.2 are all payments from one sector to another; every item that is an inflow (+) into one sector must be an outflow (−) from some other sector. If one disregards the sub-totals in lines 8 and 13 and the totals in line 15, it will be seen that for the most part every single item with a + entry in one part of the table reappears with a − entry in some other part. The exceptions fall into two groups:

(1)   The items $GDPM^*$, M^*, X^*, CND^*, $CDUR^*$, $IPRD^*$, ICP^*, SB^*, $CGPO^*$, IPU^* and CGE^* do not cancel out. But equation (95) in the model defines the gross domestic product at market prices as being made up of personal consumption, government consumption, investment including stock building, and the excess of exports over imports. Making use of equation (95), these items cancel out.

(2)   The items $DDIRPE$, $DDIPCP$, $DDIPGG$, $CIPD$ and $DIPD$ do not cancel out in the table. But equation (47) in the model states in terms of these elements of interest and dividend payments that the payments by one sector must be equal to the receipts by another; and making use of equation (47) enables these items also to be eliminated.

*The table is constructed on the convention that the only transactions with foreigners that involve real goods and services are in respect of payments by foreigners for goods that are actually exported (X^*) or payments to foreigners for goods that are actually imported (M^*). If in fact a UK resident purchases a real asset (e.g. a machine) overseas, does not import it, and operates it overseas, this purchase must be represented in the table as if the UK resident had purchased a share in a foreign company that had invested in a machine. And similarly, *mutatis mutandis*, for a foreigner purchasing a real asset in the UK.

It follows that the sum of all the items in all the columns combined is equal to zero. Since $NAFPE + NAFCO + NAFPU + NAFOS$ in line 15 also measures the sum of the items in all the columns, this sum in turn must be equal to zero.* This expresses the simple and obvious fact that if one sector is purchasing financial assets some other sector must be selling those assets.

The economic model used in this volume makes great use of the monetary flows between the sectors that are displayed in Table A.2. But it does not go on to examine the monetary and financial markets in which the amounts and prices of the various types of financial asset will be determined (e.g. quantity of cash, deposits, bills, short-dated and long-dated debt, ordinary shares, etc., and the rates of interest or yields on them). The reason is that those financial prices that are relevant in determining the payments that are shown in Table A.2 (in particular the short and long rates of interest and the rate of foreign exchange) are either assumed in the Base Run model to be what they are (i.e. exogenously given) or in the Control Run model to have been set by the authorities at whatever level may be desired on policy grounds.

This last assumption itself rests on the assumption that the authorities are able, on what one might call buffer-stock principles, to set rates of interest and of foreign exchange at the desired level. In other words, having offered to buy or sell given categories of security or foreign exchange at set prices they can meet the resulting demand (or take in the resulting supply) out of (or into) a stock of such assets. (See Chapters IV and V above.) The basic assumptions are that the policy behaviour is sufficiently restrained and sensible and the institutional arrangements sufficiently developed for this to be possible. An extensive analysis of the conditions of demand and supply for financial assets in the money and capital markets, involving such matters as the liquidity preferences and expectations of the various potential holders, would be necessary only if either (1) it were considered not possible or sensible that the authorities should set rates of interest and foreign exchange at predetermined levels but that they should rather attempt to control the quantity of money or of some other financial asset of that kind or else (2) out of simple but idle curiosity it were desired to enquire into the amounts of the various assets that it would be necessary for the authorities to provide from, or take into, their financial buffer stocks in order to set rates at the desired levels.

3.   Notation and Layout of the Model

In the following model all money flows are measured in units of million pounds per quarter, either in constant 1975 prices (sometimes called

* It is thus a relationship that is implied by the other relationships in the model and is not to be treated as an additional independent equation.

volumes) or current prices (sometimes called values). Employment is measured in thousands, and earnings are measured in earnings per man (thus to find total earnings in £m. it is necessary to divide the product of employment and wages by 1000). Prices are measured in index numbers having a value of 100 over the year 1975. The model shows the values of the variables quarter by quarter; and the following operators are used in the various equations:

$g^i X$ represents the value of X, i quarters ago; thus $g^4 X$ is the value of X
   four quarters before the present quarter. g alone stands for g^1.
$\Delta_i X = (1 - g^i)X$ and $\Delta_4 X$ thus measures the increase in X since four
   quarters before the present quarter. Δ alone stands for $\Delta_1 = (1 - g)$.
y is an operator converting an interest rate expressed at an annual percentage rate to a quarterly proportional one.

The model is laid out in the following order. First come equations for the determination of money costs (wages costs and import costs) and money prices for goods. These equations enable the flows of goods in the model to be valued. Next come the equations for income, expenditure and net acquisition of financial assets, for each of the sectors distinguished in the model:

(1)   overseas;
(2)   company (including banks and other financial institutions);
(3)   personal;
(4)   government (including public corporations).

Finally, there are certain equations defining the national income.

4.   Equations of the Model

(i)   *Money Prices and Costs*

(a)   *Import prices*
Three categories of imports are distinguished: imports of intermediate goods, imports for consumption final demand, and imports for investment final demand (see Treasury, 1979, Sections 6 and 17 and Group 22, and Treasury, 1980, Group 22).

$$(1) \quad PMQ = \mathrm{Exp}\left[\sum_{i=0}^{3} \beta_i g^i \ln \left(\frac{UKCP \times a}{RXD} \right) + \sum_{i=0}^{1} \gamma_i g^i \ln \left(\frac{PWHO}{1 + TM} \right) \right] \times r$$

$$\beta_0 = .4656 \qquad\qquad\qquad \gamma_0 = .0635$$

$$\beta_1 = .3092$$

$$\beta_2 = .0761 \qquad\qquad \gamma_1 = .0409$$

$$\beta_3 = .0447 \qquad\qquad \text{with } \Sigma\gamma = .1044$$

$$\text{with } \Sigma\beta = .8956 \qquad\qquad a = 2.22$$

The pre-tariff price of intermediate exports (PMQ) depends largely upon world prices ($UKCP$) converted into domestic currency by the sterling–dollar exchange rate (RXD) but also upon domestic wholesale prices ($PWHO$) (after adjustment for the average rate of tariff, TM). We expect the equation to be homogeneous of degree one in prices. If intermediate imports in world markets were in perfectly elastic supply, the weights on world prices would sum to unity and those on home prices would be zero; if intermediate imports were perfect substitutes with domestic products for domestic absorption, the weights on home prices would sum to unity and those on foreign prices would be zero. If there is not perfect substitution in either market, one expects something in between, and this is what equation (1) shows. The sum of the weights on foreign prices is .8956 and on home prices is .1044. The coefficient a in this and the following equations is a scaling factor such that $RXD \times a/UKCP$ has a value of unity in 1975 (see Treasury, 1980, Group 22).

(2) $UKCP$, world prices, is exogenous.

(3) TM, the rate of import duty, is exogenous and is assumed to be the same for all types of import.

(4 Base)
RXD, the dollar–sterling rate of exchange is exogenous.

(4 Control)
RXD follows the policy rule described in Section 6 below.

(5)
$$PMC = \text{Exp}\left\{\alpha\left[\beta \ln\left(\frac{UKCP \times a}{RXD}\right) + \gamma g \ln\left(\frac{PWHO}{1 + TM}\right)\right]\right.$$

$$\left. + (1 - \alpha)\sum_{i=0}^{1} \epsilon_i g^i \ln\left(\frac{WPFF \times a}{RXD}\right)\right\} \times r$$

$$\alpha = 0.4054 \quad \beta = .5964 \quad \gamma = .4036 \quad \epsilon_0 = .6667$$

$$\epsilon_1 = .3333$$

$$\text{with } \Sigma\epsilon = 1.0$$

(6) *WPFF*, world food prices, is exogenous.

(7)
$$PMI = \text{Exp}\left[\beta \ln\left(\frac{UKCP \times a}{RXD}\right) + (1-\beta)g \ln\left(\frac{PWHO}{1+TM}\right)\right] \times r$$

$$\beta = .596$$

The price of imports of investment goods (*PMI*) depends upon world prices (*UKCP*) (converted into domestic currency by the sterling–dollar exchange rate, *RXD*) and also partly on domestic wholesale prices (*PWHO*) after allowing for the average rate of tariff (*TM*) for reasons similar to those discussed for equation (1). The equation is homogeneous of degree one in prices. (See Treasury, 1980, Group 22, equation (17).)

(b) *Export prices*

(8)
$$PX = \text{Exp}\left[\sum_{i=0}^{6} \alpha_i g^i \ln UKCP + \sum_{i=0}^{6} \beta_i g^i \ln\left(\frac{a}{RXD}\right)\right.$$

$$\left. + \sum_{i=0}^{2} \gamma_i g^i \ln\left(\frac{PWHO}{1-TX}\right)\right] \times r$$

$\alpha_0 = .297$	$\beta_0 = .294$	$\gamma_0 = .580$
$\alpha_1 = .042$	$\beta_1 = .061$	$\gamma_1 = -.035$
$\alpha_2 = .029$	$\beta_2 = .057$	$\gamma_2 = -.035$
$\alpha_3 = .016$	$\beta_3 = .040$	with $\Sigma\gamma = .510$
$\alpha_4 = .016$	$\beta_4 = .024$	
$\alpha_5 = .031$	$\beta_5 = .010$	
$\alpha_6 = .059$	$\beta_6 = .004$	
with $\Sigma\alpha = .490$	with $\Sigma\beta = .490$	

Export prices (*PX*) are modelled as depending on competitors' prices (*UKCP*) converted into home currency via the exchange rate (*RXD*) and on domestic wholesale prices (*PWHO*) after allowing for the effects of any export tax or subsidy at the rate (*TX*). (See Treasury, 1979, Section 17 and Groups 20 and 24.) This equation is homogeneous of degree one in prices. If exports were in world markets perfect substitutes for competitors' goods, then the weights on competitors prices would sum to unity and those on domestic wholesale prices would sum to zero. If exports were instead perfect substitutes for home-produced output, the weights on competitors' prices would sum to zero and those on domestic wholesale prices would sum to unity. The full weight of the coefficient on home prices is equal to .51 and that on foreign prices is equal to .49. (The actual coefficients are taken from Horton, 1980, Group 1, equation (7).)

(9) TX, the rate of export tax, is exogenous.

(c)   *Earnings*
(10 Base)

$$ERPR = (gERPR) \times \left\{ 1 - \rho + \beta \times \frac{PEXPW}{100} - \gamma \sum_{i=1}^{8} \alpha_i g^i \left[\frac{rr}{g(rr)} - 1 \right] \right.$$

$$- \delta(1 + g) \ln (UNUKP \times 0.01)$$

$$\left. - \epsilon(1 + g) \left(\frac{UNUKP}{gUNUKP} - 1 \right) \right\} \times r$$

$\rho = .01452 \quad \epsilon = .0125$

$\beta = 1.0 \quad$ and the αs are as in equation (17)

$\gamma = .7$

$\delta = .00313$

with $rr \equiv (ERPR) \times (ECP + EG) \times 10^{-3} - TYPP - NIPE/(ERPR \times (ECP + EG) \times 10^{-3})$ where ECP, EG, $TYPP$ and $NIPE$ are defined in equations (37), (80), (65) and (63) respectively.

The equation for earnings per head $(ERPR)$ is a price expectations augmented Phillips curve. This relates earnings $(ERPR)$ as a ratio of previous earnings $(gERPR)$ to the expected rate of price inflation $(PEXPW)$, to the rate of growth of the ratio of earnings retained after payment of tax and national insurance (rr), to the level, and also to the rate of change, of the unemployment percentage $(UNUKP)$. It has the property that at 5 per cent unemployment an increase in the level of unemployment by one percentage point to 6 per cent reduces the underlying rate of earnings growth by 0.5 per cent and also brings about a once-for-all reduction in earnings per head of 0.5 per cent. The term in the growth of rr shows an increase in the proportion of income retained after tax as feeding through into decrease in wage inflation with a coefficient of 0.7. (See Treasury, 1979, Group 4, equation (2).)

(10 Control)

$ERPR$ follows the equation in Section 6 below.

(d) *Wage costs per unit output*

(11)
$$WI = \alpha \times \left[ERPR + (YPNIR + TXNI + OCR) \times \frac{1000}{ECP + EG} \right] \times r$$

$$\alpha = .6416$$

Wage costs per unit output (WI) depend upon wages per man ($ERPR$) and upon the ratio of employers' national insurance contributions ($YPNIR$), national insurance surcharge payments ($TXNI$) and other national insurance contributions (OCR) per employee, to employment (excluding self-employment) whether in the private sector (ECP) or the public sector (EG). (See Treasury, 1979, Group 5, equation (2).) In the Treasury Model, wage costs also depend upon (exogenous) trend productivity, which in the present model will be absorbed into the residuals (r) in equation (11), these residuals showing a fall from period to period in so far as they are influenced by a rising productivity trend. It makes no essential difference to the model whether this productivity trend is absorbed in equation (11) into the residuals or whether it is separately accounted for with a corresponding addition to the residuals. In connection with equation (37) below, an approximate exogenous rate of increase of productivity of 2 per cent per annum is deduced from the relationship between output and the demand for labour. This figure tallies reasonably well with the behaviour of the residuals in equation (11) on the average over the whole period. The coefficient α is a scaling factor necessary because of the units in which WI is defined.

(e) *Domestic wholesale prices*

(12)
$$PWHO = \left[\beta \sum_{i=0}^{7} \gamma_i g^i (WI)(1 - \alpha) + \sum_{i=0}^{6} \delta_i (PMQ)(1 + TM)\alpha \right] \times r$$

$\alpha = .24632$ $\beta = .211689$ $\gamma_0 = .1441$ $\delta_0 = .2984$

$\gamma_1 = .2215$ $\delta_1 = .5328$

$\gamma_2 = .2240$ $\delta_2 = .0886$

$\gamma_3 = .1664$ $\delta_3 = .0477$

$\gamma_4 = .1300$ $\delta_4 = .0253$

$\gamma_5 = .0990$ $\delta_5 = .0037$

$\gamma_6 = .0111$ $\delta_6 = .0035$

with $\Sigma \delta = 1.0$

$$\gamma_7 = .0039$$
$$\text{with } \Sigma\gamma = 1.0$$

Domestic wholesale prices (*PWHO*) depend upon domestic wage costs (*WI*) and post tariff (*TM*) prices of imports of intermediate goods (*PMQ*). The equation is homogeneous of degree one in prices; the weight on import prices is .24632 and on home wage costs is .75368. (The coefficients come from Horton, 1980, Group 1, equation (6); the coefficient β is a scaling factor necessary because of the units in which *WI* is defined.)

(f) *Prices of goods delivered to domestic final demand*

Consumption prices

(13)
$$PC = \frac{(1 + TC) \times [PWHO \times (CND + CDUR + CGPO - MC) + MC^* \times (1 + TM)]}{CND + CDUR + CGPO} \times r$$

Consumption prices (*PC*) are represented by the value of the domestically produced consumption goods plus the value of imports of consumption goods, after payment of indirect taxation (*TC*), divided by the total amount of consumption goods whether non-durable goods (*CND*) or durable goods (*CDUR*) for personal consumption or goods for public consumption (*CGPO*). The pre-tax value of domestically produced consumption goods is the pre-tax price of such goods (*PWHO*) multiplied by the total quantity of consumption goods excluding imported goods (*MC*), and the value of imported consumption goods (*MC**) is calculated after payment of import duty (*TM*).

(14 Base)
    TC, the rate of indirect tax on consumption, is exogenous.

(14 Control)
    TC follows the equation in Section 6 below.

Investment prices
(15)
$$PIF = \frac{[PWHO \times (ICP + IPRD + IPU - MI) + MI^* \times (1 + TM)]}{ICP + IPRD + IPU} \times r$$

Investment prices (*PIF*) are treated in a similar manner to consumption prices. *ICP, IPRD* and *IPU* are the total amounts of final investment in the company sector, in the personal sector and in the government sector respectively, MI being the quantity of imports of investment goods included in such investment and MI^* being the value of such imports that is raised by the rate of import duty (TM).

Prices of stocks
(16) $PS = [(1 - \alpha)PWHO + \alpha PMQ \times (1 + TM)] \times r$

$$\alpha = .24632$$

Prices of stocks (PS) are modelled as dependent on the price of home output ($PWHO$) and the price of imported inputs (PMQ) after payment of import duty (TM). The index has fixed proportions, owing to the assumed fixed proportions between home and foreign sources of supply (cf. equation (19) for imports of intermediate goods). The weight on foreign sources of supply is equal to the weight in the equation for imports of intermediate goods, i.e. .24632.

(g) *Price inflation expectations*
There are two price-inflation expectations terms in the model

(17)
$$PEXPW = \left[\sum_{i=1}^{8} \alpha_i g^i \left(\frac{PC}{gPC} - 1 \right) \right] \times r$$

$\alpha_1 = 16.0 \qquad \alpha_5 = 8.0$

$\alpha_2 = 22.0 \qquad \alpha_6 = 7.0$

$\alpha_3 = 25.0 \qquad \alpha_7 = 6.0$ $\qquad$ with $\Sigma\alpha = 100.0$

$\alpha_4 = 12.0 \qquad \alpha_8 = 4.0$

Inflation expectations for wage bargaining measured at a quarterly rate ($PEXPW$) are taken to depend upon the rates of rise of the cost of consumption goods (PC) over the last eight quarters, the sum of the lag coefficients being unity. (See Treasury, 1979, Group 4, equation (2), coefficients a_i.)

(18)
$$PEXPC = 100 \times \left[\frac{(\alpha + \beta g) \Delta_4 \ln PC}{1 + \gamma g} \right] \times r$$

$\alpha = +.436 \qquad \beta = -.240 \qquad \gamma = -.804$

Inflation expectations for consumer durables expenditure measured at an annual rate ($PEXPC$) depends on a lag distribution on past growth in consumer prices (PC). An increase in consumer price inflation of, say,

1 per cent initially gives rise to an increase in expected inflation of 0.436 per cent but this figure gradually increases to 1 per cent since $(\alpha + \beta)/(1 + \gamma) = 1.0$. (See Treasury, 1979, Group 11, and Treasury, 1980, Group 11.)

(ii) Foreign Sector Incomes and Expenditures

(a) Imports

Imports, as noted above, have been divided into three categories: intermediate imports, consumption goods imports and investment goods imports.

Imports of intermediate goods
(19)
$$MQ = \frac{\alpha}{1 - \alpha}(YM + SB)$$

$$\alpha = .24632$$

Imports of intermediate goods (MQ) are related to the output of domestically produced goods and to stockbuilding in the following way. $YM + MQ$ measures the volume of domestically produced output, including the output of goods added to stocks, since YM measures the domestic factor element in such output and MQ measures the imported intermediate goods embodied in such output. SB measures the volume of total stockbuilding of which a proportion α is assumed to be imported directly so that a proportion $(1 - \alpha)$ is therefore the amount that is already included in the output $YM + MQ$. It is assumed that a proportion α of total home output represents imported intermediate goods. It follows that such imports consist of (1) the amount embodied in domestic output, namely $\alpha(YM + MQ)$ plus (2) the amount imported directly for stockbuilding, namely αSB, so that $MQ = \alpha(YM + MQ + SB)$. The proportion α is here assumed to have the same value .24632 as that in the equation for wholesale prices $PWHO$ (equation 12), so that $\alpha/(1 - \alpha)$ (= .3268) measures the marginal propensity to import intermediate products. This produces an average propensity to import intermediate goods much larger than that which actually obtains and the difference is met by adjustment of residuals. Relative prices are absent from the equation for MQ, partly because only a small amount of price sensitivity of imports of intermediate products is present in the Treasury Model, and partly for theoretical reasons. To introduce them would mean that the ratio of intermediate imports to total final output of home-produced goods could change as substitution took place between intermediate imports and home-produced intermediate goods. But if this happened the ratio of gross output (i.e. of final output plus output of intermediate products) to final output would change and so would the ratio of factor demands for labour and capital to final output change (since factor demands must depend on gross rather than final output). Such a possibility suggests that for consistency there should be an identification of gross as well as final output suggesting a need to complicate the model unduly. To avoid the complexity whilst preserving consistency, a constancy of the ratio of imports of intermediate goods to final output was imposed. See Vines (1979) for a model in which this complexity is added.

$$(20) \quad MQ^* = MQ \times \frac{PMQ}{100} + r$$

The value of intermediate imports MQ^* is obtained as price times quantity.

Imports of consumption goods

$$(21) \quad MC = \beta \left\{ \text{Exp} \left[\sum_{i=0}^{4} \gamma_i g^i \ln (CND + CDUR) \right] + CGPO \right\} \times$$

$$\left\{ \text{Exp} \left[-\eta \left(\sum_{i=0}^{6} \mu_i g^i \ln \left(\frac{PMC(1 + TM)}{PWHO} \right) \right) \right] \right\} \times r$$

$\beta = .120458$	$\eta = 1.00$	$\mu_0 = .0833$
$\gamma_0 = .126$		$\mu_1 = .1429$
$\gamma_1 = .208$		$\mu_2 = .1786$
$\gamma_2 = .245$		$\mu_3 = .1904$
$\gamma_3 = .237$		$\mu_4 = .1786$
$\gamma_4 = .184$		$\mu_5 = .1429$
with $\Sigma\gamma = 1.0$		$\mu_6 = .0833$
		with $\Sigma\mu = 1.00$

Imports of consumption goods (MC) are related to quantities of durable $(CDUR)$ and non-durable (CND) consumption goods with appropriate time lags. Government consumption $(CGPO)$ is supposed to have the same import content, but any lag has been omitted. The full elasticity of consumption imports with respect to total consumption is constrained to unity, and the relative price effects $(PMC(1 + TM)/PWHO)$ are constrained to have an elasticity of 1.0. (See Treasury, 1979, 1980, Group 22, equation (6).) The average propensity to import final consumption goods is set at the value for 1975 of .1205 and subsequent time trends are dealt with in residuals. (Recall that the import propensity for intermediate goods is approximately .3268; this gives a full marginal propensity for total consumption expenditures of approximately 45 per cent, which is not implausible.)

(22)
$$MC^* = MC \times \frac{PMC}{100} + r$$

The value of consumption imports (MC^*) is equal to price (PMC) times quantity (MC).

Imports of investment goods

(23)
$$MI = \beta \, Exp \left\{ \gamma \ln (IPU + ICP) - \sum_0^8 \delta_i g^i \ln \left[\frac{PMI(1 + TM)}{PIF} \right] + \epsilon T \right\} \times r$$

$\beta = .002821$ $\quad$ $\delta_0 = .081$ $\quad$ $\delta_5 = .165$

$\gamma = 1.429$ $\quad$ $\delta_1 = .137$ $\quad$ $\delta_6 = .135$

$\epsilon = .02279$ $\quad$ $\delta_2 = .171$ $\quad$ $\delta_7 = .096$

$\delta_3 = .185$ $\quad$ $\delta_8 = .050$

$\delta_4 = .182$ $\quad$ with $\Sigma \delta = 1.202$

The imports of investment goods (MI) are modelled as having an elasticity with respect to final demand (consisting of government (IPU) and company (ICP) investment) equal to 1.43 and a full elasticity with respect to relative prices ($PMI(1 + TM)/PIF$) equal to 1.202. (See Treasury, 1979, 1980, Group 22, equation (7).) The time trend in this equation is partly modelled explicitly by ϵT (where T stands for time) and partly taken up by the multiplicative residuals; which of these is done does not matter for the simulation properties of the model.

(24)
$$MI^* = MI \times \frac{PMI}{100} + r$$

Total imports
(25) $M = (MQ + MC + MI) + r$

(26) $M^* = (MQ^* + MC^* + MI^*) + r$

The volume (M) and the value (M^*) of total imports are obtained by summing the components.

(b)   *Exports*

(27)
$$X = \text{Exp}\left[\alpha + \sum_{i=0}^{2} \beta_i g^i \ln \frac{WT}{100} - \sum_{i=0}^{17} \gamma_i g^i \ln \left(RXD \times \frac{WI}{\epsilon WCF}\right)\right] \times r$$

$\alpha = 9.0111$	$\gamma_4 = .0584$	$\gamma_{12} = .0242$
$\beta_0 = .6067$	$\gamma_5 = .0602$	$\gamma_{13} = .0216$
$\beta_1 = .3206$	$\gamma_6 = .0640$	$\gamma_{14} = .0194$
$\beta_2 = .0103$	$\gamma_7 = .0596$	$\gamma_{15} = .0179$
with $\Sigma\beta = .9376$	$\gamma_8 = .0349$	$\gamma_{16} = .0173$
$\gamma_0 = .0328$	$\gamma_9 = .0327$	$\gamma_{17} = .0179$
$\gamma_1 = .0477$	$\gamma_{10} = .0300$	with $\Sigma\gamma = .6764$
$\gamma_2 = .0583$	$\gamma_{11} = .0271$	$\epsilon = 10.489$
$\gamma_3 = .0524$		

Export volume (X) is modelled as depending upon world trade (WT) with an elasticity of .9376 and upon the ratio of home wage costs (WI) after adjustment for the foreign-exchange rate (RXD) to world wage costs (WCF) with a long-run elasticity of .6764. (See Treasury, 1979, Group 20; these coefficients are taken from Horton, 1980, Group 1, equation (4).)

This relatively low elasticity (only .6764) of export volume in respect of wage costs implies a much higher elasticity of foreign demand for the country's exports in respect of the price charged for them. When the wage cost (WI) falls by 1 per cent the price of home-produced goods $(PWHO)$ falls by only 0.7692 per cent, mainly because wage costs make up only .75368 of the total costs (equation (12)) and to a lesser extent because the price of imported intermediate goods (PMQ), which makes up the remaining .24632 of total costs, itself falls slightly in sympathy with the fall in domestic prices $(PWHO)$ (equation (1)). But the price of exports (PX) falls by only .51 times the price of home-produced goods $(PWHO)$ (equation 8)). Thus, when the wage cost falls by 1 per cent, we have an increase in the volume of exports of .6764 against a fall in the price charged for exports of only .51 × .7692, which implies a price elasticity of demand for exports of .6764/(.51 × .7692) = 1.724.

Given this price elasticity of demand of 1.724 for the country's exports and given (from equation (21)) a price elasticity of demand of unity for the country's imports of consumption goods, which constitute some 28 per cent of total imports, it is clear that the balance of trade is in the long run quite sensitive to price changes but only after the considerable time lags for export and import volumes shown in equations (27) and (21).

(28) *WT*, the volume of world trade, is exogenous.

(29) *WCF*, world wage costs, is exogenous.

(30)
$$X^* = X \times \frac{PX}{100} + r$$
The value of exports, X^*, is equal to price (*PX*) times quantity (*X*).

(c) *Interest payments and dividends*
(31) *CIPD*, the inflow of interest and dividends from overseas, is treated as exogenous.
Amongst other things this ignores changes in interest payments that result from the changes in foreign-exchange reserves caused by New Keynesian policies. This requires further work, along with the problems noted in Chapter I and below equation (32).

(32) $DIPD = gDIPD + g[y(RLG)(CIL + DBGS)] + g[y(RSH)CIS]$
Outflows of interest (*DIPD*) are modelled as being built up from payments of interest on long-term capital inflow into government bonds (*DBGS*) and into other investments (*CIL*), both of which are supposed for simplicity to earn the long-term rate of interest (*RLG*), and from payments on short-term capital inflow (*CIS*), which is supposed to earn the short rate (*RSH*). One problem with this formulation is that it does not allow for any changes in the interest rate ruling on the existing debt; it would not be easy to do this without introducing explicit stock variables and greatly complicating the model. The variables *CIL*, *DBGS* and *CIS* are treated as *exogenous* in the present model, although not in the Treasury Model, and so there is here no adequate treatment of higher interest obligations incurred through the attracting or repelling of foreign capital flows with higher or lower interest rates. The maintenance of a constant real rate of interest in the Control Run approximates to conditions that would not attract or repel such capital flows; as noted in Chapter I there is no modelling of the process of attracting the capital funds required to cover the deficits and surpluses produced on the current account of the balance of payments produced by New Keynesian policies. By an oversight the exogenous variables *CIL*, *DBGS* and *CIS* have been omitted from the present variable listing, although data on them were of course required for the construction of the model.

(33 Base)
    RSH, the short-run rate of interest, is exogenous.

(33 Control)

    RSH follows the policy rule described in Section 6 below.

(34 Base)

    RLG, the long-run rate of interest, is exogenous.

(34 Control)

    RLG follows the policy rule described in Section 6 below.

(d)   *Transfers*

(35) *NTD*, transfer payments by the government to overseas, is exogenous.

(e)   *Balance of payments on current account and overseas net acquisition of financial assets*

(36) $NAFOS = M^* - X^* + DIPD - CIPD + NTD + r$

Any excess of imports over exports $(M^* - X^*)$ plus any excess of interest and dividends paid to overseas over receipts from overseas $(DIPD - CIPD)$ plus any net transfers by the government to overseas (NTD) measures the deficit on the UK's balance of payments on current account, which, as shown in column 4 of Table A.2, must be equal to the net acquisition of financial assets by foreign owners $(NAFOS)$.

(iii) *Company sector incomes and expenditures*

(a)   *Factor demands*

(37)
$$ECP = \text{Exp}\left(\sum_{i=0}^{7} \beta_i g^i \ln ECPD \right) + r$$

$\beta_0 = .17544$	$\beta_4 = .10378$	
$\beta_1 = .20517$	$\beta_5 = .06155$	with $\Sigma\beta = 1.0$
$\beta_2 = .19774$	$\beta_6 = .06765$	
$\beta_3 = .15760$	$\beta_7 = .03107$	

Employment in the company sector (ECP) shows such employment adjusting towards a desired level $(ECPD)$ with a lag representing short-period overhead labour. (The lag profile comes from Horton, 1980, Group 2, equation (1).)

(38) $ECPD = (YM/RPT)^{\phi}$

$$\phi = .67263$$

The desired level of employment in the company sector (*ECPD*) is related to the company sector's final output (*YM*) after correction for an exogenous productivity trend (*RPT*) and after allowing for very considerable economies of scale represented by $\phi = .6726$, which implies that a 10 per cent increase in the volume of output causes a need for only 6.726 per cent more labour. (This coefficient comes from the sum of the coefficients in equation (1) of Group 2 in Horton, 1980.) There is some apparent inconsistency (mirroring that in the Treasury Model) between this assumption and the formulation in equation (12) of the factors determining selling prices (*PWHO*), which makes no allowance for the effect of scale of output upon costs, but it is possible to argue that prices are set on the basis not of actual output but of a 'normal' scale of output, while the need for labour per unit of output varies with actual output.

(39) $RPT = \mathrm{Exp}\,(\alpha + \beta T) \times r$

$$\alpha = .015237 \qquad \beta = .004952$$

The productivity trend (*RPT*) is represented by the exogenous time trend βT. It was fitted for the present model over the period 1973Q3–1979Q1, largely by finding a value for *RPT* that would most nearly result in elimination of the residuals that would otherwise appear in equation (37). The resulting constant upward trend of productivity of 0.4952 per cent per quarter (2 per cent per annum) is broadly compatible over the period concerned with the average rate of increase of productivity, which can be inferred from a comparison between labour earnings and labour cost. (See the comment on equation (11).)

(40) $KCPD = \alpha YM$

$$\alpha = 1.7$$

The desired level of the capital stock (*KCPD*) is assumed to bear a constant ratio to the level of output (*YM*).

(41)
$$ICP = \mathrm{Exp}\left(\sum_{i=0}^{9} \alpha_i g^i \ln KCPD \right) - (1 - \beta)gKPR + r$$

$\alpha_0 = .08825 \qquad \alpha_4 = .13529 \qquad \alpha_8 = .05882 \qquad \beta = .066982$

$\alpha_1 = .10588 \qquad \alpha_5 = .12353 \qquad \alpha_9 = .03529$

$\alpha_2 = .12353 \qquad \alpha_6 = .10588 \qquad \qquad$ with $\Sigma\alpha = 1.0$

$\alpha_3 = .13529 \qquad \alpha_7 = .08824$

The equation describing the company sector's gross investment (*ICP*) is of an orthodox capital-stock adjustment kind, showing the capital stock adjusting to its desired level (*KCPD*) after allowing for depreciation on the existing capital stock (g*KPR*).* The depreciation term ($\beta = .066982$) was set at its extremely large value so that investment could be explained without recourse to a constant term.

$$(42) \quad KPR = ICP + (1 - \beta)gKPR + r - r(ICP)$$

$$\beta = .066982$$

The capital stock (*KPR*) depends upon last period's capital stock (g*KPR*) less depreciation of that stock (βg*KPR*) plus additions by new investment (*ICP*).

$$(43) \quad SB = (1 - g)ST + r$$
Stockbuilding (*SB*) is expressed as the change in stocks (*ST*).

$$(44)$$
$$ST = \text{Exp}\left[\alpha + \sum_{i=1}^{3} \beta_i g^i \ln ST + \sum_{i=0}^{3} \gamma_i g^i (Y - \Delta ST) + \delta T \right] + r$$

$$\alpha = -.274872 \qquad \beta_1 = 1.0759 \qquad\qquad \gamma_0 = -.0327$$

$$\beta_2 = -.1373 \qquad\qquad \gamma_1 = .2114$$

$$\beta_3 = -.0701 \qquad\qquad \gamma_2 = -.0135$$

$$\text{with } \Sigma\beta = .8685 \quad \gamma_3 = -.0013$$

$$\text{with } \Sigma\gamma = .1639$$

$$\delta = .000914$$

Stocks (*ST*) are modelled as a *lagged* adjustment to desired levels, these desired levels being related to the level of output (*Y*) excluding stockbuilding (ΔST). But a *current* increase in such production leads to some involuntary reduction in stocks ($\gamma_0 < 0$), an effect that is extremely important for the simulation properties of the model. (This equation comes from Horton, 1980, Group 1, equation (3).)

*This equation was used in preference to that in the Treasury Model because the equation in the 1980 version of the Treasury Model, although very carefully estimated, has the unsatisfactory long-run property that an *x* per cent increase in output leads to an *x* per cent increase in investment (rather than in the capital stock) leaving the level of the capital stock undetermined (see Bean, 1979, Table 3). The lag structure in this equation, the long-run capital to output coefficient of 1.7 and the elasticity of capital with respect to output of unity were obtained with slight modification from an earlier small model built in the Treasury by G. Meen and D. Grubb, which took its investment equation from an earlier Treasury Model that did have a capital-stock adjustment formulation of the investment equation.

$$(45) \quad ICP^* = ICP \times \frac{PIF}{100} + r$$

$$(46) \quad SB^* = SB \times \frac{PS}{100} + r$$

Values of investment (ICP^*) and stockbuilding (SB^*) are obtained as price times quantity.

(b) *Other company sector current payments*

Company net payments of debt interest and dividends
$$(47) \quad DDIPCP = DDIRPE - DDIPGG - CIPD + DIPD + r$$
Company payments of interest and dividends (*DDIPCP*) are modelled as the residual resulting from the other flows of dividends and debt interest: personal sector receipts (*DDIRPE*), government sector payments (*DDIPGG*) and net payments from overseas (*CIPD − DIPD*). This is in a sense un-natural: persons in fact receive what the other sectors give them, but in the main Treasury Model it is the company sector's net payments of debt interest that are the residual. (See Ritchie, 1980, p. 21.)

Employer national insurance payments: ordinary contributions
$$(48) \quad YPNIR = \left(ERPR \times \frac{EG + ECP}{1000} \right) \times EMNI + r$$

$$(49) \quad TXNI = \left(ERPR \times \frac{EG + ECP}{1000} \right) \times SNI + r$$

Employer contributions (*YPNIR*) and surcharge (*TXNI*) are modelled as implicit rates (*EMNI* and *SNI* respectively) times wages per man (*ERPR*) times government plus private employment (*EG + ECP*). Both government and private payments are aggregated together since (because of the way company profits are constructed as a residual in equation (57)) it is not necessary to distinguish between them in the model.

(50) *EMNI*, the rate of employers' national insurance contribution, is exogenous.

(51) *SNI*, the rate of surcharge on employers' national insurance contri-bution, is exogenous.

Employers' other insurance fund contributions
$$(52) \quad OCR = \alpha \times ERPR \times \frac{EG + ECP}{1000} + r$$
$$\alpha = .03815$$

Employers' other contributions (*OCR*) include such items as employers' contributions to pension funds and are also modelled as an implicit rate ($\alpha = .03815$) times wages per man (*ERPR*) times government plus private employment (*EG + ECP*). For the same reason as in equation (48), government and company payments are not distinguished. But for the private sector, public corporations and local authorities, 'other contributions' consist of employers' contributions to funded pension schemes, whereas for central government (where pensions are unfunded) employers' contributions consist of the actual pensions paid, which will not vary with current levels of employment. The marginal rate of contribution coefficient ($\alpha = .03815$) has been set rather lower than that in Horton (1980, Group 5, equation (1)) to allow for this.

Dividends

$$(53) \quad DVPCO = gDVPCO \times \text{Exp} \left\{ \sum_{i=0}^{3} \alpha_i g^{4i} \Delta \left[\beta \ln (1 - TCPRO) \right. \right.$$
$$\left. \left. + \Delta \ln \sum_{j=1}^{4} g^j (FYCPR - SAC) \right] + \gamma \ln \delta \right\} + r$$

$\alpha_0 = .569 \qquad \beta = .666 \qquad \gamma = -.274872 \qquad \delta = 1.0759$

$\alpha_1 = .245$

$\alpha_2 = .106$

$\alpha_3 = .08$

with $\Sigma \alpha = 1.0$

Corporate distributions (*DVPCO*) are related to trading profits net of stock appreciation and to a variable related to the basic rate of tax on company incomes (*TCPRO*) designed to allow for changes in the tax structure. The profits variable is entered as maximum retainable earnings before tax (*FYCPR*) but after deducting stock appreciation (*SAC*). The equation is based on the Feldstein partial adjustment model, and comes direct from Treasury (1979), Group 12, equation (7).

(54) *TCPRO*, the rate of corporation tax, is exogenous.

Tax payments by companies

$$(55) \quad TCP = \sum_{i=2}^{9} \beta_i g^i [TCPRO \times (FYCPR - DDIPCP + DVPCO - SAC)$$
$$- DVPCO \times TPBR] + r$$

$\beta_2 = .215 \qquad \beta_6 = .060$

$$\beta_3 = .190 \qquad \beta_7 = .040$$
$$\beta_4 = .195 \qquad \beta_8 = .045$$
$$\beta_5 = .200 \qquad \beta_9 = .055$$
$$\text{with } \Sigma\beta = 1.0$$

Company tax payments (TCP) are modelled as levied at the corporation tax rate (TCPRO) upon company profits (FYCPR) after deduction of allowances for stock relief (SAC). As a simplification, allowance for investment relief has not been made, but this is much less important quantitatively than allowances for stock relief. Net payments of interest and rent are deducted from the profit tax base; and since DDIPCP represents the total net distribution of dividends, interest and rent by the company sector while DVPCO represents their distribution of dividends, DDIPCP − DVPCO measures their net payments of interest and rent. Tax credits equal to personal income tax (TPBR) on dividend payments to the personal sector (DVPCO) are deducted from company tax liabilities.*

(c) *Company sector profits and net acquisition of financial assets*

(56) $SAC = gST \times \dfrac{\Delta PS}{100} + r$

Stock appreciation (SAC), which is a component of profits, is modelled as depending on the lagged level of stocks (ST) and the change in their price over the period (ΔPS).

(57) $FYCPR = GDPM^* - r(GDPM^*) - RN - YPNIR - TXNI - FYG$
$- OCR - SE + SAC - TXPD - TXC - TXX$
$- \dfrac{(ECP + EG) \times ERPR}{1000} + r$

Profits (FYCPR) are calculated by subtracting from estimated gross domestic product at market prices (GDPM* − rGDPM*) the estimates of income from employment ((ECP + EG) × ERPR/1000) and from self-employment (SE), public sector trading surpluses (FYG), employers' insurance and other contributions (YPNIR, TXNI and OCR), rent incomes (RN), and indirect taxes on imports (TXPD), on exports (TXX), and on consumption (TXC), and then adding stock appreciation (SAC).

(58) $NAFCO = FYCPR + \alpha RN - DDIPCP - ICP^* - SB^* - TCP$
$- SAC + r - r(NAFPE) - r(FYCPR)$
$- r(NAFOS) - r(NAFPU)$

$$\alpha = .080$$

*This equation is an aggregation of those in the Treasury Model, and the lag parameters are obtained from the work by Meen and Grubb referred to in the footnote on p. 272.

Company net acquisition of financial assets ($NAFCO$) is equal to company profits ($FYCPR$) plus company rental income (modelled as a simple proportion, α, of total rent, RN) minus net company sector payments of dividends and interest ($DDIPCP$), the value of outpayments for investment goods (ICP^*), stockbuilding (SB^*), taxes (TCP), and also stock appreciation (SAC). The residuals of the net acquisition of financial assets by the other sectors, i.e. by the personal sector ($NAFPE$), by the public sector ($NAFPU$) and by the overseas sector ($NAFOS$), are also added to this equation to ensure that the overall accounts add up.

(iv) Personal Sector Incomes and Expenditures

(a) *Incomes*

(59) $ES = \alpha + r$

$$\alpha = 1886.0$$

(60) $SE = \alpha \times (GDPM^* - TXC - TXX - TXPD - TXNI) + r$

$$\alpha = .095723$$

The number of self-employed (ES) is treated as exogenous (see Treasury, 1979, Group 3, equation (1)) and income from self-employment (SE) is included as a simple proportion of GDP at market prices ($GDPM^*$) after deducting indirect taxes on consumption (TXC), on exports (TXX) and on imports ($TXPD$) and the employers' national insurance surcharge ($TXNI$). (The coefficient is taken, with slight amendment, from Horton, 1980, Group 5, equation (2).)

(61) $DDIRPE = gDDIRPE - c_1 g\{y[f_1 RSH + (1 - f_1)RLG]NAFPU\}$
$\qquad\qquad\quad + (1 - g)DVPCO - c_2 \times g[y(RLG) \cdot CIL] + r$

$$c_1 = +.800 \qquad f_1 = .47 \qquad c_2 = +.230$$

Personal sector net receipts of dividends and interest ($DDIRPE$) are modelled explicitly (using an aggregation of the equations found in Treasury, 1979, Group 63, and Horton, 1980, Group 4). Again as with the overseas interest and dividend flows, the method used, in the absence of a comprehensive set of appropriate stock variables, means using last periods flow plus (or minus) the new debt times the current interest rate. As has already been pointed out, this means that there is no easy way to make allowance for changes in the rate of interest ruling on outstanding debt. The personal sector is modelled as taking up a fixed proportion ($c_1 = 80$ per cent) of the increase in public sector debt ($-NAFPU$) and the personal sector is supposed to receive 80 per cent of the debt interest paid by the government sector; part of their holdings of government debt ($f_1 = 47$ per cent) are assumed to receive the short-term rate of interest (RSH)

and the remainder to receive the long-term rate (RLG). (See Treasury, 1979, Group 63, equation (18).) The personal sector receives the whole of the dividend payments by the company sector ($DVPCO$) and is modelled as paying a proportion ($c_2 = 23$ per cent) of the interest on long-term capital inflow (CIL). There is no explicit treatment of the payment of interest to the company sector on bank borrowing since this is largely offset by holdings of interest bearing bank deposits.

$$(62) \quad YPDY^* = \frac{ECP + EG}{1000} \times ERPR + SE + \alpha RN + OCR$$
$$+ DDIRPE + YPCG^* - TYPP - NIPE + r$$
$$\alpha = .59$$

Personal sector disposable income ($YPDY^*$) includes employment incomes (($ECP + EG$) $\times ERPR$), and a proportion ($\alpha = .59$) of rent (RN) as well as interest and dividends ($DDIRPE$). In addition there are employers' other contributions (OCR, see equation (52)) and transfer payments from the public sector ($YPCG^*$). To obtain personal sector disposable income it is necessary to subtract personal sector national insurance contributions ($NIPE$) and personal sector taxes ($TYPP$).

$$(63) \quad NIPE = ERPR \times \frac{ET \times EENI}{1000} + r$$

Personal sector national insurance contributions ($NIPE$) are the implicit rate of employees' national insurance contributions ($EENI$) times total earnings, which are represented by earnings per head ($ERPR$), times total employment inclusive of self-employment (ET). (This makes some allowance for the Class 2 and Class 4 contributions of the self-employed.) The rate $EENI$ is calculated implicitly as the rate that would cause the formula to yield the employee national insurance contributions that actually were paid.

(64 Base)
    $EENI$, the rate of employees' national insurance contribution, is then treated as exogenous in the Base Run.

(64 Control)
    $EENI$ follows the equation described in Section 6.

$$(65) \quad TYPP = TPBR \times (YPDY^* + TYPP + NIPE - YPCG^*)$$
$$\times \left(1 - \frac{TPAL}{ERPR}\right) + r$$

Personal tax payments (*TYPP*) are modelled as the basic rate of income
tax (*TPBR*) times taxable income after subtraction of allowances. Taxable
income is equal to personal disposable income (*YPDY**) plus personal tax
payments (*TYPP*) plus personal national insurance contributions (*NIPE*)
but after deduction of tax-free transfer payments from the public sector
(*YPCG**). A proportion (*TPAL/ERPR*) of taxable incomes is then
deducted to represent tax allowances. This personal tax allowance (*TPAL*)
is calculated implicitly as the amount of allowance per worker that would
cause the formula to yield the taxes that actually were paid. This procedure has the advantage of being much simpler than that adopted in the
Treasury Model but on the other hand it makes no attempt to model the
rest of the progressivity of the tax system. (It follows a suggestion by
Ritchie, 1980, p. 19.)

(66)   *TPAL*, the personal tax allowance, is then treated as exogenous.

(b)   *Expenditures*

(67) $$CND = \mathrm{Exp}\left[\ln g^4 CND + \sum_{i=0}^{3} \alpha_i g^i \Delta_4 \ln z + \beta g^4 \ln \left(\frac{z}{CND}\right)\right.$$
$$\left. + \gamma \Delta_1 \Delta_4 \ln UNUKP + \delta \Delta_4 \ln PC\right] \times r$$

$\alpha_0 = .24261$ $\beta = .12134$ $\gamma = -.028487$

$\alpha_1 = .13680$ $\delta = -.20558$

$\alpha_2 = .061097$

$\alpha_3 = .015496$

with $\Sigma \alpha = .456003$

where

$$z \equiv \frac{YPDY^*}{PC} \times 100$$

The equation for non-durable consumption, *CND, is taken unamended
from the Treasury Model (Treasury, 1979, Group II, equation (9)) and is
based on the work of Davidson and Hendry. The equation is a general one
consistent with a number of alternative theories. It can be interpreted as
having the following features. The form of the dependent variable and the
first two terms on the right-hand side imply that the rate of growth of
consumption increases by 46 per cent of any increase in the rate of growth
of income, with a short time lag spread out over just three quarters. The
third term on the right-hand side is a slower acting one that ensures that
over a longer period of time the rate of growth of consumption increases
by a full 100 per cent of any increase in the rate of growth of real income

thus establishing a long-run average propensity to consume independent of the level of real income. The price term (with coefficient δ) is interpreted as capturing a wealth effect such that consumption will be lower the lower is the real value of past savings. The unemployment term (with coefficient γ) shows that an increase in unemployment causes a temporary fall in consumption, by acting on expectations of future unemployment. This equation dominates the behaviour of the whole model, since consumption is such a large component of total final expenditures.

$$(68) \quad CDUR = \alpha(\beta - \gamma)g^2 CDUR + (\beta - \gamma - \alpha)gCDUR + (1 + \gamma g)\delta z$$
$$+ (1 + \alpha g)(1 + \gamma g)(\epsilon RSH + \eta - PEXPC)$$
$$+ \lambda \left(gNW^* \ \frac{100}{PC} \right) + \mu\Delta(1 + \alpha g)(1 + \gamma g) UNUKP$$
$$+ \rho + r \qquad \text{where} \quad z = \frac{YPDY^* \times 100}{PC}$$

$$\alpha = -.5689 \qquad \eta = 0.0$$
$$\beta = -.05321 \qquad \lambda = .005$$
$$\gamma = -.9485 \qquad \mu = -100.0$$
$$\delta = .0752 \qquad \rho = -43.36$$
$$\epsilon = -6.76$$

Durable consumption ($CDUR$) is derived from a standard stock-adjustment model, relating durable consumption to real disposable income ($YPDY^*/PC$), real interest rates ($RSH - PEXPC$), and real wealth (NW/PC). The wealth variable (NW) is a cumulant of personal savings (see equation (69)); and it is assumed that two-thirds of personal sector wealth is held in non-money fixed assets and revalued along with inflation. In the durable consumption equation (as in the equation for non-durable consumption) an increase in unemployment ($UNUKP$) causes a temporary fall in consumption. The term in unemployment has subsequently been eliminated from the durables equation in the Treasury Model, and in the present model μ has a value only two-thirds of that reported in Treasury (1980), Group 11, equation (3) (to damp swings in durable consumption caused by unemployment); otherwise the coefficients are taken direct from an earlier version of that equation.

$$(69) \quad NW^* = gNW \left(1 + \alpha \ \frac{PC - gPC}{gPC} \right)$$
$$+ \left(\frac{YPDY^* - PC \times CND}{100} \right) + r$$
$$\alpha = .67$$

Net wealth of the private sector (NW) is given by last quarter's net wealth (gNW) with an allowance for the rate of price inflation $((PC - gPC)/gPC)$ on a proportion $(\alpha = .67)$ of it, with the addition of current savings, which consist of personal disposable income $(YPDY^*)$ less expenditure on non-durable consumption $(PC \times CND)$. (This equation is taken direct from Treasury, 1979, Group 11, equation (12).)

$$(70) \quad IPRD = \alpha + \beta gIPRD + \gamma gRSH + r$$

$$\alpha = 110.0 \qquad \beta = .7872 \qquad \gamma = -1.6258$$

Private sector investment in residential dwellings $(IPRD)$ is treated in a similar but simpler way than that in Treasury (1979), Group 11, equation (10). It is simply modelled as dependent on the short-term rate of interest (RSH).

$$(71) \quad CND^* = CND \times \frac{PC}{100} + r$$

$$(72) \quad CDUR^* = CDUR \times \frac{PC}{100} + r$$

$$(73) \quad IPRD^* = IPRD \times \frac{PIF}{100} + r$$

The values of personal sector non-durable consumption (CND^*), durable consumption $(CDUR^*)$ and residential investment expenditures $(IPRD^*)$ are obtained as prices times volume.

(c)   *Acquisitions of financial assets*

$$(74) \quad NAFPE = YPDY^* - CND^* - CDUR^* - IPRD^* + r$$

Personal sector acquisitions of financial assets $(NAFPE)$ are obtained as disposable income $(YPDY^*)$ minus the value of personal expenditures on non-durable consumption (CND^*), on durable consumption $(CDUR^*)$ and on investment in housing $(IPRD^*)$.

(d)   *Employment*

Equations for total employment and unemployment of persons are appropriately grouped with the personal sector.

$$(75) \quad ET = ES + ECP + EG + r$$

Total employment (ET) is the sum of self-employment (ES), corporate employment (ECP) and employment by government (EG).

(76) $UNUK = \alpha + \beta(D - ECP - EG) + \dfrac{\beta}{\delta}$

$$\times \left(\dfrac{1}{\gamma} - \dfrac{1}{\beta}\right) \ln\left[\beta + (\gamma\epsilon)\exp(-\delta UNUK)\right] + r$$

$$\alpha = -1600 \qquad \delta = .004467$$
$$\beta = .7 \qquad \epsilon = 66.53729$$
$$\gamma = .3$$

Unemployment ($UNUK$) depends upon the labour supply (D) less corporate and government employment ($ECP + EG$) and allows for variations in the registration rate of those without a job according to the pressure of demand in the labour market as indicated by unemployment ($UNUK$). (See Treasury, 1979, Section 14. The coefficients are from Treasury, 1980, Group 3, after alteration of the constant α.)

(77) D, the labour supply, is exogenous.

(78) $UNUKP = \dfrac{100 \times UNUK}{UNUK + ET - ES} + r$

The unemployment percentage ($UNUKP$) expresses unemployment ($UNUK$) relative to the number of employed (ET) plus unemployed ($UNUK$) but abstracting from self-employment (ES).

(v) *Government Sector Expenditures and Incomes*

(a) *Expenditures*
(79) CGE, the wages and salaries part of general government consumption volume at 1975 prices, is exogenous.

(80) $EG = \text{Exp}(\alpha + \ln CGE) + \delta ECP + r$

$$\alpha = .29787 \qquad \delta = .104$$

Government employment (EG) is projected to grow at the same rate as the wages and salaries element in government consumption volume at 1975 prices (CGE) and the employment variable is defined to include employment by nationalised industries, which is not properly treated as exogenous and so, for simplicity, is set at a constant proportion ($\delta = .104$) of private employment (ECP).

(81) $CGE^* = (EG - \delta ECP) \times \dfrac{ERPR}{1000}(1 + EMNI + SNI) + r$

$$\delta = .104$$

The value of government wages and salaries including employers' national insurance contributions (CGE^*) is dependent on wage rates $(ERPR)$ together with rates of employers' national insurance contribution $(EMNI)$ and surcharge (SNI) and on government employment (EG) which like CGE is defined exclusive of employment in nationalised industries (δECP).

(82) $CGPO$, the government general procurement volume, is exogenous.

(83) $CGPO^* = CGPO \times \dfrac{PC}{100} + r$

The value of such procurements $(CGPO^*)$ is price (PC) times quantity $(CGPO)$.

(84) IPU, the volume of public investment, is exogenous.

(85) $IPU^* = IPU \times \dfrac{PIF}{100} + r$

The value of such investment (IPU^*) is price (PIF) times quantity (IPU).

(86) $YPCG^* = UB \times (\alpha + \beta UNUK) + r$

$$\alpha = 96.0 \qquad \beta = .0065$$

Grants to persons including all social security benefits and not just unemployment benefits $(YPCG^*)$ are modelled as a constant, α, times an implicit rate of weekly benefit (UB) where with 13 weeks in a quarter and $\alpha = 96.0$ this corresponds to $96/13 = 7.4$ million in receipt of this benefit. If receipt of benefit moved *pari passu* with unemployment $(UNUK)$ the coefficient β would be set at 13 (for the number of weeks) times .001 (to convert to £m.); but to make this equation simulate more like that in the full Treasury Model, the sensitivity of $YPCG^*$ to unemployment was cut in half $(= .0065)$. The implicit rate of benefit (UB) was calculated from data for $YPCG^*$ and $UNUK$ using equation (86); it is not at all sensitive to the value of β.

(87) UB, the rate of benefit, was then treated as exogenous.

(88) $DDIPGG = gDDIPGG - g\{y[f_1 RSH + (1 - f_1)RLG]NAFPU\} + r$

$$f_1 = .47$$

Payments of debt interest by general government $(DDIPGG)$ are modelled by deriving the flows from last period's flow $(gDDIPGG)$ plus or minus the short-term (RSH) or long-term (RLG) rate of interest on the new debt $(-NAFPU)$. For simplicity it is assumed that 47 per cent $(f_1 = .47)$ of new debt incurs an obligation to pay the short-term rate of interest (as in Treasury, 1979, Group 63, equation (7)).

(b) *Receipts*

General government receipts are made up of taxes on persons and companies and national insurance contributions, as already discussed. In addition, rental incomes of the government are obtained as a residual from total rent and rental receipts of the other sectors. This leaves the public sector's trading surplus, protective duties, taxes on exports and taxes on consumption.

(89) $FYG = \alpha(FYCPR) + r$

$$\alpha = .2168$$

The public sector's trading surplus (FYG) is modelled as a simple proportion of aggregate trading profits $(FYCPR)$. (This is necessary because, although the Treasury Model has separate equations for nationalised industry behaviour, these are not reproduced here.)

(90) $TXPD = TM \times M^* + r$

The revenue from protective duties $(TXPD)$ is obtained as an implicit rate of tariff (TM) times the value of imports (M^*).

(91) $TXX = TX \times X^* + r$

The revenue from taxes on exports (TXX) is modelled as an implicit rate (TX) times the value of exports (X^*).

(92) $TXC = \left(\dfrac{TC}{1 + TC}\right) \times (CND^* + CDUR^* + CGPO^*) + r$

The revenue from taxes on consumption (TXC) (principally VAT, excise duties and rates) is modelled as an implicit rate (TC) times the value of consumption, both personal $(CND^* + CDUR^*)$ and governmental $(CGPO^*)$.

(c) *Government financial deficit and acquisition of financial assets*

(93) $NAFPU = -[CGE^* + CGPO^* + IPU^* + YPCG^* + DDIPGG$
$\qquad\qquad - (1 - \alpha - \beta)RN + NTD - TYPP - TXPD - TXX$
$\qquad\qquad - TXC - TCP - YPNIR - TXNI - NIPE - FYG] + r$

Government net acquisition of financial assets $(NAFPU)$ is equal to the government financial surplus (see column 3 of Table A.2). The obverse

$(-NAFPU)$ is the financial deficit. It is obtained by subtracting revenues from expenditures. Revenues consist of rent $((1-\alpha-\beta)RN)$, personal direct taxes $(TYPP)$, protective duties $(TXPD)$, taxes on exports (TXX), indirect taxes on consumption (TXC), company tax payments (TCP), employers' national insurance contributions $(YPNIR)$ and surcharge $(TXNI)$, employees' national insurance contributions $(NIPE)$, and the surplus from government trading (FYG). Expenditure includes the cost of government employment (CGE^*), of government consumption $(CGPO^*)$, of government investment (IPU^*), of transfer payments to the personal sector $(YPCG^*)$, of interest payments $(DDIPGG)$, and of transfer payments to overseas (NTD), the whole of which are here ascribed to the government.

(vi) *Various National Income Variables*

(94) $GDPM = CND + CDUR + IPRD + ICP + CGE + CGPO$
$+ IPU + SB + X - M + r$

The gross domestic product at market price valued at constant prices $(GDPM)$ is derived from the sum of demands for personal consumption $(CND + CDUR)$, government consumption $(CGE + CGPO)$, personal, company and government investment $(IPRD + ICP + IPU)$, stockbuilding (SB), and the excess of exports over imports $(X - M)$.

(95) $GDPM^* = CND^* + CDUR^* + IPRD^* + ICP^* + CGE^* + CGPO^*$
$+ IPU^* + SB^* + X^* - M^* + r$

The gross domestic product at market prices valued at current prices comprises the same elements, each valued at its current price.

(96) $Y = GDPM - FCA + r$

(97) $FCA = \alpha(CND + CDUR + CGPO) + \beta M + \gamma X + r$

$\alpha = .12577 \qquad \beta = .01878 \qquad \gamma = .02683$

In order to obtain the gross domestic product at factor cost (Y) it is necessary to deduct from the gross domestic product at market price $(GDPM)$ a factor cost adjustment (FCA), which depends upon the rates of indirect tax $(\alpha, \beta$ and $\gamma)$ in the base year, 1975, on consumption $(CND + CDUR + CGPO)$, on imports (M) and on exports (X), respectively.

(98) $YM = Y - CGE$

For some purposes it is useful to consider (YM), i.e. 'production' exclusive of the activity of government employees, which is derived simply by subtracting such employment (CGE) from total output (Y).

(99) $RN = \beta GDPM^* + r$

$$\beta = .017275$$

Rent (including imputed rent accruing to households) is shown as moving slightly with the money value of total domestic production, to an extent obtained by simulation of the full Treasury Model.

5. Dynamic Multipliers

This section briefly portrays the properties of the model by presenting some key dynamic multipliers. Each of the figures that follow shows the outcomes that occur when there is a sustained change in one of the policy instruments, whilst at the same time the other control instruments remain unchanged.* The outcomes are shown for Money GDP (at factor cost), the wage bill, unemployment, the current account of the balance of payments and price level. All of these variables are measured in percentage deviations from their Base Run historical trajectory, except unemployment, which is measured as the difference in the percentage unemployment rate, and the current balance, which is measured as a percentage of Base Run Money GDP. The changes were applied to the model in 1975 quarter 3, and the effects were measured for seven-and-a-half years.

Figure A.1 shows the effect of an increase in the rate of indirect taxation of 5 percentage points, and Figure A.2 shows the effect of an increase in the rate of employees' national insurance contributions, also of 5 percentage points. In Figure A.1 the consumption price level rises by 4.4 percentage points (this is equal to the percentage increase in indirect taxation); in Figure A.2 the price level does not rise at all (since of course the money wage is exogenous). Otherwise the outcomes are very similar and easily understood. Real GDP falls by nearly 2 per cent in both cases after five quarters. The fall is somewhat faster in the first case because of the negative effect of higher prices on consumption (see equation (67) in Section 4); the fall is as rapid as it is because, although consumption takes time to respond (the short-run elasticity of consumption with respect to real income in equation (67) is less than one-half and only about 80 per cent of the long-run fall in consumption is achieved by the fifth quarter),

---

*We examine 'step multipliers' for ease of interpretation, whereas those used to linearise the model were impulse multipliers (see Chapter XIV, Section 2). We have also corrected an error in equation (5) of the version of the model linearised and used for the analysis of Chapter XIV. This error slightly altered the longer-term influences of indirect taxes on the outputs — particularly the balance of payments — away from the correct ones shown here. But it had little influence on the performance of the policy rules and, because of the presence in the rules of integral control (which corrects for such errors), an imperceptible effect on the rerun of history.

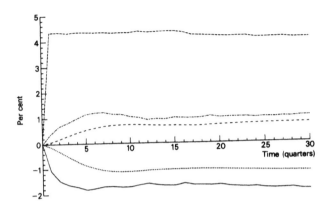

Fig. A.1 Effect of a Sustained Increase in the Rate of Indirect Taxation by 5 Percentage Points

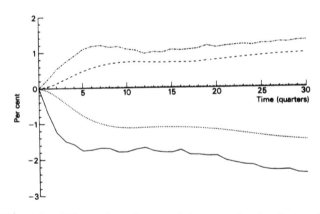

Fig. A.2 Effect of a Sustained Increase in the Rate of Employees' National Insurance Contributions by 5 Percentage Points

Key to Figures A.1 – A.5.

————	Money GDP (at factor cost, defined in equations (4Ciii) in Section 6 below)
– – –	percentage rate of unemployment (equation (78))
············	wage bill (obtained from equations for earnings and employment)
- - - - -	price of consumers' expenditure (equation (13))
.—.—.—	current account of the balance of payments (equation (36))

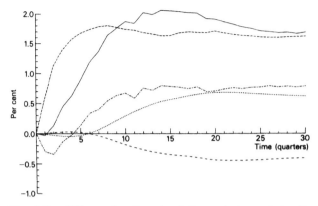

Fig. A.3 Effect of a Sustained Depreciation of the Exchange Rate by 5 Per Cent

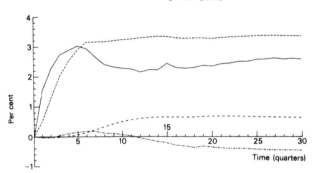

Fig. A.4 Effect of a Sustained Increase in the Rate of Money Earnings by 5 Per Cent

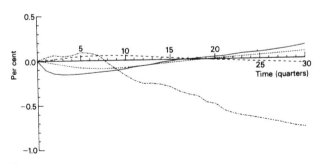

Fig. A.5 Effect of a Sustained Increase in the Short-Term Rate of Interest by 5 Percentage Points and in the Long-Term Rate of Interest by 2.5 Percentage Points

the accelerator humps of investment and (after a lag) of stockbuilding temporarily fill the gap. The percentage fall in the wage bill is about two-thirds of the percentage fall in Money GDP because of the low elasticity of employment with respect to output in equation (37), and the fall in employment lags that in GDP. This fall is mirrored by a rise in unemployment that is of even smaller proportional magnitude because of those who do not register as unemployed (see equation (76)). The contraction of economic activity shows a small tendency to cumulate in the case of the increase in national insurance contributions because of the lower interest obligations that result from a lower national debt. (There is no explicit wealth effect in the Treasury's main non-durable consumption function, which explains why this cumulative effect is not stronger.) This effect is cancelled out in the case of higher indirect taxes because an indirect tax rate higher by 5 percentage points throughout the simulation represents a smaller proportionate increase in indirect taxes in the later part of the simulation simply because the Base Run rate of indirect tax was higher in the latter part of the simulation.

Figure A.3 shows the effect of a 5 per cent depreciation of the exchange rate. The price of consumption goods rises gradually to an extent equal to about one-third of the depreciation; its rate of rise is governed by the lags in equations (1) and (12). Real GDP is lower than Base Run for four quarters, reflected in a higher level of unemployment, because the fall in consumption due to lower real income initially predominates over the slow-acting substitution effect in favour of net exports. Exports are ultimately higher by about 3 per cent or by about 1 per cent of GDP. The fall in personal disposable income caused by the higher price level more than counteracts any positive multiplier effects on consumption, and consumers' expenditure falls. But substitution away from imports and a higher level of investment cancels the resulting effects of this on real GDP at factor cost: this also increases by 1 per cent. The wage bill and unemployment mirror the change in real activity. The trade balance improves by about 0.75 of GDP, less than the increase in net exports because of the terms-of-trade loss. Money GDP rises by only a little more than the consumption price index; this is consistent with the rise in real output because the GDP deflator rises less than consumption prices, again due to the terms-of-trade loss.

Figure A.4 shows the effect of a 5 per cent increase in the rate of money earnings per man. (The effect on the wage bill, which obviously initially rises by 5 per cent and whose subsequent movement can be inferred from the behaviour of unemployment, is not shown.) The price level rises to an extent equal to about two-thirds of the increase in money earnings. Initially real GDP rises and unemployment falls slightly, but subsequently the loss of competitiveness predominates and aggregate demand falls. The trade balance first slightly worsens because of increased consumer spending, then improves slightly because of the improved terms of trade, then (after three years) goes into deficit because of the loss of competitiveness. The long-term real outcomes of Figure A.4 are not simply the reverse of those displayed in Figure A.3, because there are some categories of income (e.g. taxes, see equation (65); interest receipts, see equation (61)) that are not indexed in the model to the price level; thus the long-term rise in consumers' real incomes associated with the 5 per cent rise in the money wage is less than the fall in consumers' real incomes associated with the 5 per cent depreciation of the exchange rate. Therefore unemployment rises by more in Figure A.4 than it falls in Figure A.3, and the deterioration in the trade balance in Figure A.4 is less than the improvement in Figure A.3.

Figure A.5 shows the effects of a 5 per cent rise in the short-term rate of interest, and a 2.5 per cent rise in the long-term rate of interest. The effects are very small, because the interest-rate linkages in the present model are very small. The current account of the balance of payments goes into deficit because of higher interest obligations on foreign holdings of UK assets; but the increased inflow of foreign capital into these assets as the result of higher interest payments is not modelled, so this effect is surely understated. Durable consumption falls, stockbuilding falls, investment falls, and both Money GDP and real GDP fall. The wage bill falls and unemployment rises; the price level is unchanged. Subsequently the positive effects of higher interest payments on consumption come to dominate other changes in expenditures and unemployment falls, very slightly.

6. Equations for the Proposed Policy Rules

The derivation of the rules used for the variation of policy instruments is discussed in Chapter XIV, and the actual rules that we propose are described in Section 5(ii) of that chapter. The components of proportional, integral and derivative action in each of the rules are also explained there. These rules are written down in Appendix B. Here we show exactly how the rules were implemented on the model laid out in Section 4, when the model was used to produce the optimistic Control Run displayed in Chapter VIII.

(4 Control) Exchange rate

$$\text{(4Ci)} \qquad RXD = \left(1 + \frac{RXDC}{100}\right) \times \alpha g \left[\frac{(1+g)WCF}{(1+g)WI}\right]$$

$$\alpha = 10.94$$

where

(4Cii) $RXDC = \sum_{i=1}^{3} \alpha_i g^i RXDC + \sum_{i=1}^{3} \beta_i g^i BPD$

$$\alpha_1 = 2.1 \qquad \beta_1 = -.68954$$

$$\alpha_2 = -1.4 \qquad \beta_2 = +.99061$$

$$\alpha_3 = .3 \qquad \beta_3 = -.33062$$

and

(4Ciii) $BPD = \left[100 \dfrac{OILBAL}{\overline{GDPFC}^*} + 1.54 \right] - 100 \dfrac{-NAFOS}{GDPFC^*}$

and

(4Civ) $GDPFC^* = GDPM^* - TC - TXX - TXPD - TXNI$
and where $\overline{GDPFC}^*$ denotes the Base Run value of $GDPFC^*$

Equation (4Ci) shows the (nominal) sterling–dollar exchange rate following a path that would preserve a constant real exchange rate (the term in square brackets) adjusted by control action away from this path. The adjustments to the nominal exchange rate in order to maintain a constant real exchange rate are performed according to a weighted average of the one- and two-period lagged ratio of foreign wage costs (variable 29) and home wage costs (found from equation (11)). This averaging slightly smooths the adjustment of the exchange rate to exogenous jumps in home or foreign wage costs, without perceptibly altering the quality of feedback control, and was judged a necessary amendment to the procedure described in Section 2 of Chapter XIV. Equation (4Cii) shows the required percentage adjustment, $RXDC$, of the real exchange rate and is obtained from the real exchange rate control rule shown in Section 3 of Appendix B, after incorporation of a one-quarter implementation delay. This adjustment depends on the difference, BPD, between the target for the current account of the balance of payments and the value actually achieved, both in equation (4Ciii) as a percent of Base Run Money GDP (at factor cost, defined in equation (4Civ)). The target for the balance of payments on current account is shown in square brackets in equation (4Ciii) as equal to the (exogenous) difference between the balance of payments on oil account as a percent of Base Run Money GDP ($\overline{GDPFC}^*$) and its value (-1.54) in 1972Q2*; the value actually achieved for the current balance of payments is shown by $-NAFOS$ (from equation (36)).

---

*In the square brackets in equation (4Ciii) from 1980Q1 onwards, 100 was replaced by 30 and the term $+1.54$ was removed.

(10 Control) Earnings per man

(10Ci) $ERPR = \left(1 + \dfrac{ERPRC}{100}\right) \times 376.1 \times 1.031026^t$

where

(10Cii) $ERPRC = gERPRC + 0.35\,UNUKD + 0.65g(1-g)UNUKD$

and

(10Ciii) $UNUKD = 3.759 - UNUKP$

Equation (10Ci) shows the money earnings per man as following a path growing at 3.1026 per cent per quarter (13 per cent per annum) from its initial value in 1972Q2, adjusted by control action away from this path. Equation (10Cii) shows the required percentage adjustment, $ERPRC$, in money earnings, and is obtained from the control rule for the wage, which is shown in Section 2 of Appendix B. This adjustment depends on the difference, $UNUKD$, between the critical percentage rate of unemployment, 3.759, which is assumed to be frictional unemployment (see Section 2 of Chapter VII), and the percentage rate of unemployment, $UNUKP$, actually achieved (which is found from equation (78)).

(14 Control) Indirect tax rate

(14Ci) $TC = \dfrac{TCC}{100} + 0.208$

where

(14Cii) $TCC = \alpha gTCC + \displaystyle\sum_{i=1}^{3} \beta_i g^i ZD$

$$\alpha = .6932 \qquad \beta_1 = -.46236$$
$$\beta_2 = -.14873$$
$$\beta_3 = .57124$$

(14Ciii) $ZD = gZD + \alpha GD$

$$\alpha = 1.0$$

(14Civ) $GD = g\left(\dfrac{13553.6 \times 1.031026^t + NSO - GDPFC^*}{\overline{GDPFC^*}}\right)$

Equation (14Ci) shows the proportional rate of indirect tax on consumption to be equal to its initial value in 1972Q2 adjusted by control action away from this value. Equation (14Civ) shows the difference, GD, between the target for Money GDP (at factor cost, defined in 4Civ) and the value actually achieved, both expressed as a percentage of Base Run Money GDP. The target for Money GDP grows at 3.1026 per cent per quarter (13 per cent per annum) from its initial value in 1972Q2, adjusted upwards by the money value of North Sea oil production (NSO). Equation

(14Ciii) shows the sum over time of the values obtained for this difference *GD*. This sum is then used in equation (14Cii) to calculate the required control adjustment, *TCC*, in the proportional rate of indirect tax. Equation (14Cii) incorporates a one-quarter implementation delay and transforms the control rule so as to express it in terms of *ZD* rather than *GD*, as in Section 2 of Appendix B. This transformation is necessary because the rate of employee national insurance contributions is used as a second tax instrument to control Money GDP, and only by expressing the adjustments of these two tax instruments as functions of the same sum of all past control errors on Money GDP can one avoid the integral control actions of the two tax instruments 'fighting' each other as a result of numerical inaccuracies.

(33 Control) Short-term interest rates

$$RSH = 4(PEXPW) + 1.0$$

(34 Control) Long-term interest rates

$$RLG = 4[0.5(PEXPW)] + 7.0$$

Equation (33) represents the maintenance of a constant short-term real rate of interest of 1 per cent per annum. The adjustment of the interest rate to price inflation is not performed instantaneously as in Part Four (see Section 2 of Chapter XIV) but is made to follow a proxy for inflation expectations (that used in the Treasury wage equation, see equation (17)). This smooths the path of the nominal interest rate. But it does not impose permanent money illusion because in the rerun of history the rate of inflation is stabilised and so it does not seem unreasonable. Equation (34) shows a similar 'sticky' adjustment of the long-term rate of interest to the rate of inflation. At the 'core' rate of inflation of 11 per cent underlying the rerun of history (equal to the 13 per cent expansion of Money GDP exclusive of North Sea oil minus 2 per cent productivity growth) the real long-term rate of interest is 1.5 per cent.

(64 Control) Rate of employees' national insurance contributions

(64Ci) $EENI = \dfrac{EENIC}{100} + 0.044$

where

(64Cii) $EENIC = \alpha g EENIC + \sum_{i=1}^{3} \beta_i g^i ZD$

$$\alpha = .6623 \qquad \beta_1 = -.79105$$

$$\beta_2 = .55526$$

$$\beta_3 = .12100$$

and where ZD is defined in (14Ciii)

Equation (64Ci) shows the proportional rate of indirect tax on consumption to be equal to its initial value in 1972Q2 adjusted by control action away from this value. Equation (64Cii) shows the required adjustment in response to the sum of differences between the target for Money GDP and the value actually achieved. This equation incorporates a one-quarter implementation delay, and expresses the control rule in terms of ZD (defined in 14Ciii) for reasons explained in connection with equation (14Cii) above.

The preceding discussion has explained the implementation of the control rules so as to produce the optimistic Control Run displayed in Chapter VIII. In order to create the pessimistic Control Run displayed there, an extra delay on BPD was inserted into equation (4Cii), an extra delay on ZD was inserted into equations (14Cii) and (64Cii), and the coefficient α in equation (14Ciii) was set equal to .67 instead of 1.0.

APPENDIX B

The Policy Rules Discussed in Chapter XIV

In this appendix we use the following notation:

g = Money GDP
b = balance of payments on current account
u = unemployment
t = rate of indirect taxation
n = rate of employees' national insurance contributions
v = real exchange rate (see Section 2 of Chapter XIV)
w = wage rate
x = an auxiliary variable
k (subscript) = kth time period
e (superscript) = 'error', i.e. difference between the reference and actual values of the superscripted variable; e.g. $g_k^e = +1.5$ denotes that, in period k, Money GDP is 1.5 per cent *below* its reference (or target) value.

Note that the following statement of the rules does *not* include implementations delays; but the outputs Money GDP and balance of payments were both delayed by one quarter to simulate the effect of a delay in implementing the feedback policy (see Section 3 of Chapter VII and Section 2 of Chapter XIV) and the rules in Section 2 below were designed also to perform adequately if these outputs were delayed by a further quarter (see Section 4 of Chapter XIV).

1. The Initial Design

$$t_k = 2.55\,t_{k-1} - 2.12\,t_{k-2} + 0.57\,t_{k-3} - 0.92473\,g_k^e$$
$$+ 0.62503\,g_{k-1}^e + 1.4239\,g_{k-2}^e - 1.1304\,g_{k-3}^e$$
$$n_k = 2.55\,n_{k-1} - 2.12\,n_{k-2} + 0.57\,n_{k-3} - 1.5821\,g_k^e$$
$$+ 2.7507\,g_{k-1}^e - 0.96402\,g_{k-2}^e - 0.21449\,g_{k-3}^e$$
$$v_k = 2.1\,v_{k-1} - 1.4\,v_{k-2} + 0.3\,v_{k-3} - 5.136\,b_k^e + 12.04\,b_{k-1}^e$$
$$- 9.8683\,b_{k-2}^e + 2.8789\,b_{k-3}^e$$

$$w_k = 1.6\,w_{k-1} - 0.6\,w_{k-2} + 0.34891\,u_k^e + 1.5339\,u_{k-1}^e$$
$$- 2.8278\,u_{k-2}^e + 1.1228\,u_{k-3}^e$$

2.   The More Robust Design

$$x_k = x_{k-1} + g_k^e$$

$$t_k = 0.6932\,t_{k-1} - 0.46236\,x_k - 0.14873\,x_{k-1} + 0.57124\,x_{k-2}$$

$$n_k = 0.6623\,n_{k-1} - 0.79105\,x_k + 0.55526\,x_{k-1} + 0.121\,x_{k-2}$$

$$v_k = 2.1\,v_{k-1} - 1.4\,v_{k-2} + 0.3\,v_{k-3} - 3.5952\,b_k^e + 8.428\,b_{k-1}^e$$
$$- 6.90781\,b_{k-2}^e + 2.01523\,b_{k-3}^e$$

$$w_k = w_{k-1} + 0.35\,u_k^e + 0.65\,u_{k-1}^e - 0.65\,u_{k-2}^e$$

3.   The Proposed Policy

As Section 2, except:

$$v_k = 2.1\,v_{k-1} - 1.4\,v_{k-2} + 0.3\,v_{k-3} - 0.68954\,b_k^e$$
$$+ 0.99061\,b_{k-1}^e - 0.33062\,b_{k-2}^e$$

References

Allen, R. G. D. (1967), *Macro-economic Theory* (London: Macmillan).
Artis, M. J. and Miller, M. H. (eds) (1981), *Essays in Fiscal and Monetary Policy* (London: Oxford University Press).
Bean, C. (1979), 'An econometric model of manufacturing investment in the UK', *Government Economic Service Working Paper*, No. 29 (HM Treasury).
Cook, S. T. and Jackson, P. M. (1979), *Current Issues in Fiscal Policy* (Oxford: Martin Robertson).
Dornbusch, Rudiger (1976), 'Expectations and exchange rate dynamics', *Journal of Political Economy*, vol. 84, pp. 1161–77.
Doyle, J. C. and Stein, G. (1981), 'Multivariable feedback design: concepts for a classical/modern synthesis', *IEEE Transactions on Automatic Control*, vol. 26, pp. 4–16.
Edmunds, J. M. (1979), 'Control system design and analysis using closed-loop Nyquist and Bode arrays', *International Journal of Control*, vol. 30, pp. 773–802.
Franklin, G. F. and Powell, J. D. (1980), *Digital Control of Dynamic Systems* (Reading, Mass.: Addison-Wesley).
Friedman, M. (1953), 'The effect of a full employment policy on economic stability, a formal analysis', in *Essays in Positive Economics* (Chicago, Ill.: University of Chicago Press).
Horton, G. R. (1980), Small Model: standard simulations, HM Treasury Academic Panel Paper, July.
Jenkins, G. E. M. and Watts, D. (1968), *Spectral Analysis* (San Francisco: Holden-Day).
Kailath, T. (1980), *Linear Systems* (Englewood Cliffs, NJ: Prentice-Hall).
Kung, S. (1979) 'A new low-order approximation algorithm via singular value decomposition', *Proc. Control and Decision Conference*, Clearwater, Florida, December.
Kwakernaak, H. and Sivan, R. (1972), *Linear Optimal Control Systems* (New York: Wiley).
Maciejowski, J. M. and Vines, D. (1982) 'The design and performance of a multivariable macroeconomic regulator', *Proceedings of IEEE Conference on Applications of Adaptive and Multivariable Control*, Hull, UK, July.
Maciejowski, J. M. and Vines, D. (1983), 'Decoupled control of a macroeconomic model using frequency domain methods', paper submitted to the *Journal of Economic Dynamics and Control*.
Meade, J. E. (1981), 'Comment on the papers by Professors Laidler and Tobin', *Economic Journal*, vol. 91, pp. 49–55.
Minister of Reconstruction (1944), 'Employment Policy', White Paper

presented to Parliament by Command of His Majesty (London: HMSO).

Mundell, R. A. (1962), 'The appropriate use of monetary and fiscal policy for internal and external stability', *IMF Staff Papers*, vol. 9, pp. 70–7.

Phillips, A. W. (1954), 'Stabilization policy in a closed economy', *Economic Journal*, vol. 64, pp. 290–323.

Phillips, A. W. (1957), 'Stabilization policy and the time-form of lagged responses', *Economic Journal*, vol. 67, pp. 265–277.

Postlethwaite, I. and MacFarlane, A. G. J. (1979), *A Complex Variable Approach to the Analysis of Linear Multivariable Feedback Systems* (vol. 12 of Lecture Notes in Control and Information Sciences), (Berlin: Springer-Verlag).

Ritchie, A. (1980), 'The small model; a shrunken version of the Treasury Model', HM Treasury UMDG Paper, April.

HM Treasury (1979), *Macroeconomic Model Technical Manual 1979*, October.

HM Treasury (1980), *The Unified Model: Specification of Equations and Listing of Variables*, January.

Vines, D. (1979), 'A complete empirical macroeconomic model for the analysis of economic policy', mimeo. Department of Applied Economics, Cambridge.

Vines, D. and Maciejowski, J. M. (1983), 'The design and performance of new Keynesian economic policies', forthcoming in *Monetarism: Traditions, Debates, and Policy*, ed. A. S. Courakis and R. Harrington (Macmillan).

Westaway, P. F. and Maciejowski, J. M. (1983), 'A comparison of frequency domain and optimal control methods for the design of a macroeconomic feedback regulation policy', paper to be presented at the fourth IFAC/IFOR Conference on the Modelling and Control of National Economies, Washington, DC, June.

Index

For Product Safety Concerns and Information please contact our EU
representative GPSR@taylorandfrancis.com
Taylor & Francis Verlag GmbH, Kaufingerstraße 24, 80331 München, Germany

www.ingramcontent.com/pod-product-compliance
Ingram Content Group UK Ltd.
Pitfield, Milton Keynes, MK11 3LW, UK
UKHW020935180425
457613UK00019B/408